TASCHEN

FAVORITE MOVIES OF THE 90s

Volume 2   Ed. Jürgen Müller

In Collaboration with
Herbert Klemens Filmbild Fundus Robert Fischer

VOLUME 1

VOLUME 2

ROMEO + JULIET

1996 – USA – 120 MIN. – LOVE FILM, LITERATURE ADAPTATION
DIRECTOR BAZ LUHRMANN (*1962)
SCREENPLAY CRAIG PEARCE, BAZ LUHRMANN, based on the drama of the same name by
WILLIAM SHAKESPEARE **DIRECTOR OF PHOTOGRAPHY** DONALD M. MACALPINE **EDITING** JILL BILCOCK
MUSIC NELLEE COOPER **PRODUCTION** GABRIELLA MARTINELLI, BAZ LUHRMANN for
MAZMARK PRODUCTIONS, 20TH CENTURY FOX
STARRING LEONARDO DICAPRIO (Romeo), CLAIRE DANES (Juliet), BRIAN DENNEHY
(Ted Montague), JOHN LEGUIZAMO (Tybalt), PETE POSTLETHWAITE (Father Laurence),
PAUL SORVINO (Fulgencio Capulet), HAROLD PERRINEAU (Mercutio), M. EMMET WALSH
(Apothecary), CARLOS MARTÍN MANZO (Petruchio), CHRISTINA PICKLES
(Caroline Montague)
IFF BERLIN 1997 SILVER BEAR for BEST ACTOR (Leonardo DiCaprio)

"Did my heart love 'till now?
For swear at sight, I never saw true beauty 'till this night."

"Two households, both alike in dignity (in fair Verona, where we lay our scene) from ancient grudge break to new mutiny, where civil blood makes civil hands unclean." The prologue of Shakespeare's *Romeo and Juliet* resounds from the television. Boys from the two rival gangs meet at a gas station. One insult leads to another, guns are drawn, and the gas station goes up in smoke. The war between the Montague and Capulet families makes the whole city hold its breath and keeps the police on their toes. Romeo (Leonardo DiCaprio), old Montague's only son moons around in his unrequited love for Rosalinde and keeps out of the fighting. He lets his friend Mercutio (Harold Perrineau) persuade him to go to a costume party at the Capulet's where his beloved is also expected to appear. Instead however Romeo finds his true love: Juliet (Claire Danes), the daughter of his archenemy Capulet.

The works of William Shakespeare (1564–1616) have inspired movie adaptations since the beginning of cinema history, but it may well be the case that no other director has set an adaptation of a Shakespeare play so radically in his own times as the Australian Baz Luhrmann (*Strictly Ballroom*, 1991)

did with *Romeo + Juliet*. The prologue is delivered by the most important news medium of the late 20th century: the television. "Fair Verona" is Verona Beach (although most of the film was made in Mexico City), a multicultural megacity with a sunny beach, smog, skyscrapers, police helicopters, and an enormous Jesus statue like the one in Rio de Janeiro. The offices of the Capulets' businesses are on one side of a wide street, those of the Montagues on the other. The rival families have been transformed into gangster dynasties. The Capulets are Hispanic Americans and the Montagues white Americans (as in *West Side Story*, another *Romeo and Juliet* adaptation). The Capulets wear black, the Montagues Hawaii shirts; one family drives cars with CAP license plates, the other with MON. Their weapons are 9 mm pistols made by the firm Sword (and can still therefore be referred to as "swords" in the script). The gangsters are like action movie heroes, their rituals reminiscent of black gangster films like *New Jack City* (1990) or *Menace II Society* (1993). The costume ball at the Capulets' is a loud, trashy party featuring an appearance by a drag queen.

1

2

In 1997, three other Shakespeare films were released in addition to *Romeo + Juliet*, one of which was Kenneth Branagh's four-hour *Hamlet*. Cinema history is full of Shakespeare adaptations, with a scene from "King John" making it to the silver screen as early as 1899. Alongside faithful adaptations, there have always been films more loosely linked to the works of the bard: for example, the sci-fi classic *Forbidden Planet* (1956) based on "The Tempest," and *10 Things I Hate About You* (1998) taken from "The Taming of the Shrew." Occasionally, the playwright puts in an appearance himself, as in *Anonymous* (2011) in which director Roland Emmerich pursues the theory that the works attributed to Shakespeare were not actually written by him.

"The language of Shakespeare, the acting of Quentin Tarantino." *Zoom*

3

1 Star-crossed lovers: a whole world separates
Romeo (Leonardo DiCaprio) …

2 … and Juliet (Claire Danes) –
but the lovers are unaware of this.

3 The priest is no longer wearing the Crucifix around
his neck: Father Laurence (Pete Postlethwaite).

4 The quarrel between the Montagues and the
Capulets – gangster warfare.

"His works had to compete with bear fights and prostitutes. He was an entertainer, mixing comedy, song, violence, and tragedy. Just like MTV today." Baz Luhrmann in *Abendzeitung*

It's not just lovingly devised, creative details like those which transpose the play into the present (and that includes today's self-referential cinema and its world of quotations) but the production as a whole. Luhrmann permits himself a playfulness that goes far beyond the formal idiom of narrative cinema and does more than nod in the direction of the aesthetic of the video clip, with techniques like quick takes, high speed panning shots, slow motion and fast forward, extreme camera perspectives (shots from great heights, shots through an aquarium or a washbasin), and a wide-ranging use of music and uneven acting styles (from serious to hammy overacting). The movie is a self-confident piece of pop culture and wallows in the superficial thrill of images that have become kitsch symbols in their own right: white doves, burning hearts, a priest with a tattoo of a cross, and Juliet going to the costume party as an angel with Romeo as her knight. Amazingly, all of this combines to make a homogenous, seductively beautiful movie that miraculously maintains the magical rhythm of Shakespeare's language and verse.

HJK

SCREAM

1996 – USA – 111 MIN. – HORROR FILM
DIRECTOR WES CRAVEN (*1939)
SCREENPLAY KEVIN WILLIAMSON **DIRECTOR OF PHOTOGRAPHY** MARK IRWIN **EDITING** PATRICK LUSSIER
MUSIC MARCO BELTRAMI **PRODUCTION** CARY WOODS, CATHY KONRAD for WOODS
ENTERTAINMENT, DIMENSION FILMS, MIRAMAX
STARRING DREW BARRYMORE (Casey Becker), NEVE CAMPBELL (Sidney Prescott),
DAVID ARQUETTE (Deputy Dewey Riley), COURTENEY COX (Gale Weathers),
JAMIE KENNEDY (Randy), MATTHEW LILLARD (Stewart), SKEET ULRICH (Billy Loomis),
ROSE MCGOWAN (Tatum Riley), W. EARL BROWN (Cameraman Kenny), LIEV SCHREIBER
(Cotton Weary)

"What's your favorite scary movie?"

It was supposed to be a cozy video evening with popcorn, boyfriend, and a scary movie. It turns into pure horror. Casey (Drew Barrymore) gets an anonymous call. It starts off like a silly boys' trick and ends fatally. The caller draws her into a horror film quiz. What's the name of the killer in *Halloween*? Who's the bloodthirsty murderer in *Friday the 13th*? It turns out that if you get the answer right, you get to stay alive: wrong answers are punishable by death. Casey gets the answer wrong.

The killer's next victim is Sidney Prescott (Neve Campbell), a classmate of the dead girl at Woodsboro High School. Ever since her mother's gruesome murder exactly a year ago, Sidney has been living alone with her father. He goes away on a business trip, and she's left on her own for a few days. The killer calls first, as before, then he stands there in a mask with a knife glinting in his hand. Sidney manages to escape, as her boyfriend Billy (Skeet Ulrich) appears and frightens the psychopath away. But then a hand falls out of Billy's pocket – is he the killer? He is arrested and kept in the local jail over-

night. He is released again in the morning: the killer struck again during the night, so it can't be him.

In the meantime all of Woodsboro is in uproar. Camera teams from all over the country have arrived, including the journalist Gale Weathers (Courteney Cox) who reported the death of Sidney's mother a year ago, starting off a media mud fight in the process. The thrill seekers find plenty of trophies as the killer leaves a bloody trail through the town. His next victims are the school director and some more teenagers.

The horror movie genre was dead until Wes Craven awoke it to brilliant new life with *Scream*. "Until now the murderers always acted as if they had just invented killing. Mine knows his predecessors." In *Scream* the killer acts with self-reflective irony, fully conscious of the conventions of the horror movie, and the result is an effective combination of horror and humor. The humor is that of a connoisseur who knows that the dead killer will get up one last time at the end; the humor of Wes Craven who in his short appearance

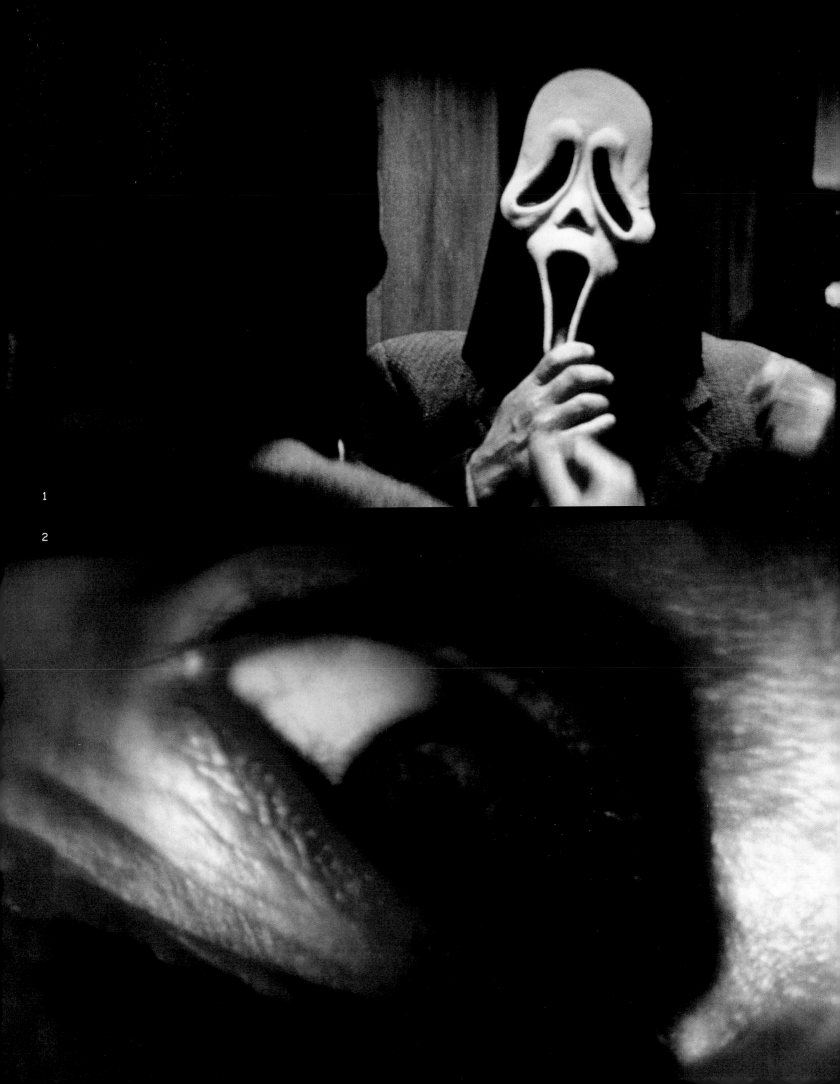

1

2

3

as a caretaker wears Freddy Krueger's striped pullover (from his masterpiece *Nightmare on Elm Street*) and even that of the bourgeois art connoisseur: the makeup is based on Edvard Munch's *The Scream*. The recognition factor is satisfying. The laughter provides brief pauses in each tense scene – the fundamental suspense, the thrill, the feverish identification with the protagonists still remain. The shock remains too: the resurrection of the killer is not just taken for granted here, it is even announced. And yet we are still shocked when it actually happens. Despite all the quotations and the games with genre conventions *Scream* never becomes a simple parody.

The protagonists are horror movie fans just like normal people, acted by youngsters already familiar from television series, like Neve Campbell from *Party Of Five* (1994–1998) and Courteney Cox from *Friends* (1994–2004). The only established film actress is Drew Barrymore, but she disappears from the scene within a few minutes – like Janet Leigh in *Psycho* (1960). The characters know what is going on. They know the rules of the teenage horror movie: no sex, no drugs, no booze, and never say you'll be back in a minute. But they don't stick to them – they have sex, they smoke, and they pass round the joints – and they have to pay the consequences.   HJK

THE SCREAM FRANCHISE "Don't kill me, I want to be in the sequel," says one girl as she tries to placate the killer. He kills her anyway, but *Scream* has had three sequels. Craven continues the insider jokes: in *Scream 2* (1997), Sidney leaves her hometown of Woodsboro to study at a film academy – giving plenty of opportunity to reflect on horror movies and their sequels. The students begin a macabre game: anyone who doesn't die must be the killer. Sidney survives and goes back to Woodsboro in *Scream 3* (2000) – not to the real town, but to a film set where her experiences are being filmed under the title *Stab 3*. In *Scream 4* (2011) Sidney is promoting her latest book on the 10th anniversary of the Woodsboro massacre and, unsurprisingly, the masked killer shows up again.

---

1 A "slasher" like *Halloween*, with the mask of Edvard Munch: Wes Craven draws on a wide range of cultural references.

2 "I don't believe in motives. Did Hannibal Lecter have a reason for wanting to eat people?"

3 Victim number one: Drew Barrymore starts chatting to a stranger on the phone about horror films, before discovering that she's talking to a lunatic.

4 For reporter Gale Weathers (Courteney Cox) all this is just part of the job – until the killer turns his knife on her.

5 Has Sidney (Neve Campbell) survived everything? Not yet: there are three sequels still to go.

"People like dying in my films. Even my lawyer asks me when he'll finally get to play a corpse."

Wes Craven in *Zeit-Magazin*

4

5

BREAKING THE WAVES

1996 – DENMARK / SWEDEN / NORWAY / NETHERLANDS / FRANCE –
159 MIN. – MELODRAMA

DIRECTOR LARS VON TRIER (*1956) **SCREENPLAY** LARS VON TRIER, PETER ASMUSSEN
DIRECTOR OF PHOTOGRAPHY ROBBY MÜLLER **EDITING** ANDERS REFN **MUSIC** JOACHIM HOLBEK
PRODUCTION PETER AALBAECK-JENSEN, VIBEKE WINDELØW for ZENTROPA
STARRING EMILY WATSON (Bess), STELLAN SKARSGÅRD (Jan), KATRIN CARTLIDGE
(Dodo), JEAN-MARC BARR (Terry), ADRIAN RAWLINS (Dr. Richardson), UDO KIER
(Sadistic Sailor), JONATHAN HACKETT (Priest), SANDRA VOE (Bess's mother),
MIKKEL GAUP (Pits), ROEF RAGAS (Pim)
IFF CANNES 1996 GRAND JURY PRIZE

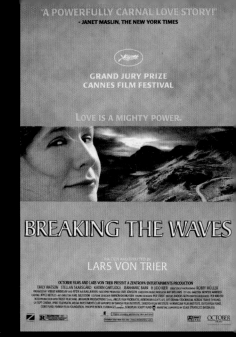

"We do not need bells in our church to worship God."

The scene is a remote coastal village in Scotland in the '70s. Bess (Emily Watson), a good-natured girl who some say has visions of God and others term mentally ill falls in love with Jan (Stellan Skarsgård), an oil rig worker, and incurs the wrath of the elders of her strict Presbyterian community. Only Dodo, her brother's widow, stands by her. As if to remind her once again of the power of the church, she is forced to watch a funeral where the elders damn the deceased for all eternity. Despite this, Bess and Jan get married and everything goes well in the first few days they spend together, particularly where their sex life is concerned.

When Jan has to return to the oil rig, Bess is overcome with yearning and desire. Once again she retreats to the church to speak to God: everything else is unimportant if only she can have Jan back with her again. In a terrible way, her wish becomes true: Jan breaks his back in an accident and is paralyzed from the neck down. Bess's mental state deteriorates so badly that

Dodo calls in the doctor. He proclaims her sane, and as Jan gets better, Bess recovers her equilibrium. One day, under the influence of the painkillers he is forced to take, Jan makes a suggestion to his wife. As he can no longer fulfil his marital duties, and as she enjoyed sex so much and he doesn't want her love for him to be dependent on what he can no longer do, she should take a lover, for his sake as well as her own. Bess takes up his suggestion and this is the beginning of her fall in the eyes of the community. Only God knows her passion, the depths of her love, and her suffering. It's a monstrous story, often bordering on the edge of madness. A bare summary of the facts makes them appear to border on the ridiculous, but Lars von Trier has exactly the right touch for the material. He develops a radical closeness to his characters and a strongly improvised, almost careless way of directing reminiscent of the Dogme films. In his TV series *The Kingdom* (*Riget*, 1994) von Trier developed a method of working in which he allows his actors to move freely and play

3

the scenes through in their entirety. The scenes are only loose structures un- til they have been through the AVID, a computerized editing program. This method, with its wildly swinging cameras, syncopated montage, and grainy, washed-out picture quality is a return to the kind of realism that began in documentary films of the '50s as "direct cinema" or "cinéma vérité." It both distances the audience from the movie's characters and emphasizes the gap between the material and the immaterial, between body and soul, the ever- widening abyss which tears Bess apart and features in songs such as Procol Harum's "A Whiter Shade of Pale" or Leonard Cohen's "Suzanne."

Von Trier emphasizes the physicality of his figures, most memorably in the beautifully frank sex scenes between Jan and Bess, and the selflessness with which Bess gives her body to other men, until it is lacerated first by a sadistic sailor then by a psychotherapist. It's impossible to say whether *Breaking the Waves* is a Catholic movie or not, as has so often been claimed. What's more important is that it's a movie about the range and spiritual depth of emotion.

OM

LARS VON TRIER Lars von Trier (*1956) shot to immediate international fame with his debut film *The Element of Crime* (1984). Along with his next two movies, *Epidemic* (1987) and *Europa* (1990), it forms a loose "Europe" trilogy, held together as much by von Trier's formal experiments as by thematic links. After the television series *The Kingdom* (*Riget*, 1994) he devoted himself to the "Golden Heart Trilogy," which comprises *Breaking the Waves* (1996), *The Idiots* (1998), and *Dancer in the Dark* (2000), all movies that examine the relationship between passion and sexuality. The controversy caused by the explicit sex and violence in the psycho-horror trip *Antichrist* (2009) and enigmatic dystopia *Melancholia* (2011) has finally established the Dane as one of the most scandalous, contentious and disturbing directors in cinema today – and one of the most exciting.

1 Everything is still fine in Jan's world … Stellan Skarsgård, probably Sweden's best-known international actor, in one of his most extroverted roles.

2 Bess in a rare moment of calm: Emily Watson ranks among the great discoveries of the 1990s.

3 Jan and Bess get married against the advice of their parents and the parish elders.

4 Heart of gold: Bess as a naturally self-sacrificing lover.

5 Sex as an existential experience: Bess recognizes divine beauty in physical love, while a satisfied Jan dreams of all the days together to come.

6 Ungodly happiness: Terry (Jean-Marc Barr) really paints the town red at his best friend's wedding.

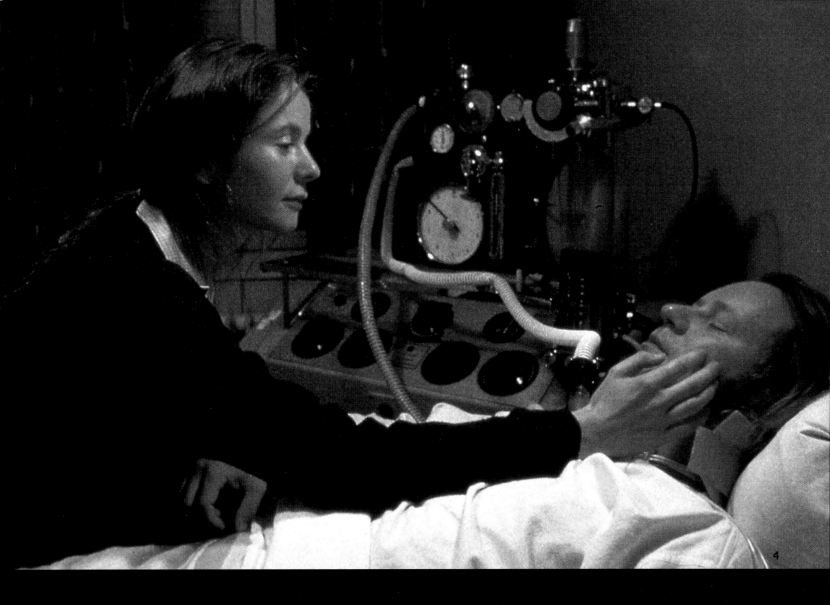

"I ... remember that Emily was the only one who came to the casting barefoot and with no makeup at all! There was something Jesus-like about her which attracted me." Lars von Trier in *Sight and Sound*

THE ENGLISH PATIENT ♟♟♟♟♟♟♟♟♟

In love, there are no boundaries.

THE
ENGLISH
PATIENT

1996 – USA – 162 MIN. – MELODRAMA, LITERATURE ADAPTATION
DIRECTOR ANTHONY MINGHELLA (*1954)
SCREENPLAY ANTHONY MINGHELLA, based on the novel of the same name by
MICHAEL ONDAATJE **DIRECTOR OF PHOTOGRAPHY** JOHN SEALE **EDITING** WALTER MURCH
MUSIC GABRIEL YARED **PRODUCTION** SAUL ZAENTZ, HARVEY WEINSTEIN, SCOTT GREENSTEIN,
BOB WEINSTEIN for SAUL ZAENTZ PRODUCTIONS, MIRAMAX
STARRING RALPH FIENNES (Graf Laszlo Almásy), KRISTIN SCOTT THOMAS (Katharine Clifton),
JULIETTE BINOCHE (Hana), WILLEM DAFOE (Caravaggio), NAVEEN ANDREWS (Kip),
COLIN FIRTH (Geoffrey Clifton), JULIAN WADHAM (Madox), JÜRGEN PROCHNOW
(Major Müller), KEVIN WHATELY (Hardy), CLIVE MERRISON (Fenalon Barnes)
ACADEMY AWARDS 1997 OSCARS for BEST PICTURE, BEST DIRECTOR (Anthony Minghella),
BEST SUPPORTING ACTRESS (Juliette Binoche), BEST CINEMATOGRAPHY (John Seale),
BEST ART DIRECTION-SET DECORATION (Stuart Craig, Stephanie McMillan),
BEST FILM EDITING (Walter Murch), BEST MUSIC, category DRAMA (Gabriel Yared),
BEST SOUND (Chris Newman, Ivan Sharrock), and BEST COSTUMES (Ann Roth)
IFF BERLIN 1997 SILVER BEAR for BEST ACTRESS (Juliette Binoche)

"The heart is an organ of fire."

The camera glides over an undulating yellow-brown surface. It looks like a desert, but in fact it's paper, and a brush starts to paint stylized human forms that swim about. We cut to a different yellow-brown surface that undulates more strongly – this time it is the desert. An airplane flies by, its shadows racing over the hillocks and valleys of the desert plain. Shots ring out, and we see that the biplane is being fired at from the ground. Dark flecks of flak dot the sky, getting ever closer, until suddenly they hit the plane. The airplane dives and bursts into flames.

The English Patient tells the story of the pilot and his great love – in an unhurried, old-fashioned way. The film unfolds gradually, slowly accumulating additional information and perspectives, and only at the end is the entire story revealed. The pilot is dubbed the "English patient" when he is delivered to an Allied hospital in Italy shortly before the end of the Second World War – he was in an English plane that was shot down by the Germans. He is deformed by hideous burns, and the flames have destroyed his face, his skin, and his lungs. He doesn't have long to live, has lost his memory, and does not even seem to know his name or nationality. The only clue is the book he carries with him – Herodotus's *History*, a Greek tale from the 5th century BC with maps, photos, and letters tucked in between the pages. He is too badly injured

to be transported any further and so French-Canadian nurse Hana (Juliette Binoche) stays behind with him in a half-ruined monastery in Tuscany. Here he spends his remaining days in peace, and gradually he recovers the memory of his great love.

The story begins in 1937. The "English patient" is Count Laszlo Almásy (Ralph Fiennes), a Hungarian aristocrat who has devoted himself to the study of the desert and joined a group of English cartographers in the Sahara. One day an English couple come to join them: Geoffrey and Katharine Clifton (Colin Firth, Kristin Scott Thomas). He is an enthusiastic pilot and she is a painter. To begin with, Katharine is dismissive and almost hostile towards the silent, introverted Laszlo. But after their car breaks down and they are forced to sit out a sandstorm together in the desert, their relationship changes. While exploring the interior of the Sahara, the group discovers a cave filled with unusual wall paintings of people swimming. The explorers are dispersed when war breaks out, but they meet again in Cairo. Love blossoms out of the friendship between Laszlo and Katharine, and they begin a passionate affair. Eventually, her husband realizes, and reacts with an act of jealous rage: he flies into the desert with Katharine to find Laszlo and tries to kill all three of them in a plane crash.

As these memories and visions return to the "English patient," life continues around him. Hana treats him lovingly, not least because she believes that she is cursed. Everyone close to her – her lover, her friend, even a fellow nurse – have all died. She has no reason not to be fond of her patient as he is going to die anyway. She wants to make his last days bearable and give him an easy death. Their solitude is short-lived however, and they are soon joined in the ruined monastery by the devious Caravaggio (Willem Dafoe), a Canadian trader of Italian descent. He was also in North Africa when the war broke out, and in contrast to Hana, he asks critical questions when the English patient's memory begins to return. Caravaggio was tortured by the Germans in the Libyan town of Tobruk, where they cut off his thumbs. Two bomb disposal experts from the British Army also take up quarters in the monastery, the Sikh Kip (Naveen Andrews) and his colleague Hardy (Kevin Whately). A fragile love affair develops between Kip and Hana, although Hana will not let herself become too involved because she still believes that she is cursed. In the meantime Laszlo lives out his love for Katharine in his memories, and images return to him with ever greater power.

English director Anthony Minghella (*Mr. Wonderful*, 1993) films Michael Ondaatje's novel as a melodramatic epic, with grandiose images of desert adventure. The movie unfolds on two narrative planes that dovetail elegantly and constantly mirror each other. The outbreak of war dovetails with its end, the burning yellow-brown of the desert is played off against the cool green of Tuscany, the great love between Katharine and Laszlo is set off against the fragile relationship between Hana and Kip, Katharine lies fatally wounded in a cave in the desert, and Laszlo faces death in the ruined monastery. The two narrative planes are not only separated by the war, but also seem to take place in entirely different eras. The cartographic exploration of the desert by the English is part of colonial history. Katharine is an aristocratic lady of the British Empire whereas practical, energetic Hana is a woman of the 20th century.

Ondaatje's 1992 novel, winner of the English Booker Prize, also works with flashbacks and dovetailing and spans the length of the Second World War. Minghella maintains the chronological framework but thins out the cast and the plot strands of what is an extensive novel. In the novel for instance

THE RETURN OF THE MELODRAMA Love in a time of war. *The English Patient* tells the story of strong emotions in a tone of complete seriousness devoid of irony. This makes it part of the long cinema tradition of melodrama that began in the silent era. Its artistic highpoint came in the '50s with the movies of Douglas Sirk, and it reached a commercial peak with the tearjerker *Love Story* in 1969. Melodramas went out of fashion in the '80s and '90s, when emotions could only be shown mixed with irony, when they weren't being ridiculed altogether. Two films at the end of the '90s brought melodrama back into cinemas: *Titanic* (1997) and *The English Patient*. The latter was perhaps the most typical of the genre, as *Titanic* is a disaster movie as well as a love story and an adaptation of a historical event. *The English Patient* on the other hand is simply the story of a great love that can only be fulfilled in death.

"Of course David Lean's *Lawrence of Arabia* comes to mind. But the comprehensive way in which Minghella tells the story, leaving nothing in his film open to doubt, is something David Lean did not permit himself." *Frankfurter Allgemeine Zeitung*

1 Count Laszlo Almásy – he finds his great love in the desert.

2 "It is principally the actors, Ralph Fiennes as the dying, ironically broken Almásy ...

3 ... and Kristin Scott Thomas, who up until now had only appeared as a wallflower, who lift this film above the average." *Zoom*

he love story between Hana and Kip plays a much more important role. The movie never denies its literary origins, however, and literature and books feature throughout, and whatever happens, Laszlo also manages to save his copy of Herodotus – Hana reads it to him, and it eventually outlives him. Hana uses books to stop the gaps in the stairs, and the Sahara itself appears in the first scene as paper, on which the love story is written.

Production of the film was an adventure story in itself. Minghella had long cherished the idea of adapting the book for the screen. After 11 producers had refused it, *The English Patient* was eventually accepted by independent producer Saul Zaentz, winner of a total of 13 Oscars and maker of seven great films over the last 20 years, including *One Flew Over the Cuckoo's Nest* (1975) and *Amadeus* (1984). All seemed well at first but a funding crisis developed when 20th Century Fox pulled out of the project. Fox's casting preferences hadn't been taken into consideration: it wanted Hollywood stars whereas Zaentz and Minghella insisted on Ralph Fiennes, Kristin Scott Thomas, and Juliette Binoche. Salvation finally arrived in the shape of Harvey Weinstein, head of Miramax. He contributed 26 of the movie's total budget of 32 million dollars and filming could go ahead. His courage was rewarded with nine Oscars.

HJK

5

THE PEOPLE VS. LARRY FLYNT

FROM THE TWO-TIME ACADEMY AWARD WINNING DIRECTOR OF
AMADEUS AND ONE FLEW OVER THE CUCKOO'S NEST
WOODY HARRELSON   COURTNEY LOVE   EDWARD NORTON

1996 – USA – 130 MIN. – DRAMA
DIRECTOR MILOŠ FORMAN (*1932)
SCREENPLAY SCOTT ALEXANDER, LARRY KARASZEWSKI
DIRECTOR OF PHOTOGRAPHY PHILIPPE ROUSSELOT **EDITING** CHRISTOPHER TELLEFSEN
MUSIC THOMAS NEWMAN **PRODUCTION** OLIVER STONE, JANET YANG, MICHAEL HAUSMAN
for IXTLAN PRODUCTIONS, PHOENIX PICTURES
STARRING WOODY HARRELSON (Larry Flynt), COURTNEY LOVE (Althea Leasure),
EDWARD NORTON (Alan Isaacman), JAMES CROMWELL (Charles Keating),
CRISPIN GLOVER (Arlo), JAMES CARVILLE (Simon Leis), BRETT HARRELSON
(Jimmy Flynt), DONNA HANOVER (Ruth Carter-Stapleton), VINCENT SCHIAVELLI
(Chester), LARRY FLYNT (Judge)
IFF BERLIN 1997 GOLDEN BEAR

You may not like what he does,
but are you prepared to give up his right to do it?

The People vs. Larry Flynt
A MILOŠ FORMAN FILM

"What is more obscene: sex or war?"

Even as a child, Larry Flynt had a good nose for business. He distilled spirits with his brother and sold them to the local farmers. And when their father drank it all himself, Larry lost his temper and threw the jug at his head. Later he became a millionaire by selling sex magazines. And when someone got in his way, he broke china in the courtroom. *Entertainment Weekly* described *Hustler* editor Larry Flynt as a "pioneer of gynecological photojournalism." Miloš Forman is somewhat free with the truth in his account of the story, but Flynt himself worked on the movie as consultant and actually appears briefly as a judge in the first court case.

In 1972 Flynt (Woody Harrelson) was running strip-tease joints in Ohio with his brother Jimmy (Harrelson's brother Brett). To improve business he started publishing a magazine where the ladies can be "surveyed" in advance, and so *Hustler* was born. Circulation figures soared when he published naked pictures of Jackie Onassis, the first lady. Flynt became rich, married his girlfriend Althea (Courtney Love), and moved into a villa that had

exactly the same number of rooms as the mansion owned by *Playboy* editor Hugh Hefner. The first of a series of court cases then began where Flynt had to appear before the judge, and where time and again the core issues were the conflict between decency and freedom of speech. He lost his first case, but won the appeal, and subsequently he began to style himself a guardian of the freedom of speech. He then formed an organization for the freedom of the press at whose meetings he alternately showed pictures of naked women and of the destruction of war and concentration camps. Bizarrely, he found an ally in the evangelist Ruth Carter-Stapleton, sister of president Jimmy Carter (played by Donna Hanover, former wife of New York mayor Rudolph Giuliani).

In Forman's film, Flynt appears in court with an American flag wrapped round his hips. He throws oranges at a judge. He has a card on his desk that reads "Jesus H. Christ, Publisher." He has an epiphany in the shape of the American national symbol, the eagle, and he makes Santa Claus and the

1 Anyone can do it! – As the embodiment of the
   American Dream Flynt (Woody Harrelson) is a
   true patriot.

2 "Courtney Love lets all the raw, untamed,
   provocative impetus of her musical career and the

   echoes of her marriage to Kurt Cobain pour into her
   role as Flynt's lover Althea." *epd Film*

characters from *The Wizard of Oz* into sex figures. He likes to have sex six times a day but after an assassination attempt is stuck in a wheelchair and impotent. Doubtless it is hard to narrate the story of a figure so colorful with utter seriousness, but Forman finds a fine balance between irony, coarseness, and a touch of mockery to describe his protagonist. Two things remain sacrosanct: Flynt's love for his wife, and his right to freedom of speech. The film makes no effort to turn Flynt into an aesthete, who makes pretty pictures of naked women (which would be far from the truth). Forman presents him honestly as a pornographer, a tasteless horror, even a mean old devil – but he still supports his right to publish his magazines. Flynt is typical of Forman's film protagonists. Forman had previously given us figures like the rebel McMurphy, played by Jack Nicholson, who ends up in a psychiatric ward in *One Flew Over the Cuckoo's Nest* (1975), and the childishly sniggering Mozart who says obscenities backwards in *Amadeus* (1984). Flynt is a fool and rogue in that tradition – a contrary spirit who questions the status quo with extraordinary nerve.   HJK

"Larry Flynt, pornographer and lowest of the low, has achieved what he never dared to hope for – a place in American history." *Frankfurter Allgemeine Zeitung*

3 "Woody Harrelson's broad smile contains a hint of the 'natural born killer' that he played for Oliver Stone." *epd Film*

4 Twenty five years imprisonment! Charles Keating's (James Cromwell) first court action against Larry Flynt is successful.

> "What distinguishes Larry Flynt from Hugh Hefner is his almost messianic obsession with pursuing sex photography to the furthest limits permitted by law." *film-dienst*

MILOŠ FORMAN Miloš Forman (*1932) studied at the Prague Film School. In 1963 he made his debut with *Cerný Petr* (*Black Peter*), an autobiographical story about a teenager in a small Czech town, and went on to become a leading figure in the Czech New Wave. He shot three films in his native land before emigrating via France to America when the Soviets arrived in 1968. His big break in America, *One Flew Over the Cuckoo's Nest* (1975), became the cult film of a generation and won five Oscars, including one for Forman as Best Director. His adaptation of the musical *Hair* was less successful, as his version of the hippie idyll simply arrived too late (1977). Eight years later he won a second Oscar for Best Director with *Amadeus*. After *The People vs. Larry Flynt* (1996) he made *Man on the Moon* (1999), a biographical film about the US comedian Andy Kaufman, and another historical film, *Goya's Ghosts* (2006).

5 His own lawyer (Edward Norton), a private jet: Flynt is almost a normal entrepreneur.

6 Flynt appears in court wearing battle dress like a freedom fighter.

7 Scantily clad girls empty out bags of dollar bills: this is how Larry Flynt pays his cash fine.

CRASH

1996 – GREAT BRITAIN / CANADA – 100 MIN. – DRAMA, THRILLER
DIRECTOR DAVID CRONENBERG (*1943)
SCREENPLAY DAVID CRONENBERG, based on the novel of the same name by JAMES GRAHAM BALLARD DIRECTOR OF PHOTOGRAPHY PETER SUSCHITZKY EDITING RONALD SANDERS
MUSIC HOWARD SHORE PRODUCTION JEREMY THOMAS, ROBERT LANTOS, DAVID CRONENBERG for ALLIANCE COMMUNICATIONS, CORPORATION IN TRUST
STARRING JAMES SPADER (James G. Ballard), HOLLY HUNTER (Dr. Helen Remington), ELIAS KOTEAS (Vaughan), DEBORAH KARA UNGER (Catherine Ballard), ROSANNA ARQUETTE (Gabrielle), PETER MACNEILL (Colin Seagrave), YOLANDE JULIAN (Prostitute), CHERYL SWARTS (Vera Seagrave), JUDAH KATZ (Car Salesman), ALICE POON (Chamber Maid)
IFF CANNES 1996 JURY PRIZE

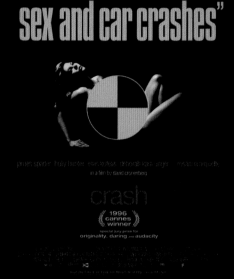

"a cool, rigorous film exploring a link between...

sex and car crashes"

"Maybe next time ... Maybe next time."

James Ballard (James Spader) and his wife Catherine (Deborah Kara Unger) are completely open to each other about their extramarital affairs. Sex with strangers stimulates their relationship. One day James has a serious car accident – a head-on collision, in which the driver of the other car is killed. James and the wife of the dead man, Dr. Helen Remington (Holly Hunter), are both badly injured. After his release from the hospital, James goes to inspect his wrecked automobile, and by chance meets Helen. He gives her a lift, and they narrowly escape being involved in a second accident. They both find this highly arousing, and so they drive to a parking garage and make love in the front seat. Helen introduces James to Vaughan (Elias Koteas), a man whose entire body is covered with scars, and who performs reconstructions of famous car crashes at illegal car shows. But for Vaughan, car accidents are

a passion in the fullest sense – as the head of a group of like-minded crash survivors, he seeks sexual fulfillment in them. James and Catherine become more and more deeply involved in this bizarre obsession. It also becomes progressively more dangerous as Vaughan loses control of his sexual urges, and searches for satisfaction outside of the stunt shows.

David Cronenberg has always been a master of provocation. As was to be expected, his film version of the novel by J. G. Ballard brought forth a storm of protest, culminating in the accusation that the film's perverse theme would inspire imitation – a curious claim, given the gloominess of the vision that Cronenberg conjures up.

Crash is far more than a quick look at a strange obsession. Cronenberg's deeper aim is to portray an essential form of human desire where the erotic

"It's like a porno movie made by a computer: It downloads gigabytes of information about sex, it discovers our love affair with cars, and it combines them in a mistaken algorithm."

Chicago Sun-Times

2

and the morbid meet. This is accompanied by transformation of the human body – a central theme in all of Cronenberg's films – manifested in *Crash* in the scarring, the prosthetics, and the bizarre orthopedic accessories of its central figures. The characters in the film are searching for total sexual fulfillment, for the most extreme experience they can possibly have. They find this in the sado-masochistic destruction of their own bodies, and in the fusion of the human body with technical apparatus. This aspect is already taken up in the title sequence, where metallic lettering advances forwards as though drilling into the spectators' eyes, an impression that is reinforced by the piercingly cold sounds of Howard Shore's brilliant film music. The music emphasizes the film's trancelike atmosphere. This impression is reinforced further by the futuristic sets, which are bathed in blue-gray lighting. They surround the human figures in the movie, making them appear driven souls whose speech is reduced to mere panting and gasping.

Cronenberg does not in any way attempt to rationalize the behavior of his figures, which is reduced to the level of pure sexual desire. And yet the behavior appears perfectly plausible, the natural consequence of our high-tech environment dominated by cars and traffic. Once, mankind dreamt of unity with nature: in Cronenberg's world, that yearning has been transformed into a sexual desire for total fusion with ubiquitous technology. The recurring image of James watching the streams of traffic through a telescope from his balcony is a symbol of that perverse longing – a longing perhaps that can only be stilled by a final crash.

JH

1 Crash-crazy: wrecked cars as the violent fusion of man and machine.

2 Metal and leather: Helen (Holly Hunter) and James seek out the close confines of the car for sex.

3 As though in a trance: the minds of the characters in Cronenberg's film are occupied only by the search for satisfaction: Catherine Ballard (Deborah Kara Unger).

4 Traffic is meaningless until there's a crash.

DAVID CRONENBERG The director David Cronenberg, born the son of a journalist and a pianist in Toronto in 1943, started writing science fiction stories as a child. His career began in 1974 with the Canadian television production *Shivers*, a film following in the tradition of Don Siegel's *Invasion of the Body Snatchers* (1956). Over the years, Cronenberg has developed an unmistakable horror style, famous for its graphic representation of bizarre transformations of the human body, which often leads to heated reactions from the public. His version of *The Fly* (1986), a remake of the horror classic by Kurt Neumann (1958), was a notable hit while *Scanners* (1980), *Videodrome* (1982), *Dead Zone* (1983), *Naked Lunch* (1991), and *Crash* (1996) all enjoy cult status among his considerable fan base. In the 2000s Cronenberg began to work outside the horror genre with films like *A History of Violence* (2005) and *Eastern Promises* (2007), two gangster action movies with existential overtones.

LOST HIGHWAY

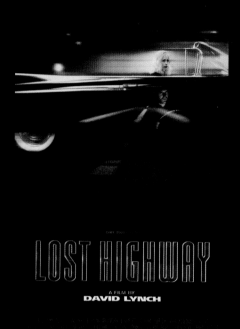

1997 – FRANCE / USA – 135 MIN. – THRILLER, NEO FILM NOIR
DIRECTOR DAVID LYNCH (*1946)
SCREENPLAY DAVID LYNCH, BARRY GIFFORD **DIRECTOR OF PHOTOGRAPHY** PETER DEMING
EDITING MARY SWEENEY **MUSIC** ANGELO BADALAMENTI **PRODUCTION** DEEPAK NAYAR,
TOM STERNBERG, MARY SWEENEY for ASYMMETRICAL, CIBY 2000
STARRING BILL PULLMAN (Fred Madison), PATRICIA ARQUETTE (Renee Madison /
Alice Wakefield), BALTHAZAR GETTY (Pete Dayton), ROBERT LOGGIA (Dick Laurent /
Mr. Eddy), ROBERT BLAKE (Mystery Man), MICHAEL MASSEE (Andy), GARY BUSEY
(Bill Dayton), NATASHA GREGSON WAGNER (Sheila), LUCY BUTLER (Candace Dayton),
GIOVANNI RIBISI (Steve "V"), HENRY ROLLINS (Henry)

"I'd like to remember things my own way. Not necessarily the way they happened."

At the beginning and at the end of *Lost Highway* we hear the same statement: "Dick Laurent is dead." Initially Fred Madison (Bill Pullman) hears it through his intercom, and at the end we realize that he is saying it at the same time as well. Lynch presents us with a paradox. Between those two events the movie switches characters and changes its mood, so much so that it can almost be considered to be made up of two separate films. The first tells the story of Fred, a saxophonist who lives with his wife Renee (Patricia Arquette with brown hair) in a villa as elegant as it is cold. He suspects that his wife is unfaithful to him and only leaves the house to go to work. He works off his angst and aggression in his playing, in free jazz solo riffs bursting with energy. The couple are sent anonymous videotapes which seem to confirm Fred's suspicions, but also cast doubt on his capacity to understand reality. The video begins with a take of their house, the camera slides in from a high angle into the house and up to their bed, and then shows Fred,

steeped in the blood of his murdered wife. Fred is condemned to death for murder.

In the "second" film, instead of Fred, we meet a young car mechanic called Pete (Balthazar Getty), who is in prison. As nothing can be proved against him, he is released, and his parents come to collect him and take him home. Somehow, Pete has changed, and he has lost interest in his former girlfriend. Instead he falls in love with Alice (Patricia Arquette, now blonde), the lover of one of his regular customers, underworld porno king Mr. Eddy (Robert Loggia). Pete and Alice begin an affair and soon it becomes clear that they will have to run away from the unprincipled Eddy. They try to get the money for their escape by robbing one of his business partners, but the plan fails.

In both movies a naive man falls victim to a femme fatale. The first movie is slow, dark and has a threatening, echoing soundtrack, while the

"*Lost Highway* isn't a journey into a man's convoluted mind; from the very beginning we are right there at the center of it." *steady cam*

1 A truly magical moment: Alice (Patricia Arquette) turns up at Pete's garage while Lou Reed sings "This Magic Moment."

2 Pete experiences worrying things on breaking into the villa – and all the while Rammstein roars: "You can see him slinking round the church."

3 "The highway leads on endlessly into the night. Leading to nowhere and back to the beginning." *Filmbulletin*

4

5

"Remote telescopy and virtual coitus: David Lynch goes to the heart of present-day cinema with a violent poetry that places us in the forefront of the spectator's condition." *Cahiers du cinéma*

second is lighter and more dynamic. Superficially it is clear how the two hang together: the male protagonist of the first movie is transformed in an incomprehensible fashion into that of the second. The female protagonists are played by the same actress.

But in fact nothing is clear. Lynch dovetails the two stories in many ways. A policeman gives Fred a bloody nose, and Pete's nose begins to bleed when he sees the photo of Alice and Renee. In his workshop, Pete hears the saxophone solo that Fred played in the club. Is the Pete story just a fantasy that Fred creates in his cell on death row, or are the arrest and Pete story a fantasy which the escaped murderer Fred dreams up? Is *Lost Highway* the story of Fred's schizophrenia? That possibility is alluded to by the pale Mystery Man (Robert Blake) who speaks to Fred at a party, and explains to him that he is both here and at Fred's house at the same time. There are various clues that point towards and away from each of these interpretations.

Lynch lays trails only to backtrack on them – and then start off on them once again. Alice seems to be a reincarnation of Renee, until we see them together on a photo. They might be sisters, but when we see the photo again, only one of them is in it.

The movie resists any one interpretation, and Lynch invites multiple interpretations by stuffing it full of quotations, from *Alice in Wonderland* and Edvard Munch's *The Scream* (in the final take) to *The Wizard of Oz* (1939). Arquette's transformation from brunette to blonde is a reference to Hollywood stereotypes of ideal female beauty, but the more individual elements we pick out, the less we succeed in forming a complete final picture of the movie. David Lynch refuses to narrate in a conventional cinematic manner and *Lost Highway* maintains its mysterious character to the very end. As Lynch said in an interview: "Many things in life are incomprehensible, but when movies are like that, people get upset."

HJK

6

DAVID LYNCH – CHAMPION OF MYSTERY From his underground debut *Eraserhead* (1974) through the movies *Blue Velvet* (1985), *Wild at Heart* (1990), *Lost Highway* (1997), and *Mulholland Drive* (2001) to TV series *Twin Peaks* (1989–1991), David Lynch has always made disturbing films about the dark side of the human soul – visually striking films with somber, distressing sound montages that maintain an essentially unresolved element of mystery. In 1999, he directed the surprisingly accessible and sensitive road movie *The Straight Story*. After years of working on the soundtracks of all his films, he made his first CD as a musician – *Crazy Clown Time* (2011).

4 Pete falls under Alice's spell at first sight, and after one night he is ready to do anything for her.

5 Mystery Man (Robert Blake): does he live in a house on the seafront – or in Fred's head?

6 Renee (Patricia Arquette in a double role): her house is as barren as a tomb, and her love for Fred has died.

7 "Pete (Balthazar Getty) meets gangster's wife Alice – a classic film noir siren." *Süddeutsche Zeitung*

"A kind of horror movie, a kind of thriller, but essentially a mystery. That's what it is. A mystery."

David Lynch in *Lynch on Lynch*

L.A. CONFIDENTIAL 🏆🏆

1997 – USA – 138 MIN. – POLICE FILM, DRAMA, NEO FILM NOIR
DIRECTOR CURTIS HANSON (*1945)
SCREENPLAY CURTIS HANSON, BRIAN HELGELAND based on the novel *L.A. CONFIDENTIAL*
by JAMES ELLROY **DIRECTOR OF PHOTOGRAPHY** DANTE SPINOTTI **EDITING** PETER HONESS
MUSIC JERRY GOLDSMITH **PRODUCTION** CURTIS HANSON, ARNON MILCHAN,
MICHAEL G. NATHANSON for REGENCY ENTERPRISES
STARRING RUSSELL CROWE (Bud White), KEVIN SPACEY (Jack Vincennes), GUY PEARCE
(Ed Exley), KIM BASINGER (Lynn Bracken), DANNY DEVITO (Sid Hudgeons),
JAMES CROMWELL (Dudley Smith), DAVID STRATHAIRN (Pierce Patchett), RON RIFKIN
(D. A. Ellis Loew), MATT MCCOY (Brett Chase), PAUL GUILFOYLE (Mickey Cohen)
ACADEMY AWARDS 1998 OSCARS for BEST SUPPORTING ACTRESS (Kim Basinger) and
BEST ADAPTED SCREENPLAY (Curtis Hanson, Brian Helgeland)

"Why did you become a cop? – I don't remember."

Sun, swimming pools, beautiful people: "Life is good in L.A., it's a paradise …" That Los Angeles only exists in commercials. In *L.A. Confidential* – set in the early '50s – the city looks quite different, and is a morass of crime and corruption. Three policemen try to combat this with varying dedication and varying motives. Ambitious young police academy graduate Ed Exley (Guy Pearce) is a champion of law and order, and his testimony against his colleagues in an internal police trial catapults him straight to the top of the station house hierarchy. Bud White (Russell Crowe) is a hardened cynic who is prepared to extract confessions with force, but cannot stand violence against women and Jack Vincennes (Kevin Spacey) is nothing more than a corrupt phony who uses his police job to get in with the entertainment

industry. He is advisor to the television series *Badge of Honor* and sets up stories for Sid Hudgeons (Danny DeVito), slimy reporter for the gossip magazine *Hush-Hush*.

Exley's first case is a spectacular bloodbath in the Nite Owl bar. Five lie dead in the bathroom, killed with a shotgun. Three black youths seen near the scene of the crime are swiftly arrested, and with his brilliant interrogation technique, Exley gets them to admit to having kidnapped and raped a Mexican girl. While White frees the victim and shoots her captor, the three suspects escape from police custody. Exley hunts them down and shoots them dead. He is hailed as a hero and awarded a medal, and it would seem that that is the end of the case. But it doesn't seem to quite add up, and Exley,

"It's striking to see how the elegance and lightness of touch in the atmosphere of *L.A. Confidential* seem both to derive from and influence the actors." *Cahiers du cinéma*

1 He may have deserved it much more for this film, but Russell Crowe didn't win an Oscar until 2001 for *Gladiator*.

2 Bud White (Russell Crowe) doesn't waste any time with the kidnapper of the Mexican girl.

3 Kim Basinger's Oscar for the part of Lynn Bracken brought her long-overdue universal acclaim.

4 A Christmas angel: Lynn out on business until late in the evening with her employer.

5 A few moments of melancholy apart, Bud White doesn't let the corruptness of the world get to him.

6 Brief moments of happiness: is there a future for Bud and Lynn's love?

7 Lynn the prostitute's little trick: she does herself up to look like 1940s glamour star Veronica Lake.

White, and Vincennes continue their investigations until they discover a conspiracy which reaches up into the highest echelons of police and city administration, involving drugs, blackmail, and a ring of porn traders.

L.A. Confidential is a reference to the first and perhaps most brazen American gossip magazine *Confidential* (1952–1957), and Hudgeons, the reporter played by Danny DeVito (who is also the offscreen narrator) is an alter ego of Robert Harrison, its infamous editor. Hudgeons gets his kicks from filth and sensationalism, and typifies the moral decadence that seems to have infected the entire city. The police make deals with criminals, the cops who uncover the conspiracy are far from blameless and even the naive greenhorn Exley loses his innocence in the course of the film.

Director Curtis Hanson conjures up the brooding atmosphere of the film noir crime movies of the '40s and '50s, but *L.A. Confidential* is far more than a throwback of a simple nostalgia trip. Cameraman Dante Spinotti shoots clear images free from any patina of age and avoids typical genre references like long shadows. The crime and the corruption seem even more devastating when told in pictures of a sunny, crisp Los Angeles winter. The plot is complex and difficult to follow on first viewing, but Hanson does not emphasize this so much as individual scenes which condense the city's amorality into striking images, like Vincennes saying he can no longer remember why he became a cop. Above all, the director focuses on his brilliant ensemble. Australians Russell Crowe and Guy Pearce, who were virtually unknown before the movie was made, make a great team with the amazing Kevin Spacey. Kim Basinger is a worthy Oscar winner as prostitute and Veronica Lake look-alike Lynn.

HJK

5

6

"When I gave Kevin Spacey the script, I said I think of two words: Dean Martin."

Curtis Hanson in *Sight and Sound*

8

JAMES ELLROY: L.A.'S RELENTLESS CHRONICLER His own life sounds like a crime story. James Ellroy was born in Los Angeles in 1948. When he was ten, his mother was the victim of a sex killer, a crime he works through in his 1996 memoir *My Dark Places*. The shock threw Ellroy completely off the rails: drugs, petty crime, and 50 arrests followed, and he came to writing relatively late. His first novel, *Brown's Requiem*, was published in 1981 and made into a movie with the same name in 1998. He then wrote a trilogy focusing on the figure of the policeman Lloyd Hopkins. The first of this series, *Blood on the Moon* (1984), was filmed in 1988 as *Cop*. Ellroy's masterpiece is the L.A. quartet, four novels on historical crimes from the period 1947 through 1960. Brian De Palma made the first volume in the series, *The Black Dahlia*, into a film with the same title in 2006. *L.A. Confidential* (1997) was based on the third volume in the series; it took director Curtis Hanson and coauthor Brian Helgeland a whole year and seven different versions to adapt this complex novel into a screenplay.

8 Tabloid reporter Sid Hudgeons (Danny DeVito) loves digging up other people's dirt.

9 Officer Vincennes (right) likes to take Hudgeons and a photographer along to his arrests.

10 Vincennes (Kevin Spacey) makes sure that first and foremost he's looking after number one.

11 Officer Ed Exley (Guy Pearce) earns praise from the press and from his boss Dudley Smith (James Cromwell, right).

9

MY BEST FRIEND'S WEDDING

997 – USA – 105 MIN. – ROMANTIC COMEDY
DIRECTOR   P. J. HOGAN (*1962)
SCREENPLAY RONALD BASS DIRECTOR OF PHOTOGRAPHY LASZLO KOVACS EDITING GARTH CRAVEN,
LISA FRUCHTMAN MUSIC JAMES NEWTON HOWARD PRODUCTION JERRY ZUCKER,
RONALD BASS for PREDAWN, TRISTAR PICTURES, COLUMBIA PICTURES
STARRING JULIA ROBERTS (Julianne Potter), DERMOT MULRONEY (Michael O'Neal),
CAMERON DIAZ (Kimberley "Kimmy" Wallace), RUPERT EVERETT (George Downes),
PHILIP BOSCO (Walter Wallace), M. EMMET WALSH (Joe O'Neal), RACHEL GRIFFITHS
(Samantha Newhouse), CARRIE PRESTON (Amanda Newhouse), SUSAN SULLIVAN
(Isabelle Wallace), CHRISTOPHER MASTERSON (Scott O'Neal)

"I am a busy girl. I've got exactly four days to break up a wedding, steal the bride's fella, and I haven't one clue how to do it."

Beautiful women can be amazingly devious. They can also sing amazingly out of tune. *My Best Friend's Wedding* is the story of a duel between two beautiful women. They fight over a man, of course. Julianne (Julia Roberts), a New York restaurant critic, is one of the two. She may be devious but she is also clueless when it comes to matters of the heart. In her high school days she dated Michael (Dermot Mulroney) and since then they have been the best of friends. She never realized that she was in love with him all along until he rings to say he has found the woman of his dreams and is going to marry her – in four days' time.

Kimmy (Cameron Diaz) is the name of the perfect creature who has come into his life, and her disastrous singing voice is her only blemish: winsome and beautiful, she even gives up her studies for Michael, who is now a sports reporter. She's rich too – her father is a Chicago businessman who owns the local baseball team and the sports channel on TV. Julianne travels to Chicago, officially as a bridesmaid, but unofficially to break up the party. The would-be wedding wrecker realizes right away how difficult her task will be when a radiant Kimmy greets her at the airport as the sister she never had and always wanted.

In his debut movie *Muriel's Wedding* (1994), the Australian director P. J. Hogan told the story of a plump young lady who aspires to social acceptance through marriage. *My Best Friend's Wedding* also plays with female stereotypes, but whereas *Muriel's Wedding* was sensitive and serious, the later movie is boisterous and full of very direct humor. Kimmy is blonde, young, and naïve, but her charm and spontaneity captivate everyone she meets. Julianne is a brunette, a little older, successful in her career and has both feet firmly on the ground. After several romantic disappointments, she

1 "In the classics of this subgenre like *It Happened One Night*, it was the man who caused the rumpus. But different tropes for different folks."
Time Magazine

2 Confounding expectations: doe-eyed Julia Roberts as the plotting and scheming Julianne Potter.

3 The embodiment of kindness: how could anyone want to harm Kimmy (Cameron Diaz)?

4 George (Rupert Everett) gives it plenty in Julianne's ridiculous game of make-believe.

5 "The film wallows enthusiastically in the brightly colored hues of the Hollywood musical and the magnificent luxury of Hollywood-style weddings."
Süddeutsche Zeitung

6 Sports reporter Michael (Dermot Mulroney) would be made if he married into Kimberley's father's business empire.

"Maybe there won't be marriage, maybe there won't be sex, but God there'll be dancing."

George in *My Best Friend's Wedding*

BURT BACHARACH The opening credits of *My Best Friend's Wedding* (1997) feature a quartet of girls singing "Wishin' and Hopin'," a clear indication of the movie's plot: only wishing and hoping can help to win someone's love. The movie is characterized by the catchy tunes of Burt Bacharach (*1928): "What the World Needs Now Is Love," playing on the radio of the delivery van rented by Julianne, and Kimmy's disastrous, meaningful karaoke song, "I Just Don't Know What To Do With Myself." Bacharach has written hundreds of songs, many performed by the singer Dionne Warwick. He has had 70 Top-40 hits in the USA and also composed film music, including the Oscar-nominated title song to *What's New Pussycat?* (1965). He won two Oscars, for Best Original Score and Best Original Song ("Raindrops Keep Fallin' on My Head") for *Butch Cassidy and the Sundance Kid* (1969), and a third for the title song for *Arthur* (1981). Bacharach had cameos in all three *Austin Powers* movies (1997, 1999, 2002), while his undying melodies remain as popular in film soundtracks as ever.

claims to be in control of her feelings. She devises a battle campaign against Kimmy, of which the most harmless element is the forced singing in a kara-oke bar. But even after the truly dreadful singing, Kimmy emerges from every encounter stronger than before. Her charm seems invincible, and Michael's love is not to be shaken. The plot is in the best tradition of old screwball com-edies like *The Philadelphia Story* (1940), and is cleverly constructed, with excellent acting and original dialogues. The movie also contains some de-lightful smaller episodes at the edge of the main action which sometimes hold up the plot, as when one of the bridesmaids at the wedding party gets stuck to a David statue made of ice – with her tongue in a prominent place.

Three boys breathe in helium instead of using it to fill balloons and sing John Denver's "Annie's Song" with Mickey Mouse voices. There is one scene of complete madness: Julianne's gay friend and boss George (Rupert Everett) comes for a day from New York, and she introduces him as her fiancé and he plays along. The party is in a lobster restaurant when he tells the hair-raising story of their first meeting, in which he manages somehow to involve the singer Dionne Warwick and promptly strikes up her song "I Say a Little Prayer." Soon the other guests join in and the waiters wave their lobster claw-shaped gloves in time.

HJK

BOOGIE NIGHTS

1997 – USA – 152 MIN. – DRAMA
DIRECTOR PAUL THOMAS ANDERSON (*1970)
SCREENPLAY PAUL THOMAS ANDERSON DIRECTOR OF PHOTOGRAPHY ROBERT ELSWIT
EDITING DYLAN TICHENOR MUSIC MICHAEL PENN PRODUCTION JOHN LYONS, LLOYD LEVIN,
PAUL THOMAS ANDERSON, JOANNE SELLAR for GHOULARDI (for NEW LINE CINEMA)
STARRING MARK WAHLBERG (Eddie Adams / Dirk Diggler), JULIANNE MOORE
(Amber Waves), BURT REYNOLDS (Jack Horner), DON CHEADLE (Buck Swope),
PHILIP SEYMOUR HOFFMAN (Scotty), JOHN C. REILLY (Reed Rotchild), HEATHER GRAHAM
(Rollergirl), WILLIAM H. MACY (Little Bill), NICOLE PARKER (Becky Barnett),
ALFRED MOLINA (Rahad Jackson)

"Everyone's blessed with one special thing."

His fans waited in vain: for years, Abel Ferrara (*Driller Killer*, 1979; *Bad Lieutenant*, 1992), iconoclast and untiring rebel of the US movie scene, invited the wildest speculations by declaring that he was going to make a film about the life of porn star legend John C. Holmes. In the end Paul Thomas Anderson got there before him. His effervescent, epic portrayal of the rise and fall of a porn star and his clique in San Fernando Valley, California, is however only loosely based on the biography of the world's most famous male porn star. Anderson was only 27 when *Boogie Nights* was made, but he succeeded in producing what is perhaps the definitive movie about the American sex film industry of the '70s and '80s, despite – or perhaps because – of conscious omissions. In *Boogie Nights* we see nothing of its Mafia structure or the organized exploitation of women that is endemic in the business. Instead, Anderson depicts a tender, sympathetic, almost romanticized portrait of a surrogate family. In *Hard Eight* (1996), the melodrama that marked his debut as a director, Anderson's solitary gambling figures sought comfort by bonding together as a replacement family, and *Magnolia* (1999), his Berlin Festival winner, also underlines the strength and uniqueness of family ties.

    Boogie Nights was not just a breakthrough for its young director, but also for its main actor. Previously known as a model for Calvin Klein underwear and as white bad boy rapper Marky Mark, Mark Wahlberg had already found a measure of success in small supporting roles, but here he conclusively proved his potential as a character actor. His character Eddie Adams is the focal point of the movie: a boy from the 'burbs who works as a bouncer in a disco, convinced that he was born both for and with greater things. His impressive penis length of 32 centimeters gets him noticed by porno producer Jack Horner, who takes him under his fatherly wing. Burt Reynolds, who made a great comeback with this role, plays Horner with wonderful coolness; he is a man with a vision. He wants to make porn films that are so entertaining and gripping that people will stay in the cinema even after they have been sexually satisfied to find out what happens next. He works on this with his new superstar Eddie under the name Dirk Diggler, with his porn muse Amber (Julianne Moore), and with the many other crew members who hang around his fashionable villa. The porn star Dirk Diggler quickly learns to take for granted all the luxurious idols of the "American way of life" which as high school dropout Eddie he could only worship on posters in his room: fast cars, hot dates, cool clothes, endless pool parties, cocktails, and coke brought to him on a tray. But in the early '80s the idyll races to a crash as the classic porn movie is replaced by videos made quickly and cheaply with anonymous

3

1 Sex sells: porn film director Jack Horner (Burt Reynolds) gambles with the secret fantasies of his viewers.

2 Group portrait with porn star: his colleagues come to be a substitute family for high school dropout and runaway Eddie Adams (Mark Wahlberg).

3 In the porn industry people have seen just about everything. But Eddie's natural talent surprises even the oldest hands.

amateurs lolling about in front of the cameras. The big stars' careers are over and the porn cinemas close. Dirk's drug consumption spirals out of control, and he is even involved in an armed robbery on a millionaire – this is one of the episodes taken from the true story of John Holmes.

Boogie Nights is a hedonistic film. It revels in the sounds of the '70s and the well-proportioned California bodies. It is provocative and politically incorrect, but as a movie it exploits neither its actors nor its theme for cheap thrills.

Dirk Diggler's greatest asset is only seen once in the final shot. This seriousness made the tragicomic melodrama a hit even in prudish America. In its wake, the cable channel HBO produced *Rated X* (2000) a mainstream film on the brothers Jim and Artie Mitchell, who began a porn revolution in the '70s with the classic movies *Behind the Green Door* (1972) and *Inside Marilyn Chambers* (1975).

AK

"It kind of got me down, watching six hours of solid fucking. You really don't have any desire to go home and kiss your girlfriend."

Paul Thomas Anderson in *Sight and Sound*

4   A star is born! With his multifaceted and sensitive portrayal ex-rapper Mark Wahlberg finally achieved his transformation into actor.

5   Horner's girlfriend Amber (Julianne Moore) leads a double life. Fascinated and tempted by luxury, drugs, and sex, she is fighting a losing battle for custody of her child…

4

5

6

6   With its disco soundtrack and garish costumes, *Boogie Nights* celebrates the hedonistic lifestyle of the 1970s.

7   Heather Graham as Rollergirl, an artificial figure she created herself. We don't find out her real name, which she disowns as she does her past, until the end of the film.

"Razor-sharp dialogue, interlocking destinies splendidly contrived, and a blend of humor and melancholy: this film might have turned out uniform gray. In fact, it's wonderful. You emerge with the conviction that a glimpse of paradise, a moment of grace has been vouchsafed." *Le nouvel observateur*

PHILIP SEYMOUR HOFFMAN   Although he claims to have become a professional actor only to impress a girl, Philip Seymour Hoffman, born in 1967 in Fairport, New York, seldom gets to play the leading man. With his massive build, dull complexion, and unruly strawberry-blond hair, he doesn't fit the image of the typical film hunk at all – and this probably gets him more exciting roles, like the drag queen in *Flawless* (1999), cursed with a homophobic neighbor played by Robert De Niro, or the snobbish Freddie in the film adaptation of Patricia Highsmith's novel *The Talented Mr. Ripley* (1999). Not that Hoffman's characters are devoid of romantic impulses: it's hard to think of any movie moment of the late '90s as touching as the scene in *Boogie Nights* (1997) when, in an ill-fitting tank top, he asks Mark Wahlberg if he can kiss him on the mouth. What must surely be his best role, which deservedly won him an Oscar, was as writer Truman Capote in Bennett Miller's biopic *Capote* (2004). In 2011, the same director cast the less than sporty-looking Hoffman in an odd bit part as a baseball trainer in *Moneyball*. He was better suited to the role of political advisor in George Clooney's thriller *The Ides of March* (2011).

LIFE IS BEAUTIFUL ♚♚♚
LA VITA È BELLA

997/1998 – ITALY – 122 (124) MIN. – TRAGICOMEDY
DIRECTOR ROBERTO BENIGNI (*1952)
SCREENPLAY VINCENZO CERAMI, ROBERTO BENIGNI DIRECTOR OF PHOTOGRAPHY TONINO DELLI COLLI
EDITING SIMONA PAGGI MUSIC NICOLA PIOVANI PRODUCTION ELDA FERRI, GIANLUIGI BRASCHI
for MELAMPO CINEMATOGRAFICA, CECCHI GORI GROUP
STARRING ROBERTO BENIGNI (Guido), NICOLETTA BRASCHI (Dora), GIORGIO CANTARINI
(Giosuè), GIUSTINO DURANO (Uncle), SERGIO BUSTRIC (Ferruccio), MARISA PAREDES
(Dora's mother), HORST BUCHHOLZ (Dr. Lessing), LYDIA ALFONSI (Guicciardini),
GIULIANA LOJODICE (Schoolteacher), AMERIGO FONTANI (Rodolfo)
ACADEMY AWARDS 1999 OSCARS for BEST FOREIGN LANGUAGE FILM,
BEST ACTOR (Roberto Benigni), BEST MUSIC (Nicola Piovani)
FF CANNES 1998 GRAND JURY PRIZE (Roberto Benigni)

"Buongiorno, Principessa!"

Telling stories about the indescribable without trivializing is a tall order. So is defending the right to liberating laughter in the face of utter inhumanity without being guilty of cynicism. Roberto Benigni got round the issue by telling a fairy tale, in the form of the story of a father who lands in the hell of a German concentration camp with his son.

Fairy-tale circumstances bring the happy-go-lucky Italian Jew Guido (Roberto Benigni) to Arezzo in the '30s to open a bookshop. On his way he meets Dora (Nicoletta Braschi) his "Princess," who literally falls into his arms from the sky. As Dora is already promised to another, whom she does not love, Guido feels obliged to abduct her from her own engagement party – a further fairy-tale motif.

Up to this point, the film has been dominated by the tricks and clowning of its hero, but all at once the amusing, bubbly style of the story becomes pointed for the first time: Guido and his Princess ride out of the hall on a horse under the astonished eyes of the guests, but their steed has been painted green by an unknown hand. The skull and crossbones painted on its flanks are accompanied by anti-Semitic slogans.

Undeterred by these first ominous signs, the two settle down and start a family. In the next scene their son Giosuè (Giorgio Cantarini) is already five years old and he is helping his father in the bookshop. All the books are half price, and the shop is obviously about to close. The town has changed, there are soldiers everywhere and little Giosuè, who can barely read, makes out the words "Out of bounds to dogs and Jews" on a sign. As usual his father saves the situation with a joke: after all, no one can stop people refusing entry to kangaroos and Frenchmen and tomorrow the shop will be closed even to spiders and Visigoths. The following day is Giosuè's birthday, but Dora comes home to find her family gone. Giosuè and his father are already on their way to a concentration camp. Dora hurries to the station and demands to be put in the train too, only to be separated from her husband and child again on arrival.

To protect the boy from the cruel reality surrounding them, Guido pretends that all the people are there to take part in a competition, whose winner will get a real tank to take home. In this way he helps his son to survive both the psychological and physical brutality of life in the camp.

In Italy La vita è bella was a smash hit, but hotly debated by critics of all political persuasions. Many people outside Italy were also uncertain as to whether it was right to laugh at a concentration camp story, and wondered whether Benigni was toning down the historical facts too much. This question arises from a fundamental misunderstanding. Whatever critics said, the movie can by no means be divided into a funny first part and a tragic second part. Benigni subtly prepares us from the very beginning for the points he plans to make in the course of the plot. His aim is not to give an accurate presentation of the Holocaust as a historical event, and so he tells us nothing about the motives of the perpetrators, who are presented either as complete

2

1 Lies in times of need: to protect him from the horror of the Nazis, bookseller Guido (Roberto Benigni) invents imaginative stories for his son Giosuè (Giorgio Cantarini).

2 Pitting humor and joie de vivre against the stupidity of inhuman brutes: Guido abducts his Principessa from her own wedding. Fascists have daubed his uncle's horse with anti-Semitic slogans.

3 Little Giosuè thinks that life in the concentration camp is a game.

4 The young family's happiness will soon be overshadowed by the first signs of war. Many shops in Arezzo are now "closed to Jews."

5 Torn between fear and hope: Dora (Nicoletta Braschi) voluntarily followed her husband and child to the concentration camp.

3

ordinary German citizens or as ridiculous figures who can do nothing but shout. There is only one scene where we can vaguely make out a mountain of corpses in the morning mist and that brief glance into hell shows us dimensions of cruelty that the movie doesn't even attempt to sound out. Its theme instead is the use of the imagination as a survival strategy in the midst of inhumanity. Benigni was well aware that he was walking the razor's edge in addressing that issue. Guido befriends the German Dr. Lessing (Horst Buchholz, who gives the best performance next to Benigni) whom he meets again in his post as camp medic. Lessing has gone insane in the face of the Nazis' incomprehensible cruelty; his madness is a protective wall against brutal reality and his own responsibility. *Life Is Beautiful* is a fairy tale that goes beyond tragedy and comedy – it also goes beyond good and evil. SH

ROBERTO BENIGNI Actor, comedian, director, and scriptwriter Roberto Benigni was born in 1952 in the Tuscan village of Misericordia. The son of a railway worker, he grew up in poor conditions. In the early '70s, Benigni started out on his career with alternative theater and one-man shows. Two roles in the films of the American independent director Jim Jarmusch brought him international recognition: he speaks pidgin English as a wheeler-dealer jailbreaker in the comedy *Down by Law* (1986) and then, in *Night on Earth* (1990), he plays a taxi driver making his confession to a passenger – a priest – who promptly suffers a heart attack and dies. In 1990, Benigni also starred in the last film made by the Italian director Federico Fellini, *The Voice of the Moon (La voce della luna)*. As well as his own movies – *Johnny Stecchino* (*Johnny Toothpick*, 1991), *Pinocchio* (2002), and *The Tiger and the Snow* (*La tigre e la neve*, 2005) – Benigni is a skilled self-publicist, a talent much in evidence in his spectacular appearance at the 1999 Oscars ceremony. Benigni married the actress Nicoletta Braschi in 1991.

"*Life Is Beautiful* relates a dream, while at the same time warning us of the danger of dreaming."
epd Film

6   Laughter in the face of terror: even in moments of the most extreme danger Guido plays the part of the joker and in doing so ultimately saves his son's life.

7   Director and leading man Roberto Benigni plays the role of his career in his own film, for which he won the most prestigious awards at Hollywood and Cannes.

6

GATTACA

1997 – USA – 112 MIN. – SCIENCE FICTION
DIRECTOR ANDREW NICCOL (*1964)
SCREENPLAY ANDREW NICCOL DIRECTOR OF PHOTOGRAPHY SLAWOMIR IDZIAK EDITING LISA ZENO CHURGIN
MUSIC MICHAEL NYMAN PRODUCTION DANNY DEVITO, MICHAEL SHAMBERG, STACEY SHER for
JERSEY FILMS
STARRING ETHAN HAWKE (Vincent/Jerome), UMA THURMAN (Irene Cassini), ALAN ARKIN
(Det. Hugo), JUDE LAW (Jerome Eugene Morrow), LOREN DEAN (Anton), GORE VIDAL
(Director Joseph), ERNEST BORGNINE (Caesar), BLAIR UNDERWOOD (Geneticist),
XANDER BERKELEY (Lamar), ELIAS KOTEAS (Antonio)

> ## "I not only think that we will temper Mother Nature.
> ## I think Mother wants us to."

A brave new world? Perhaps. *Gattaca*'s director, New Zealander Andrew Niccol, made television commercials for ten years before turning to full-length movies, and the vision he gives of the future is a world where expectant parents no longer have to worry about their offspring's health. Thanks to the genetic testing of every fertilized egg, they know not only the sex, eye and hair color of their baby, but also its present and future state of health, and even its likely life expectancy. Death is thus a factor before the baby's birth and the selection of a genetic elite has become part of everyday life. No system is perfect however, and alongside the designer babies there are still those who were not conceived in a test tube but quite conventionally on the backseat of a Cadillac. Babies like Vincent (Ethan Hawke). Seconds after his birth, a DNA test showed with 99% certainty that he had a weak heart and was unlikely to survive beyond the age of 32. With genes like his, the state decides not to invest in his education, his health, or his life. The likes of Vincent are never allowed to become an astronaut, no matter how much they dream of conquering outer space. Vincent ends up cleaning the bathrooms in the AIDS and cancer-free futuristic paradise of the space travel company Gattaca.

Like most science fiction movies, *Gattaca* tells of mankind's urge to push back the frontiers of space exploration and conquer faraway planets. But rather than vast expanses of space, the opening sequence shows us microscopic particles like treacherous beard stubble, skin cells, and eyelashes. Every morning Vincent scrubs and washes his body until it hurts. Despite all the obstacles and discrimination, he has managed to become a top engineer at Gattaca. To continue to do this he has to destroy all traces of his identity every day, and use borrowed blood, urine, and hair samples to pretend he has the genetic makeup of Jerome (Jude Law), an Olympic swimmer who was paralyzed in an accident and suffers from depression. Their identity swap seems to work and Vincent is eventually chosen for a mission to outer space. His dreams are about to be fulfilled and the spacecraft is on the point of departure when a murder interrupts Gattaca's customary calm and suddenly the company is swarming with police.

The movie is an appeal for chance instead of planning and for open-mindedness rather than clinical diagnoses. When Vincent's girlfriend Irene (Uma Thurman) and the company's doctor decide not to betray his secret, emotions win over sterility and individuality triumphs over conformity. The

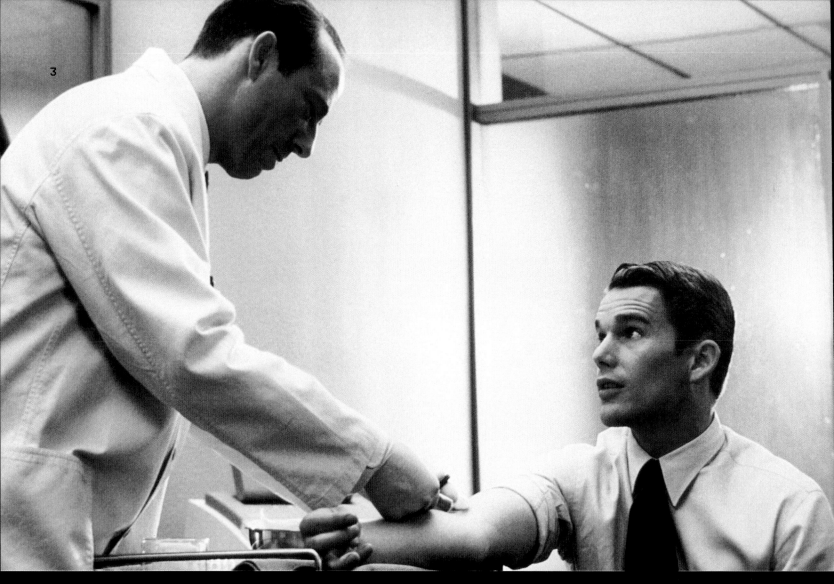

2

3

4

"Niccol provides us with the one thing sci-fi films are almost always lacking: interesting characters."

Libération

warning tone of the film is reminiscent of other futuristic detective classics such as *1984* (1956) and *Fahrenheit 451* (1966), from whose super-cool optics it also takes its aesthetic reference points. The plot unfolds, as a sub-title tells us, in "the not-too-distant future," but the dark suits and closely tailored outfits are very much in the style of the '40s and the minimalist architecture is '60s. *Gattaca* has a retro charm whose rigorous restraint is completely at odds with typical '90s action movies and their ever bigger, ever brighter, and ever louder special effects that minimize plot and maximize spectacular computer-generated pictures. In contrast to all of that, *Gattaca* depends entirely on calculated coolness and tells its story with such under-statement that many allusions and hints, like the significance of the charac-ters' names, are easily missed. Vincent is a subversive rebel who beats state surveillance with his own resources: his surname is Freeman. Jerome's middle name is Eugene, which comes from the Greek word *Eugenik* meaning the science of selective breeding, which is the main theme of the movie; and Irene's surname is Cassini, like the Franco-Italian astronomer Jean Domi-nique Cassini, who had a life-long fascination with Saturn – just like Vincent.

AK

UMA THURMAN Anyone who grows up with the name of a Hindu goddess is likely to lead an eventful life. Uma Thurman does not stand out from other American actresses solely on account of her willowy height of 5 ft 11 in (1.8 m) or her elegantly translucent beauty, reminiscent of screen goddesses like Greta Garbo and Lauren Bacall. She also happens to be one of the most intelligent actresses currently on the scene. In 1988, she made her screen breakthrough with Stephen Frears's film of the Choderlos de Laclos novel *Dangerous Liaisons;* John Malkovich, her partner in the movie, described her as having "Jayne Mansfield's body and a horrifying great brain." She has played colorful parts, ranging from a human gift in *Mad Dog and Glory* (1993), a dance-mad gangster's wife in *Pulp Fiction* (1994), Poison Ivy in *Batman & Robin* (1996), and a Swedish sex bomb in *The Producers* (2005) to the dumped superheroine intent on revenge in *My Super Ex-Girlfriend* (2006). She has been immortalized, however, through her role as the silent, tenacious assassin in Quentin Tarantino's two *Kill Bill* movies (2003, 2004).

1 The irony of casting: it just had to be ladies' heart-throb and cinema pinup Ethan Hawke who acted the part of Vincent, branded an outsider because of his genetic makeup.

2 Irene (Uma Thurman) doesn't know what to make of her colleague Jerome – but she suspects that she will fall in love with him.

3 The brave new world of genetic design is in reality a surveillance state, where blood tests are the order of the day.

4 Her intelligence, loyalty, and not least her supercool self-controlled elegance make Irene the perfect employee for the Gattaca group.

5 Vincent tries to beat the system with a fake heart-beat recording. Only those who are fit are selected for missions in outer space.

GOOD WILL HUNTING ♟♟

1997 – USA – 126 MIN. – DRAMA
DIRECTOR GUS VAN SANT (*1952)
SCREENPLAY MATT DAMON, BEN AFFLECK **DIRECTOR OF PHOTOGRAPHY** JEAN–YVES ESCOFFIER
EDITING PIETRO SCALIA **MUSIC** DANNY ELFMAN, JEFFREY KIMBALL
PRODUCTION LAWRENCE BENDER, KEVIN SMITH, SCOTT MOSIER for BE GENTLEMEN,
A BAND APART (for MIRAMAX)
STARRING ROBIN WILLIAMS (Sean Maguire), MATT DAMON (Will Hunting), BEN AFFLECK
(Chuckie), MINNIE DRIVER (Skylar), STELLAN SKARSGÅRD (Gerald Lambeau),
COLE HAUSER (Billy), CASEY AFFLECK (Morgan), JOHN MIGHTON (Tom),
RACHEL MAJOROWSKI (Krystyn), COLLEEN MCCAULEY (Cathy)
ACADEMY AWARDS 1998 OSCARS for BEST ORIGINAL SCREENPLAY (Matt Damon, Ben Affleck)
and BEST SUPPORTING ACTOR (Robin Williams)

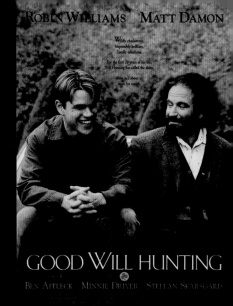

"Real loss is only possible when you love something more than you love yourself."

Matt Damon and Ben Affleck love throwing red herrings to journalists when asked in interviews for the secret of their successful collaboration: "We're lovers" is the invariable reply. The two boyhood friends, who grew up just a few houses away from each other, have every reason to joke about things. *Good Will Hunting* was received enthusiastically by critics and fans alike. Robin Williams was by far the movie's biggest star, but it was still basically their movie, despite the controlling hand of cult director Gus Van Sant *(Drugstore Cowboy, My Own Private Idaho)* and the fact that cinema tycoons Bob and Harvey Weinstein saved the movie by buying the rights for their company Miramax. The two young shooting stars do more than play main parts, they also wrote the screenplay – and it took Bob and Harvey Weinstein to recognize the potential of this atmospherically intense drama about a rebellious but emotionally isolated genius.

Matt Damon, who himself studied at Harvard and left the elite university shortly before graduating, plays Will Hunting, a cleaner at MIT. The cleaning job is one of his probation orders, for Will can't keep out of trouble. Whenever the opportunity for a fight or a quick buck presents itself, he's there. He spends almost as much time in the young offenders' center as he does in his run-down apartment in the center of Boston.

But Will is a many-sided character. When Professor Lambeau (Stellan Skarsgård) discovers the answer to a difficult math problem on the board and none of his students will own up to having solved it, he sets out to find the mysterious mathematical genius – and finds him of all places in the boy who cleans the institute's floors. Lambeau saves Will from another stay in prison by taking him under his wing and making sure he goes to the therapy sessions the court has decreed with an old friend from his student days, psychologist Sean Maguire (Robin Williams). While Will and Lambeau work together in euphoric harmony on complicated mathematical equations, Maguire has his work cut out breaking through Will's emotional defenses. Williams plays the widowed Maguire without pathos, and shows him to be an affectionate yet saddened man with the smallest of gestures. Befriending his stubborn patient is a lengthy process, but Maguire quickly realizes

that behind Will's rebellious and angry façade an unhappy and vulnerable boy is hiding.

As so often in Hollywood, success didn't arrive over night, not just in the movie but in real life as well. Damon and Affleck wrote the screenplay years previously on a scriptwriting course and several Hollywood studios had even shown an interest in it. Damon and Affleck's condition however was that they should both star in the movie, and as they were completely unknown at the time, none of the studios accepted. That changed instantly with Damon's great success in the main role of Francis Ford Coppola's film of the Grisham novel *The Rainmaker* (1997).

Miramax finally bought the rights to *Good Will Hunting* after its authors took the advice of their experienced colleagues Rob Reiner, Terrence Malick, and William Goldman, cutting the suspense element and adding love interest to the plot. In the revised version, Will, the social outsider, falls in love with Skylar (Minnie Driver) a British medical student who is the daughter of a respectable family. The emotional conflict which dominates Will's life is intensified by the love Skylar offers him and which he finds almost impossible to accept. Maguire gives him the courage to let his cynical, smart-aleck mask fall and face his feelings – even if this means that the world will have to do without the next Albert Einstein. AK

4

5

"A heart-warming, credible piece of cinema full of human impressions and sparkling wordplay." *Neue Zürcher Zeitung*

MATT DAMON Born in Cambridge, Massachusetts, in 1970, Matt Damon's breakthrough was the starring role in Francis Ford Coppola's adaptation of John Grisham's legal bestseller *The Rainmaker* (1997), in which he played a young, inexperienced, but indomitable lawyer who fights a dishonest insurance company. Everything Damon has done in Hollywood since has been a success. With his boyish charm and understated good looks, he seems predestined to play the sensitive heroes of American cinema. He received enthusiastic reviews for the title role in Steven Spielberg's *Saving Private Ryan* (1998) and fascinated critics with the contrast between his innocent boyish face and cynical indifference as the cold-blooded murderer in the film of Patricia Highsmith's novel *The Talented Mr. Ripley* (1999). Damon's subsequent appearances have included the *Bourne* and *Ocean's* series. His filmography also reveals extremely interesting roles in the films of quite a few famous directors. As well as Steven Spielberg, they include Terry Gilliam (*The Brothers Grimm*, 2005) and Clint Eastwood (*Invictus*, 2009). The Coen brothers gave the still-boyish charmer a wonderfully ironic role as Texas Ranger LaBoeuf in *True Grit* (2010).

1 Hollywood clown Robin Williams is brilliant in his role as psychologist Sean Maguire, acting with an earnestness that is not merely by chance reminiscent of Peter Weir's *Dead Poets' Society* (1988).

2 Knowledge as power? All the knowledge he has picked up from books has given Will (Matt Damon) a feeling of superiority – but hasn't brought him happiness.

3 Medical student Skylar (Minnie Driver) embodies

4 Professor Lambeau (Stellan Skarsgård) discovered Will's genius. But how honorable are his motives?

5 Shortly before a brawl: Will is still sitting peacefully with his mates (Ben Affleck, right) watching a baseball game.

MEN IN BLACK 🏆

1997 – USA – 98 MIN. – SCIENCE FICTION, COMEDY
DIRECTOR BARRY SONNENFELD (*1953)
SCREENPLAY ED SOLOMON, based on a MALIBU comic by LOWELL CUNNINGHAM
DIRECTOR OF PHOTOGRAPHY DON PETERMAN **EDITING** JIM MILLER **MUSIC** DANNY ELFMAN
PRODUCTION WALTER F. PARKES, LAURIE MACDONALD for AMBLIN ENTERTAINMENT,
COLUMBIA PICTURES
STARRING TOMMY LEE JONES (K), WILL SMITH (J), LINDA FIORENTINO (Laurel),
VINCENT D'ONOFRIO (Edgar), RIP TORN (Zed), TONY SHALHOUB (Jeebs),
SIOBHAN FALLON (Beatrice), MIKE NUSSBAUM (Gentle Rosenberg), JON GRIES
(Van Driver), SERGIO CALDERÓN (José)
ACADEMY AWARDS 1998 OSCAR for BEST MAKEUP (David LeRoy Anderson, Rick Baker)

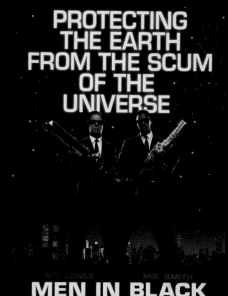

PROTECTING
THE EARTH
FROM THE SCUM
OF THE
UNIVERSE

MEN IN BLACK

JULY 2

"There are approximately 1500 aliens on the planet, most of them right here in Manhattan."

Sylvester Stallone is an alien. Elvis isn't dead, he's just gone home. And every word you read in the *National Enquirer* is true. If you've ever had the feeling that you have to deal with aliens in your terrestrial life, this movie is the confirmation you've long been waiting for: "Sometimes there are up to 1500 aliens on earth, most of them here in Manhattan." Two things are necessary to ensure that humans and aliens can coexist peacefully: cover-up jobs and ceaseless vigilance. The "Men in Black" are responsible for both of these as black-clad agents from the INS, Division 6. They do everything to stop the humans from realizing that they are not alone on their blue planet, and make sure that the guests from outer space don't step out of line. At an interstellar airport the MiB supervise the arrival of creatures from far-off planets. They inspect their luggage and grant them entry permits to limited areas of New York and the world. If they try to travel to other parts, the agents fetch them back or shoot them dead. Alien civil rights are fairly low down on the agenda.

We see an example of this on the Mexican border. Police hold up a dilap-idated truck full of illegal immigrants from the neighboring Latin American country. State officials muscle in on their local colleagues: "Man in Black" K (Tommy Lee Jones) and a colleague take over and release all the refugees except one – he comes from further afield than Mexico. Under his poncho he is hiding a slimy body and tentacles, and the blue ooze in his veins sprays out all over one of the sheriffs when K summarily blows the creature up with a "de-atomizer." With a gadget known as a "neuralizer" which looks like a pen with a light instead of a nib, the agent then wipes all trace of the incident from the sheriff's memory.

In New York another policeman is chasing someone right through Manhattan, without realizing of course that he is an alien. Cop James Darrel Edwards (Will Smith) stays hot on the criminal's heels even when he runs up the wall of the Guggenheim museum like a fly. James stops him on the roof, but the runaway avoids capture by throwing himself to his death. This attracts K's attention to James. And since the cheeky cop often clashes with the authorities, he's a good candidate to be K's new partner. Edwards passes an absurd test in which he is the only competitor and is taken on. The ends of his fingers are cauterized to stop him leaving any fingerprints.

3

"Mind you, the best thing is the two stars Will Smith and Tommy Lee Jones, whose humor is so bone-dry that they can deliver lines and keep their cool, where others would let the lines die on their lips." *Süddeutsche Zeitung*

He is fitted up with the black uniform and given dark glasses and a new name. Henceforth he is J, reduced like his colleagues to a single letter of the alphabet. Anonymity is their name, silence their language.

J and K's very first assignment is big. An alien bug has landed secretly on earth, a dangerous species that would never have been given an entry permit in the first place. The bug has killed Farmer Edgar (Vincent D'Onofrio), sucked out his entrails and put on his skin. He manages – more or less – to pass himself off as a human and is looking for the Galaxis, a valuable jewel worn by the son of the Aquilians' ruler who is living unobtrusively on earth disguised as a jeweler. K and J's assignment becomes really difficult when

the Aquilians decide they want the jewel back. If they don't get it, they're going to destroy the world. The time limit is a stellar week – a mere 60 earth minutes!

Men in Black is an almighty parody. Goggle-eyed, slimy aliens like the monsters in '50s movies, secret government organizations reminiscent of the television series *The Man From U. N. C. L. E.* (1964–1968) and the uncanny modern mystery series *The X Files* (1993–2002), the *Blues Brothers'* black gear, (1980) and *Casablanca*'s escape scenario (1942) – it's all there. Director Barry Sonnenfeld creates a funny, exciting mix from these quotations, and then goes a step further and adds historical dates and real events: the steel

1   They have to make sure they keep their shades on, otherwise the neuralizer would wipe the memories of the "Men in Black" as well.

2   Edwards (Will Smith, left) wins through in the aptitude test, against candidates who follow the regulations.

3   "Here come the Men in Black" – the song performed by Will Smith in the film also became a hit.

4   Perfectly disguised among humankind: son of the ruler of the Aquilians.

5   Dry humor and futuristic mega-weapons were the secret of *Men in Black*'s success.

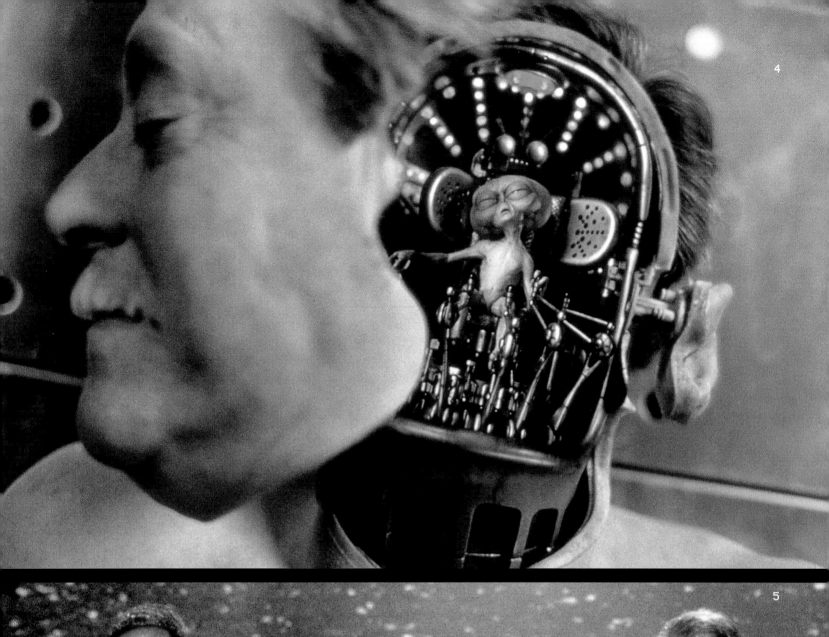

4

5

6　Useful aliens: at MiB headquarters they dish out coffee along with cheeky comments.

7　Disguised as a Mexican: an extraterrestrial immigrant tries to get into the USA, but he can't fool K.

8　Aliens bring some strange luggage with them on their trip to earth.

remains of the 1964 world's fair in Queens are nothing less than the remnants of a spaceship. The New York powercuts of 1977 were caused by … aliens. Microwaves, zippers, and silicon implants were all invented somewhere in another galaxy, and confiscated from alien tourists when they arrived on earth. Elvis lives. We learn that we are surrounded by aliens – not only are Sylvester Stallone and the Republican politician Newt Gingrich aliens, but so is singer Dionne Warwick. Sonnenfeld and his scriptwriter Ed Solomon take the game with facts and outrageous UFO fantasies to the extreme when the headlines of a gossip magazine read: "Aliens stole my husband's skin!" – tabloids are an important source of information for the MiB.

Men in Black is also a buddy movie. Rapper Will Smith – best known as an actor for the television series The Fresh Prince of Bel-Air (1990–96) – is seen here in his first main role as an energetic, go-getting action character. Tommy Lee Jones is the wise old-timer experienced in the alien business, and the two of them make an irresistible team. With stoicism and laconic humor, they go about their daily alien work; their immaculate black suits are spattered with one burst of slime after another. K is eaten alive by an alien

and J helps deliver an alien baby. Although it often conjures up the charm of old B features, Men in Black is actually a huge modern production with a 100 million dollar budget and effects by George Lucas's Industrial Light and Magic company. Rick Baker (Gremlins), perhaps Hollywood's most brilliant monster creator, made the aliens. His creativity was allowed free rein: one bug-eyed alien in human form grows a new head every time it is shot off; a quartet of curious beings – naked pipsqueaks on two legs – live by the coffee machine in the MiB headquarters and make sarcastic wisecracks; a tiny creature with enormous eyes operates a huge machine from a control tower – the machine is a human body and the control tower is its head. Baker won a well-deserved Oscar for the makeup effects.

The efforts were well rewarded, as the production was by far the most successful movie of 1997. It had millions of viewers in Europe and was a box-office smash in the USA where it earned over 250 million dollars. In the same year a television series started with the alien hunters as cartoon figures. In 2002, Men in Black 2 premiered in theaters, and the third film in the series, Men in Black 3, followed ten years later.　　　　　　　　　　　　　　　H JK

7

"In the best sci-fi movie tradition, *Men in Black* gets straight to the point in the very first scene." *epd Film*

BARRY SONNENFELD With comic adaptations *The Addams Family* (1991) and *Men in Black* (1997, 2002, 2012), the Hollywood novel *Get Shorty* (1995), and the television series *Wild Wild West* (1999) Barry Sonnenfeld has made a name for himself as a specialist in pop culture. He studied politics and then film and began his career as a cameraman, first of all for documentaries. He made his first feature film *Blood Simple* (1983) for his former classmates the Coen brothers, and worked with them on two more movies, *Raising Arizona* (1987) and *Miller's Crossing* (1990). Sonnenfeld made his directorial debut in 1991 with the first Addams Family film. He was asked to direct *Forrest Gump* (1994) and refused; Robert Zemeckis took over and the film won six Oscars. But Sonnenfeld's disappointment didn't last long. He filmed the Elmore Leonard adaptation *Get Shorty*, which was a huge hit and became his ticket to the upper echelons of Hollywood.

CONSPIRACY THEORY

1997 – USA – 135 MIN. – THRILLER
DIRECTOR RICHARD DONNER (*1939)
SCREENPLAY BRIAN HELGELAND DIRECTOR OF PHOTOGRAPHY JOHN SCHWARTZMAN EDITING KEVIN STITT,
FRANK J. URIOSTE MUSIC CARTER BURWELL PRODUCTION JOEL SILVER, RICHARD DONNER
for SILVER PICTURES, SHULER-DONNER PRODUCTIONS
STARRING MEL GIBSON (Jerry Fletcher), JULIA ROBERTS (Alice Sutton), PATRICK STEWART
(Dr. Jonas), CYLK COZART (Agent Lowry), STEVE KAHAN (Wilson), TERRY ALEXANDER
(Flip), ALEX MCARTHUR (Cynic), BRIAN J. WILLIAMS (Clarke), ROD MCLACHLAN (Guard),
GEORGE AGUILAR (Piper)

"A good conspiracy is unprovable."

Jerry Fletcher (Mel Gibson) is a man on a mission – he's got to let people know. Fluoride is added to the water to rob them of their willpower. The Vietnam War happened because Howard Hughes lost a bet against Aristotle Onassis. Earthquakes are triggered from space and one will soon kill the President of the US. Fletcher, a New York cab driver, shares discoveries like these with his passengers. He also publishes them in his newspaper "Conspiracy Theory," which only has five subscribers. He has uncovered a gigantic conspiracy, and "they" are behind it all. He doesn't know exactly who "they" are, but he does know that they are out to get him. That's why he lives in a fortress and places an empty beer bottle on the door handle as an early warning system against intruders.

Fletcher feels misunderstood and lonely. Like the hero of J. D. Salinger's *Catcher in the Rye*, a book he compulsively buys wherever he sees it, he can't find anyone who understands him. He trusts no one, with the sole exception of Alice Sutton (Julia Roberts), who is an employee of the Justice Department.

Jerry regularly tells her his latest revelations. He secretly watches her in her apartment, and he is in love with her. Jerry is crazy alright.

America loves conspiracy theories like "Elvis is alive" or "the Mafia had John F. Kennedy killed." Director Richard Donner, of *Lethal Weapon* fame (1986,1988,1992,1997) and scriptwriter Brian Helgeland (*L.A. Confidential*, 1997) spin a tale about such theories in a deliberately deceptive way. Fletcher, their protagonist, wins the audience's sympathy and tugs at their heartstrings, but he is undeniably mad. He suffers from full-blown paranoia, and we can only shake our heads at its more extreme manifestations. And then, suddenly, Fletcher is right. The conspiracies really do exist, although they are not quite as widespread as Fletcher imagines, nor are they motivated by the same reasons. Nonetheless, "they" do exist, and they want to kill him.

Together with Alice, who initially thinks it's all nonsense, we are drawn into Fletcher's world. We observe his insanity, but gradually we start to notice that some of his claims seem to be true, at least in part. Helgeland's deftly

"Madness and reality are two sides of the same coin in this film." *Süddeutsche Zeitung*

constructed story shows how Alice slowly begins to believe Jerry, to the point where she too trusts no one and ends up putting an empty beer bottle on her door handle. The President's narrow escape from an earthquake finally convinces her that it's not all mere coincidence.

Director Richard Donner evokes a number of previous movies. Travis Bickle, the taxi driver from Martin Scorsese's film of the same name, is present – he was no conspiracy theorist, but a paranoid schizophrenic of the first order. Oliver Stone, who gives us his own personal Kennedy theory in *JFK* (1991), is one of the "greats" in Fletcher's pantheon: "Stone practices disin-

formation for 'them.'" Finally, John Frankenheimer's *Ambassador of Fear* (*The Manchurian Candidate*, 1962) is used in *Conspiracy Theory* to explain what is really happening. Donner even includes his own fantasy film *Ladyhawk* (1985), which is playing in the cinema where Fletcher hides from his pursuers.The film, however, can be enjoyed independently of all these in-jokes. Mel Gibson's brilliant one-man-show, together with Julia Roberts's wide-eyed charm and cameraman John Schwartzman's wonderful pictures of New York are pleasure enough on their own.

HJK

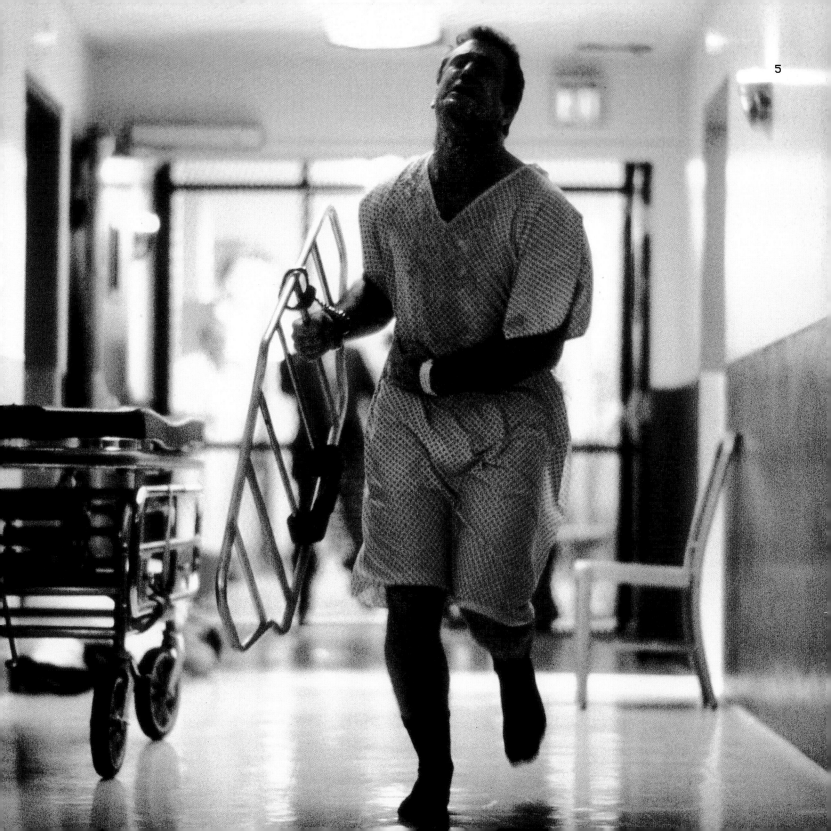

5

THE FULL MONTY

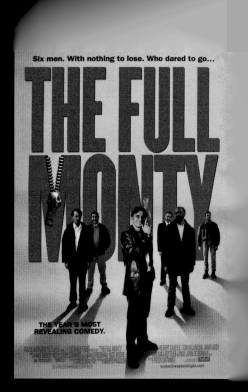

997 – USA / GREAT BRITAIN – 91 MIN. – COMEDY
DIRECTOR PETER CATTANEO (*1964)
SCREENPLAY SIMON BEAUFOY DIRECTOR OF PHOTOGRAPHY JOHN DE BORMAN EDITING DAVID FREEMAN,
NICK MOORE MUSIC ANNE DUDLEY PRODUCTION UBERTO PASOLINI, POLLY LEYS for
REDWAVE FILMS, CHANNEL FOUR, FOX
STARRING ROBERT CARLYLE (Gaz), TOM WILKINSON (Gerald), MARK ADDY (Dave),
LESLEY SHARP (Jean), STEVE HUISON (Lomper), PAUL BARBER (Horse), EMILY WOOF
(Mandy), HUGO SPEER (Guy), DEIRDRE COSTELLO (Linda), BRUCE JONES (Reg),
WILLIAM SNAPE (Nathan)
ACADEMY AWARDS 1998 OSCAR for BEST MUSIC, category COMEDY/MUSICAL (Anne Dudley)

"We dare to bare!"

Laboring steelworkers, shopping malls full of people, a lively swimming pool – urban paradise? According to a '70s promotional film, "thanks to steel Sheffield really is a city on the move" (*City on the Move*, 1971). Twenty-five years on, the boom is well and truly over and South Yorkshire is deep in crisis. The steelworks have closed down, and Gaz (Robert Carlyle) and his friend Dave (Mark Addy) are unemployed. Their attempt to earn some money with a rusty steel beam leaves them out of pocket and dripping wet from an unintentional swim in the river.

The queue is always long at the unemployment benefit counter. One particular day however there is an even longer queue outside the local club, as women wait for a performance by a troupe of male strippers. Dozens of shrieking women have turned up to be entertained. As the club is temporari-

more to lose. Guy (Hugo Speer) can't dance, but he has a definite advantage over the others when it comes to the final act of the striptease show. The six dancers – and Gaz's son Nathan who works the cassette recorder – practice together in the deserted steelworks. But there are still plenty of difficulties to be overcome before they appear on the stage of the local that they have hired: self-doubt, stage fright, and a police raid.

Time and time again, English movies try to transform difficult social conditions with dance. *The Full Monty* is the first movie that does this with a striptease, and here, taking your clothes off in front of other people is anything but humiliating. On the contrary, the men regain their self-esteem and take control of their lives, in the way that they desperately need to do. The financial situation portrayed in Peter Cattaneo's cinematic debut is not utter-

When the men strip, showing their scrawny chests, their aging bodies or their fat bellies, it says just as much, just as eloquently, about the humiliation of being unemployed and permanently hard-up." *Süddeutsche Zeitung*

KITCHEN SINK CINEMA The mine has shut, but the miners' band keeps playing bravely on; they may have lost their jobs, but no one can take their music away. *Brassed Off* tells a story of the struggle against hopeless circumstances that is not dissimilar to *The Full Monty*, also released in 1997. Since the socialist realist "kitchen sink" dramas of the '60s, themes like poverty and unemployment have been a regular feature of British cinema. Ken Loach, a "working class" director (*Looking for Eric,* 2009) began his career in the '60s with the BBC – as did Peter Cattaneo 20 years later. Loach found kindred spirits in directors like Mike Leigh (*Another Year,* 2010) and Stephen Frears (*The Van,* 1996) – as well as filmmakers like Cattaneo and the director of *Brassed Off,* Mark Herman, who season their commitment to social issues with a generous dash of humor.

1   There is seriousness behind the dancing: Gaz (Robert Carlyle) dances to win back his self-respect and the right to see his son again.

2   Playing football all day brings little satisfaction to the unemployed men.

3   Practice makes perfect: a disused steelworks can be used for anything.

4   "The entire film was shot in original locations in Sheffield. The strip club was a real strip club and the women in the audience were women from Sheffield."
Peter Cattaneo in *Zoom*

FACE/OFF

1997 – USA – 138 MIN. – ACTION FILM
DIRECTOR JOHN WOO (*1946)
SCREENPLAY MIKE WERB, MICHAEL COLLEARY DIRECTOR OF PHOTOGRAPHY OLIVER WOOD
EDITING STEVEN KEMPER, CHRISTIAN WAGNER MUSIC JOHN POWELL
PRODUCTION DAVID PERMUT, BARRIE M. OSBORNE, TERENCE CHANG,
CHRISTOPHER GODSICK for DOUGLAS-REUTHER PRODUCTION, WCG ENTERTAINMENT
STARRING JOHN TRAVOLTA (Sean Archer), NICOLAS CAGE (Castor Troy), JOAN ALLEN
(Eve Archer), ALESSANDRO NIVOLA (Pollux Troy), GINA GERSHON (Sasha Hassler),
DOMINIQUE SWAIN (Jamie Archer), NICK CASSAVETES (Dietrich Hassler),
HARVE PRESNELL (Victor Lazarro), COLM FEORE (Dr. Malcolm Walsh), CCH POUNDER
(Dr. Hollis Miller)

"In order to catch him, he must become him."

Sepia pictures, images in someone's memory. A father rides with his son on a carousel horse. A shot rings out. The father is wounded and the son is killed. Six years later L.A. cop Sean Archer (John Travolta) still hasn't caught up with Castor Troy (Nicolas Cage), the psychopathic sharp shooter who killed his son. He gets another chance at a private airfield. Castor and his brother Pollux (Alessandro Nivola) are about to take off, and Archer tries to stop them.

A shootout ensues where Pollux is arrested and Castor is injured and falls into a coma. But Archer still hasn't shaken off Castor Troy's evil legacy. His brother is carrying a disc that contains information on a gigantic bomb attack in Los Angeles, but the whereabouts of the bomb is a mystery. Pollux insists that he will only speak to his brother. To find out the truth about the bomb, a team of scientists from a secret project make Archer an unbelievable offer.

The parallel between hunter and hunted is a well-worn theme: the cop has to empathize with the criminal in order to predict his next move. Many movies have used this device, perhaps none so systematically as *Heat* (1995), where cop Al Pacino and gangster Robert De Niro meet for a tête-à-tête. *Face/Off*'s director John Woo takes the motif to new heights when he turns the cop into the gangster. With the help of the latest medical technology, Archer is given the face, stature, and voice of the gangster Troy. He already knows more than enough about Troy's story, deeds, and accomplices as he has been chasing him for years. To get the information out of him, Archer is admitted to the high security prison where Pollux is being kept. The mission remains a secret, and not even Archer's boss or his wife know anything about it. At any time, with the help of the same techniques, he can be given back his own body. But suddenly that escape route is suddenly blocked. Troy wakes out of his coma and appears in the prison – as Archer.

1

2

3

4

1　A shock: police officer Archer (John Travolta) wearing the face of the villain he has been pursuing like a man possessed for the last six years.

2　"Ridiculous chin," says Castor (Nicolas Cage) when Archer's face is fixed onto his.

3　The parallel between the hunter and the hunted is a well-known film motif, but nobody has ever taken it as far as John Woo.

4　It's not easy for Archer: locked up in the body of Castor in a high-tech jail.

5　The moment of truth: Archer (as Castor) runs his archenemy to ground.

6　Sean and Eve Archer (Joan Allen) have lost their son. Their grief lends a dark mood to the whole film.

JOHN TRAVOLTA　John Travolta's career began in 1975 when he played Vinnie in the popular television series *Welcome Back, Kotter*. After his enormous success in the dance movies *Saturday Night Fever* (1977) and *Grease* (1978) – based on his clichéd image as the handsome heartthrob – Travolta practically disappeared from the screen in the 1980s. He wasn't able to return to Hollywood's premiere league until Quentin Tarantino cast him as the temperamental hit man Vincent Vega in *Pulp Fiction* (1994). Since then, Travolta has established himself as a versatile character actor. A star of action films (*Broken Arrow*, 1995), existential dramas (*Mad City*, 1996), and comedies (*A Lovesong for Bobby Long*, 2004), he has worked with stellar director Terrence Malick (*The Thin Red Line*, 1998) as well as action specialist John Woo (*Face/Off*, 1997). In *Michael* (1996) he played an angel and in *Hairspray* (2007) he was kitted out in a "fat suit" as an obese woman.

He has had the cop's face put on and shot the scientists and the people who witnessed the "swap." Archer manages to escape from the prison and has to make his way as an outlaw while Troy lives in his comfortable home with his wife and daughter.

Two movies gave new life to the Hollywood action film genre in the '90s: *Speed* (1994) and *Face/Off*. *Speed* is a fast-paced, light-footed celebration of pure movement, whereas *Face/Off* – despite its virtuoso action scenes – has dark, elegiac undertones and a much more complex plot. Archer is a tragic figure from the outset, first losing his son and then his life. The idea of changing bodies might seem far-fetched, but it offers the director plenty of opportunities to play with the hunter/hunted motif. John Woo goes through all

of them one by one. Troy in Archer's body becomes a more subtle kind of gangster: he defuses his own bomb, becomes a hero, and decides he wants to run the whole police department. Archer in Troy's body holds Troy's son in his arms as he used to hold his own. And Archer's wife Eve is delighted with the reawakened passion of her husband, who seems like a new man.

The doppelgänger motif reaches a visual highpoint in the scene where Archer and Troy stand on two sides of a mirror and aim their pistols at their own reflections, each of them wearing the face of their archenemy. The visual stylization typical of Woo is everywhere in the movie – like the white doves in a church, or the slow motion billowing overcoat.

HJK

6

"Woo is such an action wizard that he can make planes or speed boats kickbox, but his surprising strength this time is more on a human level." *New York Times*

THE ICE STORM

1997 – USA – 113 MIN. – DRAMA
DIRECTOR ANG LEE (*1954)
SCREENPLAY JAMES SCHAMUS, based on the novel of the same name by RICK MOODY
DIRECTOR OF PHOTOGRAPHY FREDERICK ELMES EDITING TIM SQUYRES MUSIC MYCHAEL DANNA
PRODUCTION TED HOPE, JAMES SCHAMUS, ANG LEE for GOOD MACHINE
STARRING KEVIN KLINE (Ben Hood), SIGOURNEY WEAVER (Janey Carver), JOAN ALLEN
(Elena Hood), TOBEY MAGUIRE (Paul Hood), CHRISTINA RICCI (Wendy Hood),
HENRY CZERNY (George Clair), COURTNEY PELDON (Billie), ADAM HANN-BYRD
(Sandy Carver), ELIJAH WOOD (Mikey Carver), KATIE HOLMES (Libbets Casey)
IFF CANNES 1997 SILVER PALM for BEST SCREENPLAY (James Schamus)

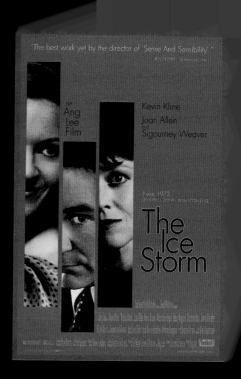

"The only big fight we've had in years is about whether to go back into couples therapy."

November 1973. Paul Hood (Tobey Maguire) travels home to his family in New Canaan, Connecticut, for Thanksgiving Day. But home is no family idyll. His parents have grown apart, and his father Ben (Kevin Kline) comforts himself with vodka or with his neighbor's wife Janey Carver (Sigourney Weaver), while his mother Elena (Joan Allen, who plays the president's wife in Stone's *Nixon*) has withdrawn completely into herself. Paul's 14-year-old sister Wendy (Christina Ricci) seems to be suffering as much from Vietnam and Watergate as she is from puberty. The parents may have lost interest in sex, but the children are just beginning to discover it. Wendy and the Carvers' two sons, 14-year-old Mikey (Elijah Wood) and his younger brother Sandy (Adam Hann-Byrd), explore each other's bodies. Paul is often interested in the girls in his class, but his roommate Francis is always one step ahead. Paul's latest love interest is Libbets, the daughter of a rich family, and one evening he goes to New York to see Libbets, while Wendy meanwhile is over at the Carvers' and the parents are at a partner-swapping party. That night, an ice storm sweeps over the country, making the roads treacherous and covering high voltage cables with icicles, and the morning after, nothing is ever quite the same again…

The Ice Storm tells a tale of puberty, of the period between the childhood and adulthood of its young protagonists. It also describes an interim period in American history. In November 1973 a cease-fire treaty was signed in the Vietnam War, ten years to the month after the shooting of President Kennedy, but the fighting still continued. The Watergate story had just broken and although Richard Nixon had resigned as president, the affair was far from over. This "interim" feeling also extends to the life of the Hood family: the parents are still married but inwardly divorced, and the children are in puberty. They live "in between" even in a geographical sense: they are not in the flatlands, but New York is still a train ride away.

Taiwanese director Ang Lee has always shown himself to be a clearsighted analyst of social relationships and family ties. Whether his subject is the world of Chinese immigrants in New York (*The Wedding Banquet*, 1993) England at the end of the 18th century (*Sense and Sensibility*, 1995)

America at the beginning of the Civil War (*Ride with the Devil*, 1999), or China shortly before its opening to the West (*Crouching Tiger, Hidden Dragon*, 2000), Lee always manages to show the social order through his protagonists without reducing them to mere symbolic ciphers. In that sense, *The Ice Storm* is typical of his other work: adults hold "key parties" (women choose car keys at random, and go home with the men whose keys they have chosen), and they discuss the porn film *Deep Throat* over canapés but they are incapable of real passion.

Paralysis, stagnation, and weariness – America's middle classes are deeply disturbed by the domestic turmoil of Watergate and the chaos of Vietnam abroad, but at the same time they believe they must live up to the sexual revolution of the none-too-distant '60s.

When Wendy puts on a Nixon mask to fool around with Mikey, the connection between sex and politics is made quite clear, and the film is full of such symbols and metaphors. The ice storm of the title is the most obvious example, but another is the characters' names: father Hood doesn't have a definitive identity, and everyone calls him something different (Ben, Benj, Benjamin). By turns bitter and grotesque, *The Ice Storm* never deteriorates into stereotypes or facile theories despite its wealth of symbols, and that perhaps the real strength of what is a virtuoso drama.

HJ

CHRISTINA RICCI Rumor has it that Natalie Portman was originally intended to play Wednesday, but her parents found the role too sexy. That said, the part of a 14-year-old desperate to experiment with her sexuality seems tailor-made for Christina Ricci (*1980). With her large, expressive eyes and mysterious air, Ricci often plays girls who don't fit the traditional Hollywood image of a carefree teenager. One of her first successes was in her role as the daughter of the horror clan *The Addams Family* (1991). After this movie, much was made of her looks, her full figure leading people to claim that she was "too healthy" to make it in a city where a waif like physique is the norm. As an adult actress, Christina Ricci has also excelled in offbeat roles: as the bleached-blonde floozy in *The Opposite of Sex* (1999) and the mysterious child-woman in *Buffalo '66* (1997). In *Monster* (2003), she falls in love with a female serial killer, while in the film adaptation of Guy de Maupassant's *Bel Ami* (2012) she gets under the covers with teen idol Robert Pattinson (*Twilight*, 2008–2012).

---

1   As Wendy Hood, Christina Ricci knows how to bring across the dark, unsettling aspects of puberty.

2   Exciting and terrifying: Mikey (Elijah Wood) and Wendy carry out their first experiments with the opposite sex.

3   Ben Hood (Kevin Kline) and Janey Carver (Sigourney Weaver): double-quick sex without the small talk.

4   A partner-swapping party – as unsettling for parents as the first sexual experiments are for their children.

5   "The story takes place during a period of crisis in the USA, the early '70s. The whole thing is like a kind of hangover from the '60s: there is no real passion any more, a kind of weariness prevails – like a transition into what America is today."
Ang Lee in *Süddeutsche Zeitung*

"The family is the antithesis of the self. The family is the void from which you came, and also the place to which you return when you die."

Paul in *The Ice Storm*

TITANIC ㅜㅜㅜㅜㅜㅜㅜㅜㅜㅜㅜ

1997 – USA –194 MIN. – MELODRAMA, DISASTER FILM
DIRECTOR JAMES CAMERON (*1954)
SCREENPLAY JAMES CAMERON **DIRECTOR OF PHOTOGRAPHY** RUSSELL CARPENTER
EDITING CONRAD BUFF, JAMES CAMERON, RICHARD A. HARRIS **MUSIC** JAMES HORNER
PRODUCTION JAMES CAMERON, JON LANDAU for 20TH CENTURY FOX,
LIGHTSTORM ENTERTAINMENT, PARAMOUNT PICTURES
STARRING LEONARDO DICAPRIO (Jack Dawson), KATE WINSLET (Rose DeWitt Bukater),
BILLY ZANE (Cal Hockley), KATHY BATES (Molly Brown), GLORIA STUART (Rose as an old
woman), BILL PAXTON (Brock Lovett), BERNARD HILL (Captain Smith), DAVID WARNER
(Spicer Lovejoy), VICTOR GARBER (Thomas Andrews), JONATHAN HYDE (Bruce Ismay)
ACADEMY AWARDS 1998 OSCARS for BEST PICTURE, BEST DIRECTOR (James Cameron),
BEST CINEMATOGRAPHY (Russell Carpenter), BEST FILM EDITING (Conrad Buff,
James Cameron, Richard A. Harris), BEST MUSIC, category DRAMA (James Horner),
BEST SONG ("My Heart Will Go On"; Music: James Horner, Lyrics: Will Jennings,
Performed by Céline Dion), BEST ART DIRECTION – SET DECORATION (Peter Lamont,
Michael Ford), BEST COSTUMES (Deborah Lynn Scott), BEST VISUAL EFFECTS
(Robert Legato, Mark Lasoff, Thomas L. Fisher, Michael Kanfer), BEST SOUND
(Gary Rydstrom, Tom Johnson, Gary Summers, Mark Ulano), BEST SOUND EFFECTS
EDITING (Tom Bellfort, Christopher Boyes)

"So this is the ship they say is unsinkable."

The sinking of the passenger ship Titanic is usually interpreted as a warning of the catastrophic end of the modern belief in progress, which was confirmed in the trenches of World War I only a few years later. The numerous film versions of the event demonstrate the fascination that the luxury liner's fate has always held. The movies themselves have had an influence on the Titanic myth, which in turn has become an integral part of our cultural memory. The story never varies: technology clashes with nature, human inventiveness with destructive natural power, arrogant presumption with impassive creation. Film versions were made almost immediately after the accident, like the long-forgotten *Saved From the Titanic* (by Etienne Arnaud, 1912) and Pier Angelo Mazzolotti's *Titanic* (1915).

Subsequently many vast and expensive films were made in which private unhappiness and technical disaster developed side by side only to fuse together in an infernal catastrophe at the end. Jean Negulesco's film version of the event was awarded an Oscar for best original screenplay in 1953. Cameron's *Titanic* cost 200 million dollars and was awarded a total of 11 Oscars – the time any film had matched the previously unbeatable *Ben Hur* (1959).

Cameron's interpretation of the Titanic myth is more proof of his talent for telling melodramatic love stories. The proletarian prince almost accidentally rescues the world-weary princess while "polite society" postures and poses to conceal its spiritual and moral decay. The megalomania that inspired the construction of a gigantic luxury liner like the Titanic is part of that modern decadence.

The film's recipe for success could be summed up as strong emotion reflected by huge disaster. And it works. The penniless painter Jack Dawson

2

3

"The scene where a lifeboat is carefully edging its way between frozen corpses floating in the water as it searches for survivors is as horrific as it is unforgettable."

Frankfurter Allgemeine Zeitung

...meets beautiful, of noble birth, but unhappy Rose DeWitt Bukater. She tries to kill herself, he saves her, and they fall in love. A passionate romance develops between this young man from the lower decks and the upper class lady from the top echelons of society. The love story becomes a social drama where class differences become apparent not just in location and decor but also in everyday life. Upstairs there is distinguished, arrogant small talk about money accompanied by pleasant string music, downstairs there is wild dancing to fast and furious Irish folk music. The class barrier becomes extremely real. Rose's fiancé Cal Hockley (Billy Zane) wants to put an end to the subversive relationship and eventually manages to have Jack forbidden from coming up to the top deck, but this is not enough to drive the two apart. Jack makes a secret drawing of Rose wearing nothing but a diamond on a chain around her neck and the social barriers to their love seem to dissolve in the magic of art. When Cal discovers this drawing in the safe, he sends out servants to track the couple down, but Rose and Jack escape into the enormous underbelly of the ship. At the same time, the captain gets the first iceberg warnings, which he ignores. Both plot strands reach a critical phase and destiny takes its course: the lovers' high spirits and the captain's arrogance combine in a tragic conclusion.

The story is told in a long flashback by the now elderly Rose after she has seen on television that a diving team has found Jack's drawing in a safe lying on the bottom of the sea. The movie takes great care to adopt a light

LEONARDO DICAPRIO Leonardo DiCaprio (*1974) began his career in commercials and TV series before getting his first big movie break with *This Boy's Life* (1993) alongside Robert De Niro. He was nominated for an Oscar for his performance as the mentally retarded Arnie Grape in *What's Eating Gilbert Grape* (1993). After a stellar performance as a youthful Romeo in Baz Luhrmann's *Romeo + Juliet* in 1996, he went on to star in *Titanic* (1997), his most successful film to date. He has now become one of the highest earning and most influential actors in Hollywood. In 2002, he began a series of collaborations with cineaste Martin Scorsese with *Gangs of New York*. He has also worked with acclaimed directors like Sam Mendes (*Revolutionary Road*, 2008), Christopher Nolan (*Inception*, 2010), and Clint Eastwood (*J. Edgar*, 2011). DiCaprio, who campaigns on environmental protection issues, produced and narrated the eco-documentary *The 11th Hour* (2007).

1 Impending disaster reflected in the lovers' eyes (Leonardo DiCaprio as Jack and Kate Winslet as Rose).

3 Humanity's presumptuousness embodied as a machine on her journey into the abyss.

4 The betrayed fiancé (Billy Zane) loses his appetite.

"The outside shots of the stern breaking up, the tidal waves inside, the drama around and in the lifeboats rank among the best special effects Hollywood has ever produced." *Frankfurter Allgemeine Zeitung*

BUFFALO '66

1997/1998 – USA – 110 MIN. – DRAMA, ROMANCE
DIRECTOR VINCENT GALLO (*1962)
SCREENPLAY VINCENT GALLO, ALISON BAGNALL DIRECTOR OF PHOTOGRAPHY LANCE ACORD
EDITING CURTISS CLAYTON MUSIC VINCENT GALLO PRODUCTION CHRIS HANLEY for MUSE,
LIONS GATE FILMS
STARRING VINCENT GALLO (Billy Brown), CHRISTINA RICCI (Layla), ANJELICA HUSTON
(Janet Brown), BEN GAZZARA (Jimmy Brown), KEVIN CORRIGAN (Goon), MICKEY ROURKE
(Bookie), ROSANNA ARQUETTE (Wendy), JAN-MICHAEL VINCENT (Sonny), JOHN RUMMEL
(Don Shanks), BOB WAHL (Scott Woods)

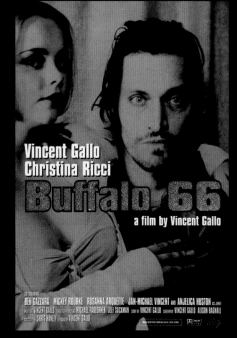

"Just don't touch me!"

Billy Brown (Vincent Gallo), an innocent man, has spent five years in Buffalo jail because of a gambling debt. When he gets out, he wants to revenge himself on Scott Woods (Bob Wahl), the man who caused his misery. Once a football star with the Buffalo Bills, Woods's poor performance in a game on which Billy bet ten thousand dollars made the Bills lose. After his release, Billy needs a good excuse for his parents (Anjelica Huston and Ben Gazzara) who have no idea where their son has spent the last five years. Billy makes a snap decision and kidnaps a young woman called Layla (Christina Ricci) and forces her to pretend to the Browns that she is his wife. "Your job is to make me look good," he instructs her. Layla throws herself into the role whole-heartedly, but we realize that Billy's parents have never really cared about him. His mother is a devoted fan of the Buffalo Bills and his father has a paranoid mistrust of his own son. It becomes increasingly clear that behind Billy's tough façade is a lonely, vulnerable young man. Layla, who soon sees through him, feels herself more and more drawn to him, although he keeps her at a distance. They leave the Browns' house together, go to a bowling alley and a fast food restaurant and finally, in a motel room that evening,

Billy seems to thaw. Everything could turn out well, but Billy still has a score to pay.

Buffalo '66 is one of that rare kind of American movies which could only have been made as the debut film of an independent filmmaker. The movie is badly proportioned, overloaded with the ideas of its director, overdramatic, autobiographical, and unrelentingly egocentric – and for exactly those reasons it has its own kind of magic. Vincent Gallo is the director, scriptwriter, and leading actor of *Buffalo '66*. Always a gifted self-publicist as an actor, artist, and Calvin Klein model, he never misses an opportunity to draw attention to the autobiographical nature of his directorial firstborn. Buffalo is Gallo's native town, and the Browns are based on his parents, or so he claims. On first viewing, the movie appears to be the self-portrait of a selfish outsider. But its fairy-tale quality is at least as important as its autobiographical aspects and its often rough and ready realism. The artificial colors, the overemphasis on narrative and cinematic effects and above all the almost parodic characterization make *Buffalo '66* a surprisingly tender tale of existential loneliness and the indispensable nature of love. From being the autistic son

"Gallo, who also wrote, directed and scored *Buffalo '66*, is a smart young filmmaker, not least in his casting. Gazzara, angrily mourning his lost career as a local lounge singer, and Huston, obsessing on the Bills' football frustrations, are glorious eccentrics. And Christina Ricci, as the tap dancer Billy forces to play his faux fiancée, is just lovely." *Time Magazine*

1 Suburban blues: Layla (Christina Ricci) on a search for love.

2 It takes some time for Billy (Vincent Gallo) to overcome his fear and open up to Layla.

3 A blond suburban angel: Christina Ricci lends a fairytale quality to Layla.

4 Buffalo can be very cold: Vincent Gallo directs himself as a tragic-romantic loner.

GUEST APPEARANCE In contrast to the cameo appearance, where famous people – often to comic effect – appear as themselves for a short moment to disturb the fictional plot of a film, a guest appearance is a small role that fits into the plot. Both were already popular in the era of silent movies. Charlie Chaplin for instance had a cameo role in King Vidor's *Show People* (1928), and he is to be found in his own film *A Woman of Paris* (1923) in a guest appearance as a porter. The difference between guest and cameo roles is sometimes rather artificial. In Robert Altman's *The Player* (1992), a satire about the film industry, various Hollywood stars can be seen in guest or cameo roles. A more restrictive definition of the term limits guest appearances to appearances by directors in movies made by their colleagues.

5

5   Two icons of independent US cinema: Christina Ricci and Vincent Gallo as distant lovers.

6   A sideways glance: Jimmy Brown (Ben Gazzara) harbours a paranoid distrust of his son Billy.

7   Her world revolves around football and nothing else: Billy's mother (Anjelica Huston) is an obsessive fan of the Buffalo Bills.

of unfeeling average Americans, Billy, with his lanky figure and his heavily shadowed, light blue eyes in an unusually pale face, becomes the ideal embodiment of a tragic-romantic loner and plump, big-eyed Layla is his blonde suburban angel.

. *Buffalo '66* is a movie full of wonderful moments and witty cinematic magic tricks. Gallo demonstrates both his artistic originality and his admiration of other creative talents from the independent scene. Ben Gazzara gets

a melancholy singing scene, Christina Ricci an introverted tap-dance number, and Anjelica Huston is stunning in the role of football-obsessed bad mother. Mickey Rourke, one of the most eccentric cult figures of US cinema in the '80s, also turns up with a guest appearance as a criminal bookie. These moments are lovingly set up and if they don't make *Buffalo '66* a masterpiece, they do make it at least a high point of American independent cinema in the '90s.   JH

6

"*Buffalo '66* is an American response to the European autobiographical film."

Neue Zürcher Zeitung

JACKIE BROWN

1997 – USA – 154 MIN. – GANGSTER FILM
DIRECTOR QUENTIN TARANTINO (*1963)
SCREENPLAY QUENTIN TARANTINO, based on the novel *RUM PUNCH* by ELMORE LEONARD
DIRECTOR OF PHOTOGRAPHY GUILLERMO NAVARRO EDITING SALLY MENKE MUSIC Various soul and
hip-hop songs PRODUCTION LAWRENCE BENDER for A BAND APART, MIGHTY MIGHTY
AFRODITE PRODUCTIONS, MIRAMAX FILMS
STARRING PAM GRIER (Jackie Brown), SAMUEL L. JACKSON (Ordell Robbie),
ROBERT FORSTER (Max Cherry), BRIDGET FONDA (Melanie Ralston), MICHAEL KEATON
(Ray Nicolette), ROBERT DE NIRO (Louis Gara), MICHAEL BOWEN (Mark Dargus),
CHRIS TUCKER (Beaumont Livingston), TOMMY "TINY" LISTER JR. (Winston)
IFF BERLIN 1998 SILVER BEAR for BEST ACTOR (Samuel L. Jackson)

Six players on the trail of a half million in cash.
There's only one question...Who's playing who?

This Christmas, Santa's got a brand new bag.

"You're not old, you look great."

Pam Grier is an icon of the Blaxploitation cinema of the '70s and, since *Foxy Brown* (1974), a black sex symbol. Quentin Tarantino tailored the role of Jackie Brown especially for her. Although the plot of the film is based on Elmore Leonard's novel *Rum Punch*, Tarantino completely ignored the fact that the book's main figure is a white woman, creating a true homage to Grier. He also featured another star of '70s cinema, Robert Forster. The whole movie is retro: the sets, decor, and music are all taken from the '70s and once again Tarantino does a lot of quoting from other movies. Ordell and Jackie remind us of figures like Joe Cabot (*Reservoir Dogs*, 1991) or Winston Wolf (*Pulp Fiction*, 1994) who try to manage other people's lives as though they had a script. In *Jackie Brown* there is also a shot from inside the trunk of a car, watching videos plays an important role, and killings are filmed with

the same gruesome nonchalance. Such things are fixed coordinates in the Tarantino universe.

His recreation of the '70s is colorful and atmospheric. It's there from the very first shot: a woman appears at the left of the scene, the camera lingers on her while she is carried along on a moving walkway in front of a multi-colored tile mosaic to the music of Bobby Womack. Psychedelic colors and forms combine with Pop Art textures and soul music to build an imaginary framework. The woman's steady gaze is fixed straight ahead, her posture suggests determination and self-confidence – we know that Jackie Brown has arrived. She is a stewardess with a small airline and improves her slim earnings by carrying money for arms dealer Ordell Robbie. When she is caught the police find a plastic bag of cocaine together with the 50 thousand

"This thriller isn't dominated by the pressure of rising tempo, nor is the escalation of events heralded by any frantic facial expressions. Instead, it is the law of inertia that rules; everything moves as slowly as possible, and faces change expression slowest of all." *Frankfurter Allgemeine Zeitung*

1 Mature sex appeal and cool charm: Pam Grier in the role of Jackie Brown. All those beautiful young Hollywood actresses were left out in the cold …

2 Whose side is cold-blooded Ordell (Samuel L. Jackson) on?

3 Solid eroticism within touching distance.

4 Filled with love beyond sexual desire: Max Cherry (Robert Forster).

dollars in the wallet she is carrying. Jackie ends up in prison. Ordell Robbie sends a bail broker named Max Cherry (Robert Forster) to visit her, and a touching affair begins. Their meetings in the prison courtyard, in a bar, and in Jackie's apartment, the almost blind trust and mutual esteem are unexpected examples of a new kind of empathy from Tarantino, the supposed master of cinematic brutality. Once again, he proves that his gangsters are nothing more than caricatures and that his criminals are merely comic figures – especially when they are "being serious." Ordell jabbers on in a macho and hypocritical manner about street credibility and then shoots his black "brother" Beaumont in cold blood. Ordell's weak right-hand man Louis (Robert De Niro) kills Ordell's girlfriend Melanie (Bridget Fonda) without thinking twice when she nags him. The trio are played by Samuel L. Jackson, Bridget Fonda, and gangster icon Robert De Niro, as though to illustrate the Tarantino philosophy of deconstructing film stereotypes through grotesque exaggeration. The interpersonal relationships between them are reduced to watching videos, smoking joints, showing off, having sex, and having fun. They form a striking contrast to the real love story in the film, the relationship between Jackie and Max.

The turning point comes when Jackie arranges to hand over some money and then plays a trick on the police with Max's help. The police want

"Where the formal rage of *Reservoir Dogs* and *Pulp Fiction* is reminiscent of Godard, *Jackie Brown's* leisureliness shows an unexpected affinity on Tarantino's part with the stylistic devices of Rohmer and – even more so – Rivette." *epd Film*

5 Echoes of *Pulp Fiction*: gangsters (Robert De Niro) are also only human.

6 Good-looking blonde Melanie (Bridget Fonda) isn't as dumb as she seems.

Ordell, and Ordell wants his money. She strikes a deal with both parties in advance but makes sure that she will be the only winner. The movie shows the handing over of the bag from the three different perspectives of Jackie, Melanie, and Max – and each one of the chronologically overlapping sequences reveals a further element of the transaction. Panning shots and circular camera movements mark the story's climax: we know that this is the decisive moment, but we don't know if Jackie's sophisticated plan will succeed or fail. All does go according to plan: Max picks up the money unnoticed, and only Ordell realizes that he has been cheated. He is then lured to Max's office where the police are already waiting, and they shoot Ordell when Jackie shouts that he has a gun. Jackie wins; the police know nothing about the rest of the money which Jackie and Max have already hidden.

The film spins this gangster story around Jackie Brown with humor and sophistication. Once again Tarantino revolutionizes the linear narrative structure typical of mainstream cinema by delaying the handing over of the money and effortlessly juxtaposing lots of seemingly unconnected story lines. Much of the charm of *Jackie Brown* comes from its '70s retro look. Part of this is the almost forgotten "split screen" technique where the screen is divided into two halves so that action taking place in different places at the same time can be shown in the same picture.

At the end of the movie, Jackie leaves with her loot – and we feel she really deserves it. Max, sad and lonely, is left behind. Pam Grier alias Jackie Brown looks thoughtful and moves her lips to the music which shows her the way "across 110th Street." BR

BLAXPLOITATION Following the civil rights movement at the end of the '60s the film industry began to work on a market segment which previously had been neglected; movies with black people both in front of and behind the cameras, dealing with things that concerned the African American population. To exploit the market potential of frustrated black employees, many low budget productions were made with tough, sexually potent heroes set in a milieu dominated by drug dealings, prostitution, and Mafia organizations, underpinned by bombastic, sentimental soundtracks. Like most "exploitation films," these crime and gangster movies, mostly set in run-down black neighborhoods, have little claim to artistic merit. Quick market success was the aim, so the films break down easily into readily identifiable sensational elements. Classics of the black exploitation movie include *Cotton Comes to Harlem* (1969), Melvin Van Peebles's angry, experimental *Sweet Sweetback's Baadasssss Song* (1971), and glamorous Hollywood productions like the extraordinarily popular *Shaft* series (1970–1975). In the final instance however, the stereotyped superficiality of these movies and their rigid separation from white culture served above all to drive black pop culture further into the ghetto.

6

THE SWEET HEREAFTER

1997 – CANADA – 112 MIN. – DRAMA
DIRECTOR ATOM EGOYAN (*1960)
SCREENPLAY ATOM EGOYAN, based on the novel of the same name by
RUSSELL BANKS DIRECTOR OF PHOTOGRAPHY PAUL SAROSSY
EDITING SUSAN SHIPTON MUSIC MYCHAEL DANNA
PRODUCTION ATOM EGOYAN, CAMELA FRIEBERG for ALLICANE FILMS,
TELEFILM CANADA, THE HAROLD GREENBERG FUND
STARRING IAN HOLM (Mitchell Stephens), SARAH POLLEY
(Nicole Burnell), BRUCE GREENWOOD (Billy Ansell), TOM MCCAMUS
(Sam Burnell), GABRIELLE ROSE (Dolores Driscoll),
ALBERTA WATSON (Risa Walker), ARSINÉE KHANJIAN (Wanda Otto),
STEPHANIE MORGENSTERN (Alison), MAURY CHAYKIN
(Wendell Walker), CAERTHAN BANKS (Zoe Stephens)
IFF CANNES 1997 JURY PRIZE

"Something terrible is happening. It's taken our children away."

The car wash has gone crazy. It holds the strange car prisoner with its brushes and water sprinklers as if it were the gatekeeper of the small Canadian settlement. Inside the car sits the lawyer Stephens (Ian Holm), who has come to the wintry mountains from the city far away because he scents an opportunity to make capital out of a tragedy. Fourteen children have just died in an accident where a school bus skidded off a slippery road and sank in an icy lake. The only survivors were the driver and the oldest schoolgirl, 13-year-old Nicole (Sarah Polley), and the lawyer wants to persuade the parents of the victims to claim compensation. In the '90s nothing happens without a reason, so someone must be legally responsible for the catastrophe: even if it's just a mechanic who failed to tighten a bolt the last time the bus was serviced, Stephens is convinced that he will find someone to pay for the children's lives. He's not the type to spend much time wondering if he is welcome or not. He breaks out of the car wash with the help of his umbrella, and then forces his way into the houses of the mourning community.

Everything is ambivalent in *The Sweet Hereafter*, nothing is clear at first sight. By day, Nicole seems like a normal teenager who looks after the neighbors' baby, but at night she fondles her father in a haystack. Even the determined lawyer turns out to be a broken man who has never got over the loss of his daughter. An HIV-positive drug addict, she vegetates in a state of living death in a strange city. Instead of dealing with his pain, he feels only bitter anger. With the words "Let me direct your rage" he gains the support of the drowned children's parents, and convinces them that he will be able to find an explanation for the tragic events. Under his influence however, that rage begins to drown out the memories of the children that they have lost.

The Sweet Hereafter is a disturbing movie about grief and loss. It's disturbing because Atom Egoyan doesn't tell his story chronologically but jumps instead back and forth between various time periods. Sometimes we see the time before the bus accident, sometimes the direct aftermath. There is also an epilogue that takes place two years later, and this fragmentary narrative

"Egoyan's films are complex and eccentric, inwardly torn and full of longing, just like people are. Although with *The Sweet Hereafter* Egoyan has for the first time adapted foreign material following a novel by Russell Banks, he has never made a richer or more profound film." *epd Film*

style makes the film resemble a fascinating mosaic. Spectators are constantly made aware that they are seeing only one of many possible truths, as Egoyan could just as easily have assembled the pieces of the mosaic in quite a different way.

The movie is beautiful to watch, with fantastic tableaux and pictures of great depth. It avoids being overly weepy despite the emotional theme. It ends with the optimistic hope of a sweet hereafter, where people will live together in peace. That place is where the Pied Piper of Hamelin led the children of the town. As it says in the Robert Browning poem which runs through the movie like a leitmotif: "a wondrous portal opened wide, as if a cavern was

suddenly hollowed / And the Piper advanced and the children followed / And when all were in at the very last / The door in the mountain-side shut fast." *The Sweet Hereafter* is a modern version of the old tale, but there is more than one piper: the bus driver, who collects children like berries, Nicole's father, who abuses his daughter, and the lawyer, who lures the parents with sweet promises of money and divides the community in two. They are all part of a society where the space available for children to be children seems to get smaller and smaller.

Egoyan's film gives no answers but it raises questions long after the curtain in the cinema has fallen. NM

ATOM EGOYAN Atom Egoyan makes movies about pictures: about the pictures from his characters' memories and about pictures from the media, made by video or film cameras. Above all, he works with the pictures we have of ourselves, which we use to form our identities, whether as individuals or communities. Atom's Armenian parents chose his unusual name because he was born in 1960, the year in which the first Egyptian nuclear power station became operational. Not long after, the family of artists moved to Canada. His movies *The Adjuster* (1991), *Calendar* (1993), and *Exotica* (1994) were well received by the critics, though not necessarily a wider public. This changed with the drama *The Sweet Hereafter* (1997) and the thriller *Felicia's Journey* (1999), where Egoyan moved from purely intellectual to psychological narrative cinema. In *Ararat* (2002) he dealt with the fate of the Armenian people. He is married to the actress Arsinée Khanjian, who appears in most of his films.

---

1   Ian Holm is outstanding in the role of angry attorney Mitchell Stephens. He stepped in at the last minute for Donald Sutherland, who was originally intended for the main part.

2   The school bus never reaches its destination: it skids off the road at the next bend and drags 14 children down to their death.

3   Nicole (Sarah Polley) survives the accident. The decision to bring charges or not all rests on her testimony.

4   A movie image like a painting. The idyll of the sleeping family represents peace and harmony, but also denotes the transitory nature of things.

5   By day Nicole's father (Tom McCamus) supports his daughter's appearances as a folk singer. By night he forces his affections upon her in the hay.

6   In Egoyan's film, the hereafter is the Promised Land, a place of transcendence. To reach the light, Nicole has only one option: to tell a lie.

AS GOOD AS IT GETS ♟♟

1997 – USA – 138 MIN. – ROMANTIC COMEDY
DIRECTOR JAMES L. BROOKS (*1940)
SCREENPLAY JAMES L. BROOKS, MARK ANDRUS based on a story by MARK ANDRUS
DIRECTOR OF PHOTOGRAPHY JOHN BAILEY **EDITING** RICHARD MARKS **MUSIC** HANS ZIMMER
PRODUCTION JAMES L. BROOKS, BRIDGET JOHNSON, KRISTI ZEA for GRACIE FILM, TRISTAR
STARRING JACK NICHOLSON (Melvin Udall), HELEN HUNT (Carol Connelly), GREG KINNEAR
(Simon Bishop), CUBA GOODING JR. (Frank Sachs), SHIRLEY KNIGHT (Beverly),
SKEET ULRICH (Vincent), JESSE JAMES (Spencer), HAROLD RAMIS (Dr. Martin Bettes),
LAWRENCE KASDAN (Dr. Green), TODD SOLONDZ (Man in bus)
ACADEMY AWARDS 1998 OSCARS for BEST ACTRESS (Helen Hunt) and BEST ACTOR
(Jack Nicholson)

BRACE YOURSELF FOR MELVIN

JACK NICHOLSON
HELEN HUNT   GREG KINNEAR
AS GOOD AS IT GETS
A comedy from the heart that goes for the throat.

"You don't love anything, Mr. Udall!"

Melvin Udall (Jack Nicholson) is eccentric, selfish, and irritating – an embittered misanthrope who tyrannizes and terrorizes those around him. It's hard to believe that he made his fortune writing syrupy romantic novels. When an enthusiastic fan asks him how he manages to describe women so well, he hesitates for a second and answers, "I think of a man. Then I take away reason and accountability."

We make his acquaintance as he sends the dwarf pinscher owned by his gay neighbor Simon (Greg Kinnear) out into the world by shoving it down the garbage chute. His heartfelt farewell is a piece of cynical advice: "This is New York. If you can make it here you can make it anywhere." When Melvin is at home, he barricades himself behind a battery of door locks. When he goes out, he makes sure never to step on the cracks between the paving stones. And when he eats in his favorite café, he brings his own plastic cutlery. The waitress Carol (Helen Hunt) is the only person at all willing to serve the quarrelsome guest and to put up with his abuse. When Simon is beaten up by a gang of burglars so badly that he has to go into hospital, it falls to Melvin of all people to take care of Verdell, his beloved dog. At first the little beast drives hygiene-obsessed Melvin to distraction, but slowly it manages to conquer his lonely heart. With astonishing results: Melvin, whose knowledge of love until now was purely theoretical, actually starts to fall in love with single mother Carol …

Jack Nicholson, the man with the diabolical grin and Hollywood's most arched eyebrows, delivers the insults with such bravura and self-irony that his portrayal of the grumbling antihero made its way not only into the hearts of the public, it also earned him an Oscar and a Golden Globe. As did the performance of his partner Helen Hunt, who as the snappy waitress matches his bitchy quips blow for blow. She counters Melvin's insults with the speed and accuracy of a machine gun: "When I saw you when you first came into breakfast, I thought you were handsome," she explains, and then pauses in barely perceptible melodramatic fashion before sending a sharp look in his direction. She delivers the punch line with dryness and charm: "Then, of course, you spoke." That hits home! Hunt had to struggle to secure the role in this feel-good Beauty and the Beast movie, which, after the sitcom *Mad About You* and the disaster Blockbuster *Twister* (1996) gave her her big breakthrough. Veteran director James L. Brooks (*Terms of Endearment*, 1983) initially had the charmingly pert Holly Hunter in mind, as she had already shone in his media satire *Broadcast News* (1987). But that plan broke down over her salary demands. Clearly it wasn't quite so hard for Brooks to persuade other prominent personalities to step in front of the camera: cameo appearances by cult directors Harold Ramis, Lawrence Kasdan, and Todd Solondz put the finishing touches to this enchanting mixture of romantic comedy and biting social satire.

1   She has the potential to play the blonde bombshell, but Helen Hunt generally feels more at home in the role of the homely girl-next-door. Here she plays waitress and single mum Carol Connelly.

2   Misanthrope Melvin Udall, grimly fighting his way through the jungle of the metropolis: a showpiece role for Hollywood veteran Jack Nicholson.

3   With his hatred of dogs, Udall proves a worthy follower of W. C. Fields, who once declared: "Anyone who hates small dogs and children can't be all bad."

"The cascades of words and succinct punch lines of this film make you realize the amount of impoverished dialogue that contemporary comedy usually fobs you off with." *Abendzeitung*

4

5   6

4   Enemies can become friends – in spite of the age
     difference there is a real spark between Carol and
     Melvin.

5   Greg Kinnear as Simon, the gay painter who is
     beaten up by a gang and forced to rely on his
     horrible neighbor for help.

6   When health is a matter of money: Carol's son
     Spencer (Jesse James) can only get the best
     medical care with Udall's financial support.

HELEN HUNT   From age six, Oscar-winner Helen Hunt (*1963) only ever wanted to be an actress. The daughter of director Gordon Hunt had her first role in a TV movie *(Pioneer Woman)* when she was nine years old. In 1986, she attracted a wider audience for the first time in the comedy *Peggy Sue Got Married*. In the TV sitcom *Mad About You* (1992–1999), Hunt was not only brilliant as the newlywed wife, but also acted as producer and occasionally took on the direction. Her first breakthrough came with Jan de Bont's disaster film *Twister* (1996). Since then "the hardest working gal in show biz" (according to fellow actor Eric Stoltz) has celebrated one hit film after another, playing alongside the likes of Kevin Spacey (*Pay it Forward*, 2000), Mel Gibson (*What Women Want*, 2000), and Woody Allen (*The Curse of the Jade Scorpion*, 2001). She made her directorial debut with the tragicomic family film *Then She Found Me* in 2007.

KUNDUN

1997 – USA – 134 MIN. – DRAMA, BIOPIC
DIRECTOR Martin Scorsese (*1942)
SCREENPLAY MELISSA MATHISON DIRECTOR OF PHOTOGRAPHY ROGER DEAKINS EDITING THELMA SCHOONMAKER MUSIC Philip Glass PRODUCTION BARBARA DE FINA for CAPPA / DE FINA PRODUCTIONS
STARRING TENZIN THUTHOB TSARONG (Dalai Lama as an adult), GYURME TETHONG (Dalai-Lama, age 12), TULKU JAMYANG KUNGA TENZIN (Dalai Lama, age five), TENZIN YESHI PAICHANG (Dalai Lama, age two), TENCHO GYALPO (Mother of the Dalai Lama), TSEWANG MIGYUR KHANGSAR (Father of the Dalai Lama), GESHI YESHI GYATSO (Lama of Sera), SONAM PHUNTSOK (Reting Rinpoche), GYATSO LUKHANG (Lord Chamberlain), ROBERT LIN (Mao Tse-tung)

"You can not liberate me, I can only liberate myself."

"Me, me...this is mine." – he is a stubborn, wild child and claims that which clearly belong to others for himself: his father's seat at the head of the table, the prayer beads of a Buddhist dignitary...and yet he is due everything, for this bright two-year-old is the reincarnation of the Dalai Lama. A high priest discovers the boy in a remote village. The child passes a test in which he chooses from a variety of ritual objects exactly those that once belonged to the 13th Dalai Lama, who passed away four years earlier.

The film *Kundun* – "Kundun" (pronounced kun-dune) is the honorific title Tibetans use when addressing their highest officials – tells the story of the 14th Dalai Lama: from his discovery in 1937 in a village on the border to China to his journey into exile to Dharamsala, India, in 1959. Together with his family, the young boy is first brought to the Tibetan Capital of Lhasa. Before he is officially crowned the new spiritual and secular leader of Tibet, he must submit to a strict and demanding education in the teachings of Buddha. Although the young boy is waited on and spoiled by high officials and servants, he must, however, also complete a myriad of tasks dictated by tradition and, last but not least, further his spiritual and religious development – a program that resembles little the childhood of a normal boy.

Over time, worldly and western influences gradually seep into the boy's upbringing. In one instance, he is given a telescope as a gift, which he uses enthusiastically and in another, he even tries to drive a car. In the paper, he reads about World War II, Hitler, and Nazi Germany. His life, however, is not truly affected by world politics until 1950, when the Chinese People's Liberation Army invades Tibet and the party's leader, Mao Tse-tung, declares Tibet part of the People's Republic of China. As a result of these events, the Dalai Lama, who was crowned ruler of Tibet three years earlier than usual at the young age of 15, seeks the support of the United States, the United Kingdom, and India and even negotiates with Mao himself in Beijing. His efforts, however, are all in vain. In the end, he flies to India.

The story is based on the biography of the real 14th Dalai Lama, Tenzin Gyatso, the internationally revered spiritual leader, who received the Nobel Peace Prize in 1989. The screenplay writer, Melissa Mathison (who also wrote, among others, the script for *E.T.: The Extra-Terrestrial*, 1982), tells the story from the perspective of a child or adolescent – a child who overnight becomes entangled in the power struggles of world politics. In an interview about his film, Scorsese said he was particularly interested in showing how a boy who grows up in a society purely based on spiritual values reacts.

1   Still a child and already a ruler, still a learner and already an advisor: the 12-year-old Dalai Lama (Gyurme Tethong).

2   At the age of five, the Dalai Lama (Tulku Jamyang Kunga Tenzin) is brought to the palace in Lhasa – his life as a normal child comes to an end.

3   His older brother, Lobsang (Tenzin Topjar, right), accompanies the Dalai Lama to Lhasa.

"Probably only a filmmaker like Mr. Scorsese, a former Roman Catholic altar boy who once considered joining the priesthood, would have made a film like *Kundun*." *The New York Times*

4 He belongs to the people and not only to his family: the Dalai Lama must even part with his brother.

5 The Dalai Lama's mother (Tencho Gyalpo) goes with her son to the palace in Lhasa.

6 In the surroundings of the bright and airy summer residence, the Dalai Lama enjoys nature. His attendant (Losang Samten, right, a sand mandala artist and former Buddhist monk) makes sure he does not stray too far.

Director Martin Scorsese (*Casino*, 1995) himself grew up in the strict catholic environment of New York's Little Italy. For a time, he attended a Jesuit school and even wanted to become a priest. After *The Last Temptation of Christ* (1988), *Kundun* is Scorsese's second biopic about a religious leader. He developed *Kundun* on two parallel levels. On the first level, the biographical story unfolds, which the film follows linearly over a span of 22 years.

The second level is incomparably stronger and more moving – here, Scorsese's film creates a meditative visual and auditory world in which we as viewers are submerged as if into a spiritual world. The cinematography of Roger Deakin's (Oscar nomination for *True Grit*, 2010) captures Tibet's harsh desert beauty in utterly overwhelming visual compositions (filming took place, however, in Morocco). Sequences of vision and symbols – for example, a large mandala out of colored sand, which emerges throughout the film as a kind of

"The film's visuals and music are rich and inspiring, and like a mass by Bach or a Renaissance church painting, it exists as an aid to worship: It wants to enhance, not question." *Chicago Sun-Times*

7 The Dalai-Lama (Tenzin Thuthob Tsarong) flees
   incognito over the peaks of the Himalayas to India.

8 Weakened by illness and tortured by horrifying
   visions, the Dalai-Lama must cross the border to
   India on foot.

9 The Dalai-Lama (under the parasol) departs on a
   long journey to Beijing to negotiate with China's
   leader Mao Tse-tung.

10 Crowned the spiritual leader of the Tibetan
   people, the Dalai-Lama (l) must also perform
   Buddhist rituals.

leitmotif – as well as the Buddhist rituals depicted in intense colors evoke a strange and, at the same time, magical atmosphere. In contrast to these the Dalai Lama's visions are interspersed throughout the film, which at times appear bizarre and brutal, and disturbingly pierce through the spiritual element of the film. Above all, these scenes reflect the extremely violent nature of the actual political situation of Tibet's occupation by Mao's soldiers.

The stunning visual world together with the hypnotic film score by Philip Glass give the film a contemplative quality. Scorsese produces a frenzy of sounds and images in which some recognize the endless circle of life as well as Buddhism's harmony with and understanding of nature. The New York Times wrote, "Martin Scorsese has come the closest he ever has to making a work of pure cinema."   HJK

PHILIP GLASS Dark ringing Tibetan horns, shimmering strings and the deep voices of monks – this is how the soundtrack of Kundun begins. And without much variation, this motif is repeated again and again. The American composer Philip Glass (*1937) is considered one of the fathers of minimal music, a style of the 20th century characterized by repetitive structures and the influence of world music. Glass has written instrumental pieces, operas, and several film scores. He became internationally popular with his soundtrack for the cult film Koyaanisqatsi (1983), a combination of experiment, documentation, and hallucinatory trip. Glass is a Buddhist and, since meeting with the Dalai-Lama in 1972, he is considered one of the most important international supporters of the Tibetan Independence Movement. He learned of Scorsese's Dalai-Lama project early on and began composing the soundtrack even before the end of filming. During the final stages of production, director Martin Scorsese edited several passages according to the rhythm and feeling of the music: a rare approach in filmmaking, which incidentally was also used by Sergio Leone for his film Once Upon a Time in the West (C'era una volta il West, 1968). Indeed, only this approach could create the close relationship between image and sound, in which the two strengthen and enrich each other. In an interview, the composer expressed this in a more humble manner: he "wanted to open a door," so that the viewer could get a feel for the setting.

THE CELEBRATION
FESTEN (DOGME 1)

1998 – DENMARK – 106 MIN. – DRAMA
DIRECTOR THOMAS VINTERBERG (*1969)
SCREENPLAY THOMAS VINTERBERG, MOGENS RUKOV
DIRECTOR OF PHOTOGRAPHY ANTHONY DOD MANTLE **EDITING** VALDÍS
ÓSKARSDÓTTIR **MUSIC** MORTEN HOLM **PRODUCTION** BRIGITTE HALD,
MORTEN KAUFMANN FOR NIMBUS FILM
STARRING ULRICH THOMSEN (Christian), THOMAS BO LARSEN
(Michael), PAPRIKA STEEN (Helene), HENNING MORITZEN (Helge),
BIRTHE NEUMANN (Mother), TRINE DYRHOLM (Pia),
HELLE DOLLERIS (Mette), BJARNE HENRIKSEN (Chef),
GBATOKAI DAKINAH (Gbatokai), KLAUS BONDAM
(Master of Ceremonies), THOMAS VINTERBERG (Taxi Driver),
JOHN BOAS (Grandfather)
IFF CANNES 1998 SPECIAL JURY PRIZE

"Here's to the man who killed my sister, a toast to a murderer."

A dogma is a religious teaching or a doctrine of belief. When four Danes got together to draw up ten commandments in 1995, they baptized them "Dogme 95" and described them as a cinematic vow of chastity, it seemed a bizarre act of self-chastisement in a postideological age. Perhaps, critics suggested, the whole thing was a bid for freedom at a time of computer animation and post-modern indifference. They wanted to do away with all the trappings of technology and get back to the basics: strict classical form following crazy, ornate Baroque. Perhaps, the sceptics replied, it was nothing more than a publicity stunt: Tarantino meets *It's a Wonderful Life*.

Nobody could have guessed at that point that the same four Danes would go on to open an agency that watched over the keeping of the commandments and distributes certificates. By the beginning of 2001 a dozen films had been adjudged worthy to promote themselves as "produced in accordance with the rules of the Dogme Manifesto." Both the manifesto and the certification process are inspired by deadly seriousness tempered with a certain dose of ironic humor, and certificates cost anything from nothing at all to 2000 dollars, according to the budget of the film in question. One of the signatories, Thomas Vinterberg, director of the first brilliant Dogme film *The Celebration*, admitted in an interview that the whole thing oscillated between being "a game and in deadly earnest."

That is also a good description of *The Celebration*'s relationship to its subject matter: whenever viewers attempt to look at it purely as a comedy or solely as drama, it is guaranteed to topple over into the opposite. Drama and comedy are most likely to meet at their extremes. *The Celebration* is not exactly a black comedy, more a bitter reckoning with the deceptive façade of the institution of family life. The best ideas often come from a new look at traditional models and the movie's departure point is very simple: patriarch Helge (Henning Moritzen) is celebrating his 60th birthday with his family at a country mansion. The party turns into a night of grim revelations and innumerable skeletons are dragged out of the family closet.

Basically, the film is about the accusations of the oldest son Christian (Ulrich Thomsen). He claims that he and his twin sister were abused by their father, and that this was the reason for his sister's recent suicide. After a shocked pause, the guests return to the festivities as if nothing had happened. At first, Christian's repeated accusations are received with the same equanimity as the table speeches of the grandfather (John Boas) who always tells the same anecdote. Later his mother (Birthe Neumann) attempts to smooth over the situation and finally his hot-tempered youngest brother Michael (Thomas Bo Larsen) explodes. It takes a message from the next world to convince those present of Christian's story.

The Discreet Charm of the Dogme Commandments

Some critics consider the Dogme commandments to be a self-important waste of time, but the rules for the use of natural sound and handheld cameras result in films that look like home movies, giving a picture and sound quality which contributes greatly to the believability of their story lines. At first sight, high-resolution video shot without artificial light and transferred onto 35 mm looks like an amateur recording of a private birthday party. The unusual, often underexposed or unfocused pictures force the audience to concentrate. Like a source of purity and liberation, they contrast with the family's repression of the party's shocking revelations. The Dogme films' rejection of skillfully produced, artificial images gives them a feeling of undiluted direct-ness and a whole new palette of expressive means. This is the attack of the documentary handheld camera on the bastion of the feature film – direct cinema as a presentation of the truth in fiction.

Once spectators get used to the grainy, wobbly pictures, which have quite a different beauty from polished Hollywood pictures, the movie itself is highly coherent both visually and dramatically. The camera angles have been chosen with extreme care: there is a bird's eye view from the corner of the room, a jump shot over a fence, and a camera hidden behind the banisters. Furniture or objects often obstruct the camera's viewfinder. There are two possible interpretations of this: firstly, a blocked viewpoint implies that the place of filming is treated spontaneously and that potential obstacles are dealt with as they arise. Secondly, obscured viewpoints give the movie a documentary feel, as if the camera were a hidden witness or a passerby. The plot follows the classic division in three acts with Christian as the hero and focal point overcoming opposition and obstacles. At the beginning he only has the

1 The patriarch Helge shortly before his fall from power: Henning Moritzen, Birthe Neumann.

2 Michael (Thomas Bo Larsen) lets himself be waited on by his ex-lover (Birgitte Simonsen).

3 "When my sister died a couple of months ago, it became clear to me that with all the baths he took, Helge was a very clean man." Christian (Ulrich Thomsen) accuses his father.

4 Chopped-off heads, blurred images, and natural lighting – camera technique applying the Dogme 95 resolutions.

5 Two brothers still fighting for their father's favor: Christian is thrown out of the house at the instigation of his younger brother Michael.

3

support of the hotel staff who have known him since he was little, like the chef Kim, who spirits away the guests' keys so that they are isolated in the country house like the guests in Buñuel's *The Exterminating Angel* (*El ángel exterminador*, 1962). But Mexico or Denmark, 1962 or 1998, bourgeois charm is revealed to be nothing but a veneer of civilization that peels away all too easily.

With great intensity and directness, Vinterberg and his actors show how the respectable bourgeois atmosphere is rapidly transformed into hate-filled racism, how finally the aggressive brother Michael changes sides and erupts against his father instead of shouting at his wife and children, his sister's black boyfriend, and his brother. The abyss in *The Celebration* lurks just below the surface: the official face of the family only just manages to conceal the grimace behind it. Vinterberg is so committed and uncompromising, he almost seems like a descendent of the iconoclasts of the '68 generation.

Vinterberg grew up in a hippy commune. In interviews, he often points out that the Catholic terminology of the Dogme Manifesto came from cosignatory Lars von Trier and has nothing to do with him. He prefers the communist component implicit in the word "manifesto." To him, this artistic manifesto is also a compelling call to revolt, a return to the basics of collective film-making and an appeal for the rejection of production hierarchies, so as a protest against the cult of the auteur, the director's name is not allowed to appear on the film. The aim above all is to reclaim film from the spirit of postmodernism. Dogma means nothing less than forgetting everything you've already seen and done, beginning again from the beginning, and reinventing cinema. Vinterberg is still filled with awe and wonder in the face of "living pictures" and he shares this with his audience.

MH

DOGME 95 **1.** Shooting must be done on location. Props and sets must not be brought in. **2.** The sound must never be produced separate from the images or vice versa. **3.** The camera must be handheld. **4.** The film must be in color. Special lighting is not acceptable. **5.** Optical work and filters are forbidden. **6.** The film must not contain superficial action. **7.** Temporal and geographical alienation are forbidden (i.e. the film takes place in the here and now.) **8.** Genre movies are not acceptable. **9.** The film format must be Academy 35 mm. **10.** The director must not be credited. For a time, the Dogme 95 movement – an avant-garde film collective initiated in Denmark by Lars von Trier – influenced independent cinema in Europe, and to an extent the US. Between 50 and 100 films are attributed to the genre; one of the last Dogme films, which was explicitly guided by the manifesto from 1995, is *Open Hearts* (*Elsker dig for evigt*, 2002, Denmark) by Susanne Bier. In March 2005 it was decided that from then on filmmakers themselves are left with the decision as to whether their work is in accordance with the principles of the Dogme 95 movement.

"Something terrible happens and everyone says, 'Let's have another cup of coffee, let's sing a song and have a dance.' That is typical of the Danes."

Thomas Vinterberg in *Zoom*

RUN LOLA RUN
LOLA RENNT

1998 – GERMANY – 79 MIN. – LOVE FILM, ACTION FILM
DIRECTOR TOM TYKWER (*1965)
SCREENPLAY TOM TYKWER DIRECTOR OF PHOTOGRAPHY FRANK GRIEBE EDITING MATHILDE BONNEFOY
MUSIC TOM TYKWER, JOHNNY KLIMEK, REINHOLD HEIL PRODUCTION STEFAN ARNDT for
X FILME CREATIVE POOL, ARTE, WDR
STARRING FRANKA POTENTE (Lola), MORITZ BLEIBTREU (Manni), HERBERT KNAUP
(Lola's father), ARMIN ROHDE (Mr. Schuster), JOACHIM KRÓL (Norbert von Au / Bum),
HEINO FERCH (Ronnie), NINA PETRI (Jutta Hansen), SUZANNE VON BORSODY
(Mrs. Jäger), LARS RUDOLPH (Kassierer Kruse), SEBASTIAN SCHIPPER (Mike)

"Ball's round. Game lasts 90 minutes. I can follow that much. All the rest is just theory."

Tom Tykwer's first films caused a stir – his elegiac debut *Deadly Maria* (*Die tödliche Maria*, 1993) and the prize-winning *Wintersleepers* (*Winterschläfer*, 1997), although naturally the interest came more from critics and impassioned art house fans than it did from the general public. *Run Lola Run* came as a surprise in every respect. Its content is as complex as his previous film, the mournful, difficult melodrama *Wintersleepers*, but formally it is exactly the opposite with its hip, contemporary look. It combines classic means of expression such as split screen, slow motion, time lapse, and animated sequences with a modern pop video aesthetic resulting in some impressive visual fireworks. Those visuals are complimented by Franka Potente and Moritz Bleibtreu, its fresh, cool, attractive young stars, but above all by its speed. *Run Lola Run* is a throwback to the childish enthusiasm inspired by the earliest cinema pictures, the simplest of all film images: a person in motion.

It's high-speed cinema. Tykwer's movie is literally a running film, and spectators are carried along with it through the streets of Berlin, where Lola (Franka Potente) races panting over the asphalt and cobblestones, over bridges, building sites and squares, puffing and gasping but determined, driven on by the pumping techno soundtrack. The movie was also a welcome surprise where the image of German films abroad was concerned. Humor is difficult to translate, and while domestic German cinema had turned out some excellent relationship comedies like *Maybe … Maybe Not* (1994) in the '90s, they had never really made it abroad. *Lola* on the other hand ran not only all over German cinema screens but was also invited to international festivals such as Venice and Sundance.

Hers is a race against time, for love: Lola has 20 minutes to find 100,000 marks. That's the amount of money that her boyfriend Manni (Moritz Bleibtreu) has lost in the subway – money which actually belonged to the gangster boss Ronnie (Heino Ferch), and if Manni doesn't deliver the sum at 12 on the dot, he's a dead man – "it's as simple as that." And so Lola runs through Berlin, first to her father, who is a bank director, then to meet Manni who is threatening to rob a supermarket.

Run Lola Run is physical, dynamic, speed-dominated action cinema. With her fire-red shock of hair, Lola runs like the Pippi Longstocking of the ecstasy generation. "I make the world how I like it …" she seems to say, and Lola's streets are empty and wide. Anyone who knows Berlin soon realizes that the routes she runs have nothing to do with the real geography of

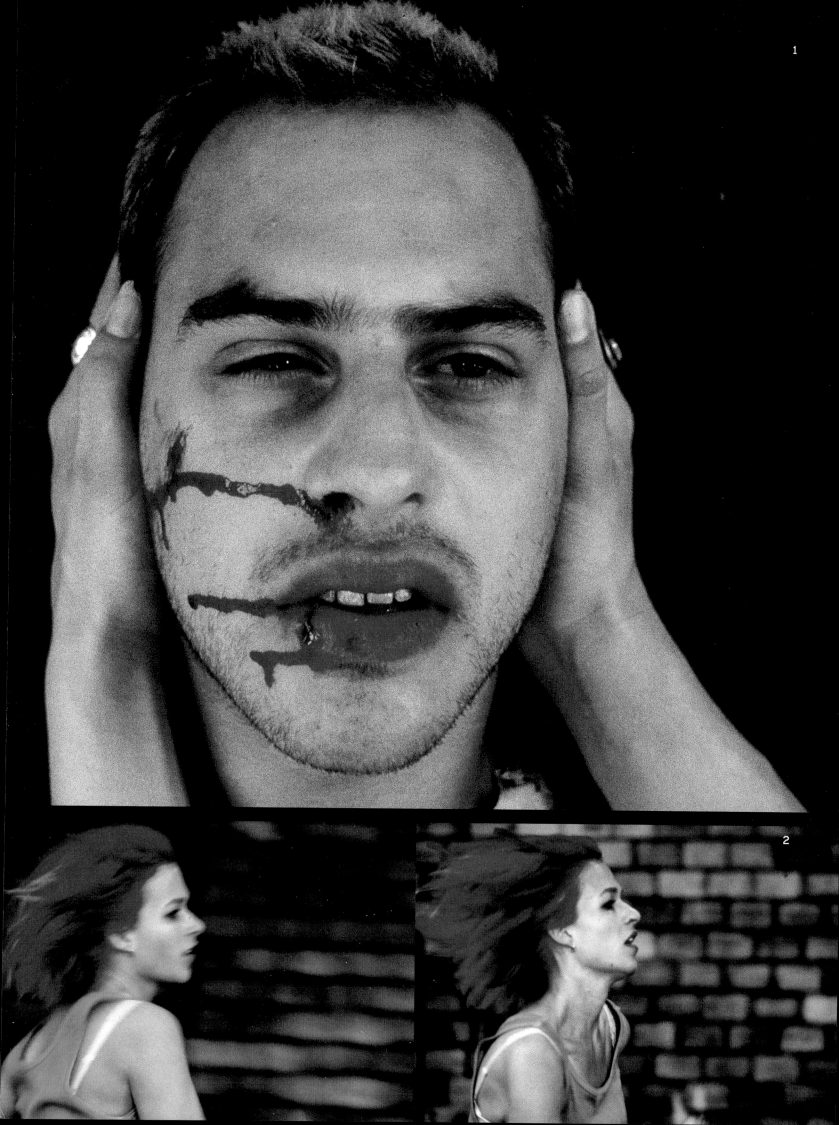

4

1 After *Knockin' on Heaven's Door* Moritz Bleibtreu's role as Manni in *Run Lola Run* finally made him a star.

2 Seventy-nine minutes of speed, 79 minutes of life in the fast lane: Franka Potente as Lola.

3 On a narrative and visual level, *Run Lola Run* is a sophisticated play of displacements, duplications, about-turns, and mirror images.

4 The film slackens its pace for a few moments during conversations about love.

5 German heartthrob Heino Ferch, barely recognizable as shaven-headed gang leader Ronnie.

6 Lola's costume, a city brat outfit representing something near permanence in the metropolitan jungle with boots, combat trousers, and vest quickly found a place in the Berlin Film Museum.

DIGITAL PICTURES With the development of the computer, a completely new world opened up for special effects experts. Pictures scanned into the computer could be changed at will: to erase a price label left inadvertently on a coffee cup; to combine actors with real historical personalities, as in Robert Zemeckis's *Forrest Gump* (1994); or to save an army of extras by copying digital images as in Wolfgang Petersen's *In the Line of Fire* (1993) and Ridley Scott's *Gladiator* (2000). Computer generated images (CGI) open up an entire new dimension for special effects. While films like Steven Spielberg's *Jurassic Park* (1993) still used a combination of CGI and camera shots, films were soon being produced entirely by digital means, such as *Final Fantasy* (2001), and more recently in 3D like *The Adventures of Tintin* (2011).

---

the city. But that's not just an error, for *Run Lola Run* is also a philosophical film, an illustration of chaos theory, a hypothetical game of "what if …" Lola sets off three times to save Manni, in three lots of 20 minutes. Her way across town is different every time, according to how she reacts to the dog that snarls at her in the stairwell of her apartment building. Does she jump over it? Is she momentarily frightened? Or does the child with the dog stick a leg out and trip her up? Every second won or lost in leaving the house changes her own fate and that of many others. The first time Lola bursts into her father's office to discover him embracing his lover, the second time he has just discovered that she is pregnant, and a third time it becomes clear that the child is not his. One time Lola dies, another time Manni dies, and there is one happy ending. This game with destiny, with possibilities, options, and their effects on time and space is also played on an emotional level in the few quiet moments of the movie. Manni and Lola lie in bed together and talk like Valentine's Day cards, asking "Well, do you love me or not?" Spectators immediately identify with the dialogues – Manni wants to find out whether Lola would still love him if he were dead or if she met someone else or if she didn't even know that he existed.

AK

"This image of the running woman contains everything: despair, emotion, dynamism – all the reasons why you actually wanted to make films ..."

Tom Tykwer in *Süddeutsche Zeitung*

THE TRUMAN SHOW

1998 – USA – 103 MIN. – SCIENCE FICTION, DRAMA
DIRECTOR PETER WEIR (*1944)
SCREENPLAY ANDREW NICCOL DIRECTOR OF PHOTOGRAPHY PETER BIZIOU EDITING WILLIAM M. ANDERSON,
LEE SMITH MUSIC PHILIP GLASS, BURKHART DALLWITZ PRODUCTION EDWARD S. FELDMAN,
ANDREW NICCOL, SCOTT RUDIN, ADAM SCHROEDER for PARAMOUNT PICTURES
STARRING JIM CARREY (Truman Burbank), ED HARRIS (Christof), LAURA LINNEY
(Meryl Burbank / Hanna Gill), NOAH EMMERICH (Marlon / Louis Coltrane),
NATASCHA MCELHONE (Lauren Garland / Sylvia), HOLLAND TAYLOR (Angela Burbank,
Truman's mother), BRIAN DELATE (Kirk Burbank, Truman's father)

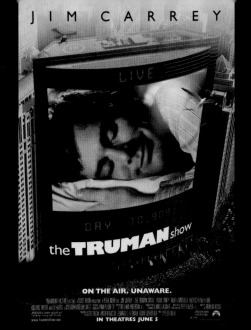

"We accept the reality of the world with which we are presented."

During our childhood, we often have the impression that the world around us was made solely for our benefit. This makes it all the more depressing when things happen to make us realize that this is not the case. Film and television have made it their task over the last hundred years to try and console us for the loss of this naive notion. It sounds like an absurd idea, but what if the world really did revolve around us? What would happen if we found out? George Orwell's fictional Big Brother in his futuristic novel *1984* was the first to make us suspicious, but now reality TV shows like *Big Brother* have confirmed that we are both observing and observed, guinea pigs in an experimental labyrinth watching other animals try to find their way around. When Truman Burbank (Jim Carrey) finds that a spotlight has fallen out of the sky

and landed at his feet, that amusing yet horrifying process of realization begins for him.

In Peter Weir's media parable *The Truman Show*, the life of Truman Bank, the main character, has been organized like an enormous soap opera that has millions glued to their screens every day – and Truman is the only person who knows nothing about it. Since his birth 30 years ago his life has taken place in a kind of TV test tube, in a huge production hall where no expense is spared to create the realistic effects that make up his world. What appears outside on the screen as fiction is grotesque reality inside, the result of the production crew's hard work. Outside nobody needs to worry about that, as they make their money out of Truman's life and his emotions.

Truman is totally financed by advertising. He is a merchandising concept, exposed without mercy, available round the clock, a genuine 24 hours a day, seven days a week star. The idea is the life's work of Christof (Ed Harris), the genius producer of the "Truman Show."

Without Jim Carrey in the role of Truman Burbank, it might have been a much more cynical movie. Truman's smooth and superficial world is beginning to crack under the strain of too much product placement and over-perfection. Carrey's comic genius saves us – luckily, some might say – from too many worrying insights. In the synthetic television world of his own show Truman is a charmingly innocent insurance agent, who wants nothing more than to relax after a stressful day at the office, and one day, to travel to the faraway Fiji islands. But that is absolutely impossible, for reasons of which he is unaware – in reality he is the prisoner of a mass media spectacle. The entire production team spends all its time trying to distract him from this thought, either with faked traffic jams or posters which warn against long journeys or discouraging travel agents.

The production team of the "Truman Show" tends to Truman's every need, every second of the day. But as the system gets bigger it becomes increasingly difficult to control. Then Truman sees a homeless bum, and he suddenly recognizes his father. A flashback explains that Truman had always believed his father to have died in a tragic accident at sea when he was still a child, and this new revelation brings his world crashing down around him.

1   Friendly, cheerful, and a bit backward: Truman Burbank (Jim Carrey) is half Forrest Gump, half Jerry Lewis.

2   The real world as a real whirl of merchandise: attractively packaged promises of happiness, shown off by a friendly nurse (Laura Linney).

3   Can Truman really trust his friend Marlon (Noah Emmerich)?

"Truman Burbank, the 'true man' from Burbank, the place in California where all the big studios are based, is completely normal, authentic down to the smallest detail, and famous the world over."

Frankfurter Allgemeine Zeitung

JIM CARREY   His performances are reminiscent of another great comedian and clown of American cinema – Jerry Lewis. Like Lewis, Carrey, who was born in Canada in 1962, favors a crazy, exaggerated, physical style of comedy. The distinguishing features of Carrey's appearances are an enormous grin and his penchant for bizarre characters and zany pranks. He became famous as the title character in the surprise hit *Ace Ventura: Pet Detective* (1993), which grossed over 100 million dollars. Many, often over-the-top, comedies followed: *Dumb & Dumber* and *The Mask* (both 1994), *The Cable Guy* (1996), *The Grinch* (2000), and *Mr. Popper's Penguins* (2011). Carrey has also, however, made regular appearances in more serious films, such as *The Truman Show* (1998) and the philosophical romantic drama *Eternal Sunshine of the Spotless Mind* (2004). Perhaps his best role to date, seamlessly combining satire and drama, was in Miloš Forman's biography of the TV comedian Andy Kaufman, *Man on the Moon* (1999).

4

"In an age where the mass media of television and film are exploiting their very own simulation strategies and how these relate to 'reality' with wavering quality, we were crying out for a satire on these media." *epd Film*

5

4 A god of artifice: director Christof (Ed Harris) as
   creator and supreme father of the world.

5 Television-style TLC.

6 The view in the mirror: who is watching whom?

He is the main character in a perfect illusion that is shattered by one of its own elementary principles, repetition. The same actor is hired to play the homeless man as played by his father in his fake yet traumatic childhood memories. Additional goofs mount up: spotlights repeatedly fall from the sky, it only rains where Truman happens to be, stage directions are broadcast on the radio by mistake and passersby and cars move at implausibly regular intervals along the same trajectories. The movie cleverly combines ironic humor and important truths. The pictures of Truman's life are framed by iris

patterns that constantly remind us of the secret observers, the voyeuristic gaze of the hidden camera which registers Truman's every move with no less than five thousand lenses.

Luckily, however, there is a limit to this entertaining yet deeply disturbing scenario. When Truman tries to escape from his home on Seahaven Island in a sailing dinghy, he crashes into the painted horizon on the scenery wall and both audiences breathe a sigh of relief. Life as a cliché in a cliché comes to a – happy – end here in the literal sense of the word.   BR

THE THIN RED LINE

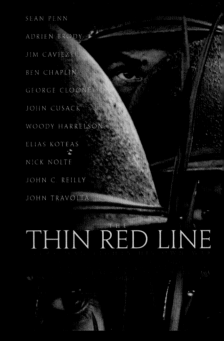

1998 – USA – 170 MIN. – WAR FILM

DIRECTOR TERRENCE MALICK (*1943)

SCREENPLAY TERRENCE MALICK, based on the novel of the same name by JAMES JONES

DIRECTOR OF PHOTOGRAPHY JOHN TOLL **EDITING** LESLIE JONES, SAAR KLEIN, BILLY WEBER

MUSIC HANS ZIMMER **PRODUCTION** ROBERT MICHAEL GEISLER, GRANT HILL, JOHN ROBERDEAU for PHOENIX, GEISLER-ROBERDEAU-PRODUCTIONS

STARRING SEAN PENN (First Sgt. Edward Welsh), ADRIEN BRODY (Corp. Fife), JIM CAVIEZEL (Priv. Witt), BEN CHAPLIN (Priv. Jack Bell), GEORGE CLOONEY (Capt. Charles Bosche), JOHN CUSACK (Capt. John Gaff), WOODY HARRELSON (Sgt. Keck), ELIAS KOTEAS (Capt. James Staros), NICK NOLTE (Col. Gordon Tall), JOHN TRAVOLTA (Brig. Gen. Quintard)

IFF BERLIN 1999 GOLDEN BEAR, SPECIAL COMMENDATION for CINEMATOGRAPHY (John Toll)

"Is there an avenging power in nature?"

War movies are characterized by much more than their own iconography and aren't limited to uniforms and airplanes, gaping wounds and amputated limbs, or helmets and weapons. They differ from other action films as they tend not to have an individual hero with a private adventure, but usually concentrate instead on a group of soldiers who have to overcome internal tensions in order to carry out a difficult mission together. This team is either played by lesser-known actors or is cast with a whole ensemble of stars, as both possibilities guarantee equality inside the team. When Hollywood outsider Terrence Malick decided to come out of a self-imposed 20-year period of seclusion by making a war movie, few expected him to stick to the established rules of the genre. *The Thin Red Line* did not disappoint these expectations. The movie tells the story of a group of soldiers on an island in the Pacific during the Second World War who are ordered to storm a hill held by the Japanese. The task seems simple and clearly defined, but the wider strategic importance of the battle is never really explained. At times, war doesn't seem to be the real theme of Malick's movie at all, and the many stars who grace the film seem to be tactically deployed, mere commercial calculations without whose presence no producer would have agree to finance the film.

The movie doesn't suffer from the typical dilemma of antiwar films that portray the horrors of war so brutally and graphically that it is impossible for them not to hold a certain fascination. Malick's recipe is antidramatization and a clear division into three parts which are as different as possible. It is almost as if *The Thin Red Line* falls apart, so different are the sections in tempo and in mood: in the first three-quarters of an hour, atmosphere is created, the characters and settings are introduced, and not one shot is fired. The main part of the film narrating the attack on the hill lasts about 75 minutes and is the part that comes closest to obeying the classic rules of plot development. The last 45 minutes are an epilogue that brings together a number of the plot strands and contains one last action sequence.

Some movies demand utter trust and self-abandonment from their audiences. They are not easy for viewers used to the standards of the typical Hollywood film, but the rewards are accordingly much higher. *The Thin Red Line* is one such movie. The perspective changes constantly and we are never sure who the actual main figures are – stars like Nick Nolte and Sean Penn or newcomers like Jim Caviezel and Ben Chaplin. The movie is more interested in the personal experiences of the recruits than it is in the actual fighting. Numerous narrative voices distract us from the action with philosophical thoughts that cause our mind to wander from the plot. The result is a clear refusal to conform to the conventional rules of drama, but what the movie loses in form, it wins in its freedom to illuminate different aspects of war

"As a visual spectacle, *The Thin Red Line* meets the expectations raised by *Badlands* and *Days of Heaven*. There's no question that Malick's ability to lend depth and texture to his images is without rival in Hollywood at the moment." *Sight and Sound*

War and Creation

The main part of the movie shows how the American soldiers try to conquer a hill occupied by the Japanese. The soldiers lose themselves in the waving grass of the hill: bent double, the scouts sneak forward through waist-high vegetation, half-crawling, half-running. The other soldiers watch anxiously and tensely. Shots ring out like whip cracks in the silence. The fallen soldiers disappear into the hill like stones dropped in a pond; the hill remains as still and seemingly untouched as before. When the weapons fall silent for a moment, nothing can be heard but the soft rustling of the wind as it blows through the blades of grass, forming a constant acoustic accompaniment to the attack. Then all hell breaks loose in a maelstrom of rockets, machine guns, grenades, shots, explosions, and shouts. In the midst of this commotion, a solider trips over a snake in the grass. For a split second the battle fades into the background and nature penetrates our consciousness with all her power. Again and again the movie turns away from the immediate threat in moments of danger or tension and shows colorful exotic birds, gnarled logs, or the tropical treetops with the sun shining brightly through them.

Malick contrasts the majesty of nature with the corruption of war and its culture of destruction. These diversions are not self-indulgently picturesque or irrelevant animal images, they serve to sharpen our eyes for the contrast between nature and culture and therefore also for war. There are unforgettable images, the likes of which are rarely seen in other war movies, like a dying bird hit by a bullet, writhing in agony, or a native striding past a jungle patrol, who shows no sign of having seen the soldiers. Another soldier stares fascinated at a bizarrely shaped leaf in the midst of the battle while his comrades die around him.

Unlike Steven Spielberg's *Saving Private Ryan* (1998), which was made at more or less the same time, the viewer is never told exactly why or for what the soldiers are fighting. The actors go through the movie seemingly without an aim or motivation. They retreat into the background for half an hour or so or leave the picture completely, then unexpectedly reappear. This makes them a symbol of the expendability of soldiers in war. It is therefore all the

1   Battle plans during a temporary lull: First Sergeant Welsh (Sean Penn), Colonel Tall (Nick Nolte), and Captain Staros (Elias Koteas).

2   Mail from home: Bell (Ben Chaplin) misses his wife, who eventually leaves him for an air force captain.

3   Captain Staros, of Greek origin, refuses to send his men into a battle they have no hope of winning, bringing great trouble upon himself.

4   Staring the high casualty rate in the eye. The natural surroundings so prominent in the film remain unmoved by the war.

5   An innocent paradise? Two blueprints for civilization collide on a Pacific island (Jim Caviezel, right).

TERRENCE MALICK When Terrence Malick (*1943) finished *Days of Heaven* in 1978, two years had passed since the end of filming. Through endless fights with the producers and Richard Gere, the movie's leading actor, the stubborn and self-willed Malick stuck to his vision. Belief in his own ideas, his sparse film output (five films in almost forty years) and last but not least his aesthetic formal language have together made Malick, who studied philosophy and directing, one of the great, enigmatic poets of cinema. Malick's movie debut was *Badlands* (1973), about a young, criminal couple fleeing through the deserted landscapes of Dakota and Montana. After *The Thin Red Line* (1998), he made *The New World* (2005) about the clash between English colonial settlers and Native Americans, and the philosophical film *The Tree of Life* (2011) – a hypnotic, elegiac drama that won Malick the Golden Palm at Cannes.

"Death appears in the endless sea of green like an episode in Nature's never-ending drama." *Die Zeit*

6 Facing death. Keck (Woody Harrelson) has
   accidentally pulled the pin from a hand grenade.

7 Commander Tall wants to capture the hill at any
   price.

8 Keck and Welsh still find something to laugh about.

more surprising that famous stars agreed to be treated this way; however, as with Woody Allen or Stanley Kubrick, working with Malick is a distinction for which many actors are prepared to waive their usual conditions.

John Travolta appears at the beginning of the movie for three brief minutes as a brigadier general who does little other than cast meaningful glances out to sea, and George Clooney appears in an even shorter scene at the end of the movie in a pastiche of the patriarchal "family man" who talks down to his soldiers as though they were children. Scenes filmed with Lukas Haas and Bill Pullman were later cut and the role planned for Gary Oldman never materialized.

At the end of the movie the survivors return on a battleship and we see new recruits arrive on the island. The movie may be over, but the war goes on.

Malick once again confirmed his place as a leading outsider in Hollywood with *The Thin Red Line*. By mixing chaotic images of war with sublime pictures of the natural world, he shows the ambivalence of human nature. The movie claims the right to ask questions which go beyond visible reality. Who are we, if we are capable of such utter madness, while still being able to appreciate and experience the beauties of nature?

MH

8

THE BIG LEBOWSKI

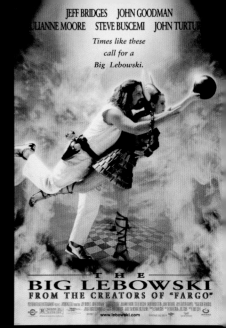

998 – USA – 113 MIN. – COMEDY
DIRECTOR JOEL COEN (*1954)
SCREENPLAY JOEL COEN, ETHAN COEN DIRECTOR OF PHOTOGRAPHY ROGER DEAKINS
EDITING TRICIA COOKE, ETHAN COEN, JOEL COEN (as Roderick Jaynes)
MUSIC CARTER BURWELL, T-BONE BURNETT PRODUCTION ETHAN COEN for
WORKING TITLE FILMS
STARRING JEFF BRIDGES (Jeffrey "The Dude" Lebowski), JOHN GOODMAN (Walter Sobchak),
JULIANNE MOORE (Maude Lebowski), STEVE BUSCEMI (Donny), DAVID HUDDLESTON
(The Big Lebowski), PETER STORMARE (Nihilist no.1), FLEA (Nihilist no. 2),
TORSTEN VOGES (Nihilist no. 3), PHILIP SEYMOUR HOFFMAN (Brandt), JOHN TURTURRO
(Jesus Quintana), SAM ELLIOTT (The Stranger), BEN GAZZARA (Jackie Treehorn)

"Quite possibly the laziest man in Los Angeles County ... which would place him high in the runnin' for laziest worldwide."

Woe betide anyone who calls him Mr. Lebowski. "I'm the Dude," he insists, "so that's what you call me. That, or Duder. His Dudeness. Or El Duderino." A hairy old hippy whose nourishment consists entirely of White Russian cocktails, likes to smoke his joints in the bathtub and listens to whale calls at great length.

It's 1991. The Gulf War rages at the other end of the world, but the Dude (Jeff Bridges) is still floating in the serene intoxication of the psychedelic 70s. The center of his life is the bowling alley where he meets his friends Walter (John Goodman) and Donny (Steve Buscemi) to prepare for the next tournament, although even there his main aim is to move as little as possible. However, these leisurely days come to an abrupt halt when some debt collectors confuse the Dude with a millionaire of the same name from Pasadena and pee on his beautiful Persian carpet as a warning. The Big Lebowski is Joel and Ethan Coen's third movie about kidnapping, following Raising Arizona (1987) and Fargo (1996); their weakness for this particular plot mechanism is because "everything can go so very wrong." Accordingly,

the Dude's life runs completely out of control when Bunny, the wife of the other Lebowski, is kidnapped. After the Dude and his bad-tempered friend Vietnam veteran Walter, have messed up handing over the money, they suddenly find themselves involved in an absolutely impenetrable tangle of interests and are threatened by a legendary porn producer, the police, and a trio of German nihilists.

Unmistakably a Coen movie, this hash-fueled comedy is filled with quotations, hints, and postmodern mannerisms. The Big Lebowski begins like a parody of the standard Western and develops into a gloriously laconic and ironic homage to the classics of hard-boiled literature. It may be a disinterested day dreamer who lopes through Los Angeles instead of a cool, hardened private detective, but the plot is just as confused as Raymond Chandler's The Big Sleep where even Philip Marlowe's creator couldn't say for sure who shot the chauffeur. At the end of The Big Lebowski nobody knows exactly what's going on, nor how the events hang together – least of all the Dude himself. The Coens are only superficially interested in establishing the

logical reconstruction of a crime, they are much more interested in indulging their weakness for bizarre characters, crazy situations, and sophisticated bluffs. Aspects of the movie are even reminiscent of the great musicals of the '30s, and one of its highlights is a flashy musical sequence that seems to have been choreographed by Busby Berkeley on acid. Under pressure from all sides, the happy hash dreams of the Dude give way to fearful fantasies where he ends up in a porn film being made by one of his enemies. With its characteristic top shots, the long legs of the glamour girls, and its symmetri-

cal choreography, his dream production (called "Gutterballs") looks like a down-market version of a famous Warner Bros. musical from the '30s. But fear creeps into the glittering arrangement of paste jewels and feathers, Saddam Hussein grins slyly in front of a shelf of bowling shoes and the German nihilists in flaming red catsuits brandish enormous scissors and threaten to remove Lebowski's "Johnson." Apparently, according to the Coen brothers, the figure of the Dude is based on an uncle of theirs – although who knows if they're to be trusted!   AK

"The Coens have an incredible sense for the crazy spirit of the contemporary age. They can't fall short of their surreal standard, and *The Big Lebowski* casts a glimmer of nightmare comedy on life." *Neue Zürcher Zeitung*

1   "The Dude" Lebowski (Jeff Bridges): one man and his drink. A White Russian is a mixture of vodka, kahlua, and cream.

2   "You said it, man. Nobody fucks with the Jesus!" – The most uptight challenger of the threesome is Jesus Quintana (John Turturro), a macho Latino dressed head to toe in purple.

3   "Losers like the Dude like hanging out at bowling alleys best. Bowling is a comfortable sport where you don't have to worry about keeping fit. We were also attracted by the design with the retro fifties and sixties feel to it." *Joel Coen*

4

5

4   When Jesus makes fun of him yet again, Walter (John Goodman) flips and pulls a gun on him. The Dude tries to calm him down, *"This is not Nam. This is bowling."*

5   Julianne Moore as the devious Maude Lebowski.

6   After his exaggerated role as the "kinda funny looking" kidnapper in *Fargo* (1996), Coen regular Steve Buscemi played Lebowski's withdrawn, almost melancholy buddy Donny.

6

OUT OF SIGHT

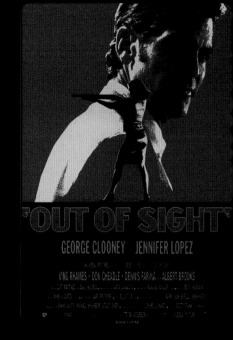

998 – USA – 123 MIN. – GANGSTER FILM, ROMANCE
DIRECTOR STEVEN SODERBERGH (*1963)
SCREENPLAY SCOTT FRANK, based on the novel of the same name by ELMORE LEONARD
DIRECTOR OF PHOTOGRAPHY ELLIOT DAVIS **EDITING** ANNE V. COATES **MUSIC** DAVID HOLMES
PRODUCTION DANNY DEVITO, MICHAEL SHAMBERG, STACEY SHER for JERSEY FILMS
(for UNIVERSAL)
STARRING GEORGE CLOONEY (Jack Foley), JENNIFER LOPEZ (Karen Sisco), VING RHAMES
(Buddy Bragg), DON CHEADLE (Maurice "Snoopy" Miller), DENNIS FARINA
(Marshal Sisco), ALBERT BROOKS (Richard Ripley), STEVE ZAHN (Glenn Michaels),
LUIS GUZMÁN (Chino)

"It's like seeing someone for the first time, and you look at each other for a few seconds, and there's this kind of recognition like you both know something."

Jack Foley (George Clooney) is a smart bank robber. He doesn't need a mask or a gun. His only weapons are his intelligence, his eloquence, and above all his irresistible charm. He's just finished relieving a bank of its earnings for the day, while still managing to give the insecure teller the feeling that she's doing a great job. There's only one thing missing from his life – luck. The getaway car fails to start up, the police are closing in, and it looks like another spell in the big house for our gentleman-gangster.

U. S. Marshal Karen Sisco (Jennifer Lopez) is a smart policewoman. She's clever, pretty, stylishly dressed, and has a soft spot for cold steel weapons. No birthday present could make her happier than the Sig-Sauer 380 that her father gives her, wrapped up in an elegantly worked box, polished and glittering like a piece of expensive jewelery.

Clearly, two such contrasting types are destined to be adversaries. Except that in Hollywood, the conventions teach us that opposites attract and that the protagonists, particularly when they are cast so ostentatiously, are bound to end up in each other's arms. When Karen and Jack meet for the first time, they are not only on opposing sides of the law, but are also quite literally separated by the trench and security fence of a prison. Jack attempts his tunnel escape from prison at the very moment that Karen is parking her car in the prison parking lot. With iron determination Karen Sisco, in a low-cut Chanel suit, loads her pump gun, sets her sights on the escapee, and walks toward him with steady pace, tough and sexy like no other film star of the past few years. But that irresistible appeal is of little use to Karen here, and seconds later she finds herself overpowered, tied up in the trunk of the getaway car, and face to face with Foley, her kidnapper. Their politely distanced conversation illuminated by the red-hot brake lights crackles with submerged tension and passion. And so it continues. Officially Karen trails the escaped criminal in order to arrest him, but in reality she just wants to be near him – to protect, to watch, to cherish, and to touch him. In this film, in an unusual reversal of the traditional gender clichés, it's the woman's fantasies that we watch on screen, and the man we are forced to see as a sex object. But Jack also longs to be with Karen. The nervous tension between attraction and separation, between intimacy and distance reminds us of classical stories of love between enemies like Achilles and Penthesilea. It is a drama of revelation and self-deception.

Steven Soderbergh's adaptation of Elmore Leonard's novel is an elegantly filmed and cleverly constructed collage. It doesn't tell a strictly linear story, but permanently shifts perspective by means of numerous jumps back and forth in time. The editing that results and the unsteady handheld camera work make *Out of Sight* a cool and stylish film that doesn't make a show of its coolness. It doesn't celebrate coolness with self-conscious pomp, like Barry Sonnenfeld's *Get Shorty* (1995) or Quentin Tarantino's *Jackie Brown* (1997, based on Leonard's novel *Rum Punch*), both of which helped bring about a Leonard renaissance. Compared with their calculated precision, the

2

1 Not even a spell in jail can dim George Clooney's image as the "sexiest man alive."

2 As a charming womanizer Clooney is reminiscent of classic Hollywood's great heroes.

3 From background dancer in musicals to highly paid Latin star: Jennifer Lopez has forged her path with determination.

4 They wanted to bring off the major coup together, but from the start the two gangs distrusted each other. Nonetheless, Jack Foley agrees to take part in the deal – with disastrous results...

JENNIFER LOPEZ Jennifer Lopez (*1969) is one of the few female entertainers to enjoy equal success as both a singer and actress. Her first two albums, *On the 6* and *J. Lo.*, both reached the top of the American charts. She was the first Hispanic actress in cinema history to break the salary barrier of a million dollars in the title role of *Selena* (1997), the biopic of an almost mythically revered Tejano singer who was brutally murdered. Her debut as a young mother in Nava's *My Family* (*Mi familia*, 1995) was a role that matched her ethnic background. Following the horror movie *Anaconda* (1996) and thrillers *U Turn* (1997) and *Out of Sight* (1998), she found her cinematic niche in romantic comedies. Her biggest hits in the genre include *Maid in Manhattan* (2002), *Shall We Dance* (2004), and *The Back-up Plan* (2010).

"As the suavest-looking thief since Cary Grant played a cat burglar on the Riviera, Clooney stares at her meaningfully, half-smiling, as he sweet-talks his way through the crime." New York Times

mannerisms of *Out of Sight* seem lighter, more playful, and almost improvised. And yet it is the more carefully staged movie as far as its overall effect is concerned.

This passionate hormone-filled thriller was a brilliant comeback for Steven Soderbergh. With *Sex, Lies, and Videotape* (1989) director and scriptwriter Soderbergh became the youngest ever award winner in Cannes. The films that followed however fell below critical and market expectations. With *Out of Sight* he seemed to find his touch again, and his next two movies, *Erin Brockovich* (2000) and *Traffic* (2000) were nominated in 2001 for an Oscar in the best film category – an honor last enjoyed by Michael Curtiz in 1939.

AK   3

HAPPINESS

1998 – USA – 134 MIN. – DRAMA
DIRECTOR TODD SOLONDZ (*1959)
SCREENPLAY TODD SOLONDZ **DIRECTOR OF PHOTOGRAPHY** MARYSE ALBERTI **EDITING** ALAN OXMAN
MUSIC ROBBIE KONDOR **PRODUCTION** TED HOPE, CHRISTINE VACHON for GOOD MACHINE
STARRING JANE ADAMS (Joy Jordan), LOUISE LASSER (Mona Jordan), LARA FLYNN BOYLE
(Helen Jordan), BEN GAZZARA (Lenny Jordan), DYLAN BAKER (Bill Maplewood),
JARED HARRIS (Vlad), PHILIP SEYMOUR HOFFMAN (Allen), JON LOVITZ (Andy Kornbluth),
JUSTIN ELVIN (Timmy Maplewood), CYNTHIA STEVENSON (Trish Maplewood),
EVAN SILVERBERG (Johnny Grasso)

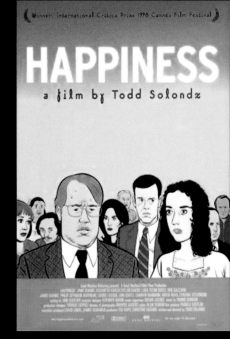

"I want kids that love me as much as I hated my mother."

The "pursuit of happiness" is a central element in American culture. The right of the individual to seek happiness after his own fashion is enshrined in the US Constitution. In his film, which is sarcastically entitled *Happiness*, Todd Solondz shows that this basic right does not always lead to success, and can easily end in its opposite. The film focuses on a disturbed relationship between three sisters. We are introduced to their crazy parents, who live in a kind of pensioners' theme park, and to a host of other eccentric characters – all of whom are engaged in the pursuit of that most elusive commodity, happiness itself. What initially sounds like a cheerful social comedy ultimately reveals itself to be a cynical and nightmarish treatment of the American Dream in all its facets. The park is filled with serial killers instead of canoodling lovers, golf courses mean heart attacks rather than relaxed recreation, and sexual delinquency replaces the suburban family idyll.

The first person we meet is Joy (Jane Adams), a lonely woman who writes songs about happiness that nobody wants to hear until her guitar is stolen by one of her lovers. She telephones her sister Helen (Lara Flynn Boyle), who cuts her short because she's busy in bed with her bodybuilder boyfriend. Yet when Helen visits her other sister Trish (Cynthia Stevenson), whose model family seems – on the surface at least – to uphold the middle-class ideal, they have a venomous debate about which of the two their unloved sister Joy trusts the most. Their parent's relationship has long been a war zone. Life is a daily battle, and normal human relations are the exception rather than the rule.

When Solondz shows us his long and carefully composed images of housing and external walls, he does this not only to characterize the lifestyles of his protagonists, but also to signal that the film is taking a look behind the scenes of this bogus bourgeois prosperity. When we peer behind the façade, things seem to be much less rosy for the middle-class people at the center of this film.

Happiness shows a nation that is threatening to suffocate under its own neuroses. The difficult theme of child abuse, which is also treated in the film, caused huge problems for its producers and distributors, and at one point

"Yes, Solondz's film is no less amusing than the best Woody Allen comedies. But it's more ambitious than that, too: it's the grave of American family values."

Le nouvel observateur

6

Happiness was in danger of being boycotted throughout the United States. The sympathetic portrayal of the father who sexually abuses the friend of his 11-year-old son had the conservative majority of Americans up in arms. What the film mercilessly reveals is the almost hysterical tendency to bring everything sexual out into the open, the disappearance of any last vestiges of shame or decency. Helen writes poems about an imaginary rape that she never suffered as a young girl. The greatest concern of Trish's son is whether he has reached sexual maturity or not, and Joy's frantic search for a boyfriend is just as pathological as Helen's promiscuity.

Whereas Solondz's first film *Welcome to the Dollhouse* (1996) shows how the pretensions of a single family are dismantled from the perspective of an 11-year-old child, *Happiness* deconstructs the entire lifestyle of middle-class suburban America. It is no accident that Trish and Allen's son is also 11 years old. Solondz portrays childhood as a kind of anteroom to hell, where we don't yet understand what's tormenting us. Things can only get worse with sexual maturity.

MH

BEN GAZZARA Ben Gazzara (1930–2012) is an actor who has never managed to achieve the fame commensurate with his acting talents. He has, however, consistently attracted the type of directors who have never entirely capitulated to the Hollywood system. The son of Sicilian immigrants, he originally studied engineering before training as an actor under Erwin Piscator and at The Actors Studio. He played the suspect in Otto Preminger's *Anatomy of a Murder* (1959) and became famous in the indie sector through his leading roles in John Cassavetes's *Husbands* (1970) and *The Killing of a Chinese Bookie* (1976). His career cooled off somewhat in the '80s, but then he was rediscovered by a new generation of innovative directors: the Coen brothers for *The Big Lebowski* (1998), Vincent Gallo for *Buffalo '66* (1997/1998), Spike Lee for *Summer of Sam* (1999), Lars von Trier for *Dogville* (2003) – and even Todd Solondz.

---

1   Three sisters: Trish (Cynthia Stevenson), her husband Bill (Dylan Baker), who has a dark secret…

2   … Joy (Jane Adams), who sings along to her guitar to cheer herself up, until she loses the instrument on a one-night stand…

3   … and Helen (Lara Flynn Boyle), who is the successful author of allegedly autobiographical sensational fiction.

4   Imprisoned by his obsession: the pedophile psychiatrist Bill watches children playing baseball.

5   Allen (Philip Seymour Hoffman) pesters his neighbor Helen with obscene phone calls.

6   Hell comes early in Solondz's world: Johnny Grasso (Evan Silverberg) and the toilet.

BUENA VISTA SOCIAL CLUB

1998/1999 – GERMANY / USA / FRANCE / CUBA – 105 MIN. – MUSIC FILM, DOCUMENTARY
DIRECTOR WIM WENDERS (*1945)
SCREENPLAY WIM WENDERS **DIRECTOR OF PHOTOGRAPHY** ROBBY MÜLLER, JÖRG WIDMER, LISA RINZLER
EDITING BRIAN JOHNSON **MUSIC** RY COODER, BUENA VISTA SOCIAL CLUB
PRODUCTION ULRICH FELSBERG, DEEPAK NAYAR for ROAD MOVIES, KINTOP PICTURES, ARTE, ICAIC
STARRING IBRAHIM FERRER, RUBÉN GONZÁLES, ELIADES OCHOA, OMARA PORTUONDO, COMPAY SEGUNDO, PIO LEYVA, MANUEL "PUNTILLITA" LICEA, ORLANDO "CACHAÍTO" LÓPEZ, RY COODER, JOACHIM COODER

"It's good not to have to pass the hat 'round anymore, but you don't forget."

Right at the beginning of the movie, we see pictures of Castro in front of the Lincoln Memorial in Washington. "David and Goliath" is the photographer's dry comment. It would be wrong however to expect *Buena Vista Social Club*, the film version of the album recorded by Ry Cooder with legendary Cuban Son musicians, to be a political movie. If the musicians portrayed are not at all concerned with material possessions, that is not because of their socialist convictions, but rather because there is only one meaning to their lives: music.

The movie came about through a series of coincidences. Producer Nick Gold and guitarist Ry Cooder had planned to record an album with African and Cuban musicians in the mid-'90s, but when they arrived in Havana for the recording they found that the Africans were stuck in Paris. Since they were already in Cuba, they looked round for alternatives and got hold of numerous old Son legends. Cooder named the demo tape of this session after the leg-

endary "Buena Vista" dance club of the '40s and '50s, and gave it to his old friend Wim Wenders. Cooder had previously written the music for two Wenders movies, *Paris, Texas* (1984) and *The End of Violence* (1997). Before the actual boom took off, Wenders accompanied Cooder to Cuba on a trip to record Ibrahim Ferrer's solo album and also filmed the only concerts the Buena Vista Social Club performed together, in the Carré Theatre in Amsterdam and New York's Carnegie Hall.

The Buena Vista Social Club ensemble did not exist before its one and only album and after these concerts, it will in all probability cease to exist. The musicians of the all-star project of popular Cuban music of past decades already knew each other well, but it was the first time they had played together in this combination. Most of them already had successful solo careers. We get to know and love many of them in the movie: the die-hard philanderer Compay Segundo, who at 90 has fathered five children and, as he says

1   Ry Cooder and his son Joachim (in the background)
    got the Buena Vista Social Club musicians
    together and set the ball rolling for one of the most
    astounding success stories in all Cuban music.

2   A lineup of old men: the Buena Vista Social Club
    takes the audience's applause.

3   Guitarist Eliades Ochoa accompanies Omara
    Portuondo singing "Dos Gardenias para ti," her duet
    with Ibrahim Ferrer.

4   A triumphal reception in the heart of the USA:
    standing ovations from the New York audience in
    Carnegie Hall.

5   Director Wim Wenders described the dilapidated
    charm of Havanna as a "submerged city of the
    future."

CONCERT MOVIES US filmmaker D. A. Pennebaker is a veteran of music documentaries, starting with the movie *Don't Look Back* about Bob Dylan's 1965 British tour. Two years later, he filmed a predecessor of the legendary Woodstock concert, *Monterey Pop*, for posterity. In 1989, he brought Depeche Mode to the screen in *101*. Perhaps the most famous "rockumentaries" ever made are *Woodstock* (1969, Michael Wadleigh), which branded the event on the collective memory, and *Gimme Shelter* (1971, David and Albert Maysles) about a Rolling Stones concert where Hell's Angels acting as stewards killed a black man right in front of the stage. Various other film auteurs have also tried their hand at the genre, for example Jean-Luc Godard with *One Plus One* (1968) about the Rolling Stones, Jim Jarmusch with *Year of the Horse* (1997, Neil Young) and Martin Scorsese with *The Last Waltz* (1978, The Band) and *Shine a Light* (2008, Rolling Stones).

with a grin, is currently working on the sixth; the gifted pianist Rubén Gonzáles who for ten years did not even possess a piano and claimed he could no longer play, the amazing Ibrahim Ferrer, who had promised himself never to sing again, and the *grande dame* Omara Portuondo. Almost completely forgotten, most of the one-time music stars of Son and Bolero of the '40s, '50s, and '60s were eking out a miserable existence in Havana.

Many little things remain unforgettable – Ferrer surreptitiously wiping tears of emotion from Portuondo's eyes during their concert duet; Portuondo striding through the streets of Havana, shot by Wenders in nostalgic pastel tones and filmed with all the charm of decay. She waves to some women who join in her song. The Cubans give a triumphant concert at Carnegie Hall,

stronghold of US music, and then wander through New York wondering at many things that we have long taken for granted. Gonzáles accompanies children's gymnastics and exercises in an old dance hall, and gradually draws them around his piano in a clumsy dance.

House walls display slogans like "The revolution will last for ever," but the musicians seem to have little interest in that. The audience in New York presents them with a Cuban flag at the end of their concert and they gather around it. However, even in the anti-Cuban United States, this doesn't resemble a political gesture so much as a symbol of belated recognition for these captivating performers and their beautiful music.

MH

"I came to Havana, because I wanted to let these musicians speak for themselves, since their music speaks so powerfully for itself."

Wim Wenders in *Sight and Sound*

5

YOU'VE GOT MAIL

1998 – USA – 119 MIN. – ROMANTIC COMEDY
DIRECTOR NORA EPHRON (*1941) SCREENPLAY NORA EPHRON, DELIA EPHRON, based on the
theater play *PARFUMERIE* by MIKLOS LASZLO and the screenplay *THE SHOP AROUND
THE CORNER* by SAMSON RAPHAELSON DIRECTOR OF PHOTOGRAPHY JOHN LINDLEY
EDITING RICHARD MARKS MUSIC GEORGE FENTON PRODUCTION LAUREN SHULER DONNER,
NORA EPHRON for LAUREN SHULER DONNER PRODUCTIONS
STARRING TOM HANKS (Joe Fox), MEG RYAN (Kathleen Kelly), PARKER POSEY (Patricia Eden),
GREG KINNEAR (Frank Navasky), JEAN STAPLETON (Birdie), DAVE CHAPPELLE (Kevin),
STEVE ZAHN (George Pappas), DABNEY COLEMAN (Nelson Fox), HEATHER BURNS
(Christina), JOHN RANDOLPH (Schuyler Fox)

"So much of what I see reminds me of something I read in a book, when shouldn't it be the other way around?"

It's clear from the beginning: such complete opposites just have to attract. She wears hand-knitted clothes and puts homemade ornaments on her Christmas tree, he buys designer suits and has someone else decorate his tree; she pours out human warmth, he cappuccino. But they both want to sell books. Her shop is old-fashioned and wittily named "Shop Around the Corner" after Ernst Lubitsch's clever 1940s comedy, which served as a model for *You've Got Mail*. His chain of shops on the other hand, the bad guy of the piece, is called Fox – the name of the main competitors of Warner Studios who made this movie.

At the outset, none of this is important. When Joe Fox (Tom Hanks) and Kathleen Kelly (Meg Ryan) get home in the evenings, they grab their laptops and write e-mails to each other. For a long time they don't know that behind the pseudonyms under which they exchange poetic comments on the chang-ing seasons and life in New York their main competitor is hiding. Conflict between them is unavoidable as Joe wants to open a book superstore right next door to Kathleen's little shop, and that is a move that is bound to ruin her. The Internet and the anonymity of e-mail as a means of communication facil-itate the unprejudiced exchange of ideas, although it's hard to transfer that into everyday life, as the movie is careful to point out.

Internet pioneers believed that its revolutionary power lay in its ability to bridge gaps of nationality, color or social status. Hollywood chooses pure love, untouched by external factors such as looks or profession. Accordingly, the movie brought the Internet into contemporary American mainstream cin-ema for once and for all – previously it had only ever provided material for science fiction movies such as *Johnny Mnemonic* (1995) and *The Matrix* (1999) or pessimistic global conspiracy thrillers like *Disclosure* (1994) and

3

1   Sleepless in New York: Joe Fox (Tom Hanks) sends
    e-mails under a pen name to …

2   … Kathleen Kelly (Meg Ryan), who thinks her
    unknown e-mail correspondent is a romantic.

3   However, in the tough business world of Manhattan
    the couple are competitors, and cannot stand each
    other.

4   Kathleen's intellectual technophobe of a boyfriend
    Frank (Greg Kinnear) still type his articles on a
    mechanical typewriter.

5   The romantic dream couple of the 1990s:
    Meg Ryan's girlish charm meets Tom Hanks's
    mischievous pragmatism.

ROMANTIC COMEDY   Back in his day, Shakespeare knew that love can be used as material for both dramas and comedies. No stranger to such considerations of course, Hollywood has perfected the art, giving us both romantic dramas like *Love Story* (1969) and comedies such as *Pretty Woman* (1989). Misunderstandings, breakdowns, and setbacks in relationships – this is the stuff these comedies are made of. Characters meet, become separated, and are then reunited after overcoming lots of problems; or, two people don't realize at first that they are made for each other. Romantic comedies – "romcoms" – have been popular in Hollywood since the comedies of Ernst Lubitsch in the 1930s, continuing through *Some Like It Hot* (1959) to *Sex and the City* (2008, 2010) and *Crazy, Stupid, Love* (2011). Movie couples like Spencer Tracy and Katharine Hepburn, Doris Day and Rock Hudson, and even Tom Hanks and Meg Ryan all owe their success to this genre.

4

"The star couple of the nineties is Ryan und Hanks, and they sell the well-seasoned comedy material in attractive, contemporary e-mail packaging." *Zoom*

The Net (1995). The Internet becomes part of the plot of this romantic comedy because people type away on their keyboards, not because of events that are taking place inside the computer. Text on the monitor is shown for its content, not for its graphics. When Kathleen checks her e-mail at night in bed or Joe fails even to register the spectacular view from his office after a meeting because he is waiting for a message from her, the result is a picture of intimacy in the '90s.

Even if Hollywood is putting in a sentimental word here for the little shop around the corner, we shouldn't forget that as businesses, the big studios are much more like the Fox chain in the movie. Hollywood in the '90s is not a cozy family firm, but a profit-oriented multinational. The movie also seems a little contrived as Meg Ryan and Tom Hanks had already played a couple who find each other through modern communication methods in the extremely popular *Sleepless in Seattle* (1993). In that film it was telephones and the radio, but the name of the director and the author of the screenplay was also Nora Ephron. This latter film depends quite heavily on the practiced interaction of Ryan and Hanks. She is dreamy and nervy, romantic and a little girlish, a mermaid in the shark tank of turbo capitalism; he is a successful businessman who has stayed a boy at heart. It's loving courtship as hostile takeover. The kisses come right at the very end – and bed is only for checking your e-mail.

MH

Harper) after they have made rich pickings at a robbery. The holdup goes off without a hitch, but for Eddie, Tom, Bacon, and Soap the problems are just beginning. From now on, all the gangs in the East End are after them.

It's difficult to reduce *Lock, Stock and Two Smoking Barrels* to one story. Five or six plot strands weave around the actions of the four friends. Director Guy Ritchie burns them off at an absurd tempo in his debut movie only to bring them back again in an equally bravura manner. The question of who will

the movies of Quentin Tarantino. The film's anarchic style would be equally unthinkable without Danny Boyle's pioneering *Trainspotting* (1996). That said, *Lock, Stock and Two Smoking Barrels* has its own form, influenced by Ritchie's background in music and commercials, where extreme speed, both visually and as far as the plot is concerned, is absolutely key. Long stretches of the movie closely resemble pop videos, characters are sketched in a split second, action is subordinated to the film music, and classic movie

"The movie is frolicsome but pushy, the triumph of flash over style." *Time Magazine*

mechanisms are deconstructed. The movie is characterized by an originality of form that seems to have been forced upon it by the outrageous behavior of its protagonists.

Despite all its emphasis of the fun factor, *Lock, Stock and Two Smoking Barrels* is also a tongue-in-cheek look at the British zeitgeist of the late '90s. Eddie, Tom, Bacon, and Soap are ideal heroes of Tony Blair's "New Labour" – creative working-class lads who pool their talents to further their careers.

Unfortunately, the free market soon turns out to be a shark-infested swamp where they have to swim desperately for their lives. When at the end the friends frantically reach for their mobile phones to try for their last chance, someone else has got there long before them. The only "professional" in the whole film is a merciless money collector (Vinnie Jones) who retires to become a banker.

JH

1. Cards on the table: Guy Ritchie's production is pure cinematic pleasure.

2. Gang leader Hatchet Harry (P. H. Moriarty) enjoys manipulating people, and plays by his own rules.

3. Classic cinema setpiece: the inevitable poker game.

4. Echoes of Tarantino: Ritchie's film is unabashed in its imitation.

5. New heroes: Soap, Eddie, and Tom embody the entrepreneurial spirit of the late 1990s (Dexter Fletcher, Nick Moran, Jason Statham).

GANGSTER FILM Originally an American genre, the classic gangster movie tells the tale of the rise and fall of a member of a criminal organization. The hero usually comes from a poor family, and therefore realizes an illegal version of the American dream for which he must pay in the end. There were already gangster movies in the era of silent film, although their golden age really began after the introduction of sound at the beginning of the '30s in the US, when the gangster became a movie hero for a public suffering under the Great Depression. The gangster movie then developed into a full-blown genre with its own conventions. Famous movies from that time include Mervin LeRoy's *Little Caesar* (1930), William Wellman's *The Public Enemy* (1931), and finally Howard Hawks' *Scarface* (1931).

THERE'S SOMETHING ABOUT MARY

1998 – USA – 119 MIN. – COMEDY

DIRECTOR PETER FARRELLY (*1957), BOBBY FARRELLY (*1958)
SCREENPLAY ED DECTER, JOHN J. STRAUSS, PETER FARRELLY, BOBBY FARRELLY
DIRECTOR OF PHOTOGRAPHY MARK IRWIN EDITING CHRISTOPHER GREENBURY
MUSIC JONATHAN RICHMAN PRODUCTION FRANK BEDDOR, MICHAEL STEINBERG,
CHARLES B. WESSLER, BRADLEY THOMAS for 20TH CENTURY FOX
STARRING CAMERON DIAZ (Mary Jensen Matthews), MATT DILLON (Pat Healy),
BEN STILLER (Ted Stroehman), LEE EVANS (Tucker), CHRIS ELLIOTT (Dom Woganowski),
LIN SHAYE (Magda), JEFFREY TAMBOR (Sully), MARKIE POST (Mary's mother),
KEITH DAVID (Mary's father), W. EARL BROWN (Warren Jensen)

*"Husband ... negative.
Children and a Labrador ... negative.
Tight little package ... affirmative."*

How about this for a nightmare experience: you pick up your dream girl for the school prom, first you get beaten up by her little brother and then you get a body part so sensitive caught in your zipper in her family bathroom that half of the town arrives to witness the rescue attempts by the police and the fire brigade. Perhaps this hasn't actually happened to many people, but generations have dreaded of this or similar disasters on their first date.

The Farrelly brothers have a passion for everyday visions of horror. They take the underside of the everyday life of moderately intelligent small town inhabitants with an average number of complexes, and then take them to extremes. They don't really care much whether their assortment of coarse, dirty jokes and grotesquely embarrassing situations is bearable for less hardened viewers or not.

Dumb & Dumber (1994) sounded the depths of absolute stupidity and *Kingpin* (1996) dared to investigate the seedy world of American professional bowling, a world of sweaty feet and damp hotel beds. In *There's Something About Mary* the Farrellys decided to try their hand at a love story. With inevitable results: painful fishing accidents, spunk as hair gel, burning dogs, gross jokes about gynecology and the disabled – let's face it, not everyone will

share the Farrellys' view of romance. But in the end, and this is what *Something About Mary* brings home with a vengeance, they do make us aware that the confused, impoverished, and disadvantaged of this world have a love life too.

Ever since the memorable bathroom fiasco, Ted (Ben Stiller) hasn't been able to get Mary (Cameron Diaz) out of his head. Years later, his monstrous braces and bowl cut have gone, but he still has a despairing conviction that a woman like Mary could never be interested in a loser like him. Dom (Chris Elliott), his best friend, is full of useful advice, and he sends Ted off to see shady private detective Pat Healy (Matt Dillon), who sets off to find Mary and promptly falls in love with her himself.

When Ted discovers that Mary is by no means the wheelchair-bound enormously overweight woman with four children that Healy describes to put him off the scent, he screws up his courage and goes to Miami to the scene of the action to try and conquer Mary's heart. He soon comes to the unwelcome realization that her hordes of admirers are larger than he thought. Before the key issue of whether he gets the girl or not is resolved, the heavy hand of fate deals Ted some mighty blows, to the delight of sadistic viewers

"Peter and Bobby Farrelly are Hollywood's 'bad boys' of the moment: two cunning confidence tricksters who have found their place in mainstream cinema with a mixture of catchy material and provocative disregard for taboos."

film-dienst

5

1 A hairstyle to the taste of the Farrelly brothers: Mary (Cameron Diaz) tries out a very unusual hair gel made from purely natural ingredients.

2 Asking for trouble: the loathsome Pat Healy (Matt Dillon) thinks he knows how to win women over and see off any annoying competition.

3 With a winning smile Ted (Ben Stiller) demonstrates his stylish but passion-killing dental adornment.

4 A little kiss for mummikins: fans of the Farrellys have to have a strong stomach.

5 Terrier in plaster: the battle over Mary leaves its mark on people and animals alike.

6 Who could resist this smile? To win the beautiful Mary as their girl, her admirers will stoop to any nastiness.

CAMERON DIAZ Born in San Diego, California, in 1972, Cameron Diaz worked as a model until the age of 21, when she got her first part in *The Mask* (1994) with Jim Carrey. Her natural and candid acting style helped in her breakthrough. The daughter of a Cuban father and German-American mother, she did not tie herself to one genre in her subsequent roles. Her range includes romantic comedies (*The Holiday*, 2006), brash adventure comedies (*Charlie's Angels:* 2000, 2003), art house films (*Being John Malkovich*, 1999), and action thrillers (*Knight and Day*, 2010).

There is no kind of silly joke or disgusting substance that the transparent plot is not prepared to feature, and it is mostly saved from banality by the unscrupulous womanizers Matt Dillon and the English stand-up comedian Lee Evans. That tricky task was carried out with great panache by Jim Carrey and Jeff Daniels in *Dumb & Dumber* and Woody Harrelson and Randy Quaid in *Kingpin*. Part of the Farrellys' success is that high-quality actors are always more than ready to work with them, even Cameron Diaz, who is as breathtakingly beautiful as ever. The music for the movie was composed by independent cinema icon Jonathan Richman. One rule seems to do for the production team and audience alike where the Farrelly brothers' movies are concerned: put aside your political correctness, good taste, and common sense, and you will have loads of fun.

SH

6

SHAKESPEARE IN LOVE ♟♟♟♟♟♟♟

LOVE IS THE ONLY INSPIRATION

GWYNETH
PALTROW
JOSEPH
FIENNES
GEOFFREY
RUSH
COLIN
FIRTH
BEN
AFFLECK
JUDI
DENCH

SHAKESPEARE IN LOVE

1998 – USA – 123 MIN. – LOVE FILM, COSTUME FILM
DIRECTOR JOHN MADDEN (*1949)
SCREENPLAY MARC NORMAN, TOM STOPPARD **DIRECTOR OF PHOTOGRAPHY** RICHARD GREATEX
EDITING DAVID GAMBLE **MUSIC** STEPHEN WARBECK **PRODUCTION** DAVIT PARFIT,
DONNA GIGLIOTTI, HARVEY WEINSTEIN, EDWARD ZWICK, MARC NORMAN for
BEDFORD FALLS PRODUCTIONS
STARRING JOSEPH FIENNES (William Shakespeare), GWYNETH PALTROW (Viola de Lesseps),
GEOFFREY RUSH (Philip Henslowe), JUDI DENCH (Queen Elizabeth), SIMON CALLOW
(Tilney), BEN AFFLECK (Ned Alleyn), COLIN FIRTH (Lord Wessex), JOE ROBERTS
(John Webster), TOM WILKINSON (Hugh Fennyman), RUPERT EVERETT
(Christopher Marlowe)
ACADEMY AWARDS 1999 OSCARS for BEST PICTURE, BEST ACTRESS (Gwyneth Paltrow),
BEST SUPPORTING ACTRESS (Judi Dench), BEST ART DIRECTION-SET DECORATION
(Martin Childs, Jill Quertier), BEST ORIGINAL SCREENPLAY (Marc Norman,
Tom Stoppard), BEST COSTUMES (Sandy Powell), BEST MUSIC, category
COMEDY (Stephen Warbeck)
IFF BERLIN 1999 SILVER BEAR for BEST SCREENPLAY (Marc Norman, Tom Stoppard)

"I know something of a woman in a man's profession."

Viola (Gwyneth Paltrow) loves William (Joseph Fiennes), and William loves Viola. This becomes clear relatively quickly and seems to be a good thing, but it's also where all the problems begin. For William's surname is Shakespeare, and being a writer in Elizabethan England is not a particularly respectable profession. Viola on the other hand is a member of the respectable de Lesseps family and is promised in marriage to the aristocrat Lord Wessex (Colin Firth), who may be in dire financial straits but can at least offer her a title. We understand immediately that there is going to be a conflict of interests as far as matters of the heart are concerned: but what we don't suspect are the questions of money and art.

Unfortunately, theater owner Philip Henslowe (Geoffrey Rush) is also in dire financial straits. He is desperate for Shakespeare to finish the play he has promised Henslowe's Rose Theatre, *Romeo and Ethel – The Pirate's Daughter*, but Shakespeare is suffering from writer's block. He only overcomes it when he meets Viola, who turns up disguised as a boy – women were not allowed

to act in Shakespeare's day – to audition for the main part of Romeo. However, Lord Wessex soon gets wind of the unbecoming plans of his future wife and decides to get rid of the inconvenient and disreputable writer.

These events are mirrored in the plot of the play that Shakespeare writes during the rehearsals in the theater. The movie's two levels are closely connected and intelligently dovetailed but never become incomprehensible, and their interaction is the driving force of the film. Art neither imitates life nor life art – the two feed off each other instead.

Against a well-researched backdrop of Elizabethan theatrical life, the plot speculates about Shakespeare's private life, which in fact remains a mystery to experts even today. The screenplay skillfully combines elements from his plays with historical fact and pure fantasy. But there's nothing dry or dusty about it, it's not only about English theater in the 16th century but is also a radical modernization of Shakespeare. Its authors were inspired by the idea that if Shakespeare lived today he would be a screenplay writer and a

3

1   Writer's block, Renaissance-style: when Shakespeare (Joseph Fiennes) isn't in love, he can't write a single line.

2   All the world's a stage and we are merely players: a stage battle becomes a real skirmish.

3   Shakespeare's enigmatic object of desire: Lady Viola (Gwyneth Paltrow).

4   "Shall I compare thee to a summer's day ..."

5   Always on his guard against creditors: Henslowe (Geoffrey Rush), the notorious bankrupt theater director.

6   Gwyneth Paltrow disguised as Thomas Kent on the way to her first Oscar.

"We had 25 million dollars, not that much for a project of this size. The set was hugely expensive. We had to build not only two theaters, but also a whole district of the city from a brothel to Shakespeare's digs, behind Shepperton Studios in London." John Madden in *Abendzeitung*

5

Hollywood star, so they fill the film with comic anachronisms and quotes from other movies: Shakespeare goes to confess on the psychoanalyst's couch, Philip Henslowe is introduced in the opening sequences as a businessman with cash flow problems, and with a sharp "Follow that boat!" Shakespeare directly quotes innumerable crime movies.

Rather than allowing the movie to be dominated by opulent costumes and imagery, director John Madden gathered a first-class ensemble whose talent shines in every scene. Judi Dench may only appear in a few scenes as Queen Elizabeth, but she is all the more impressive for that. Joseph Fiennes is convincing as the bard and Gwyneth Paltrow as his muse, particularly in her breeches role. The rest of the ensemble, from Geoffrey Rush and Ben Affleck to a brief but memorable appearance from Rupert Everett as Christopher Marlowe, lend great naturalness and texture to the wonderful recreation of 1590s London.

Shakespeare in Love is intelligent and well-made entertainment cinema. It was rewarded with a shower of Oscars, not least because Hollywood was flattered to see the US film industry portrayed as the legitimate heir to Shakespeare's theater.

MP

7   A queen with a natural wit: Judi Dench as Queen Elizabeth, with scowling villain Lord Wessex (Colin Firth).

8   Their world is the Globe Theatre, as the ill-fated love of William and Viola can only exist on stage.

GWYNETH PALTROW Some found her enchanting, others insufferable: when Gwyneth Paltrow won an Oscar for her performance as Viola in *Shakespeare in Love* (1998), her acceptance speech was delivered in copious floods of tears. Born in Los Angeles in 1972, the daughter of TV producer Bruce Paltrow and actress Blythe Danner, she mainly became famous for her roles in costume movies and literary adaptations: *Mrs. Parker and the Vicious Circle* (1994), *Emma* (1996) based on the novel by Jane Austen, and the Dickens's adaptation *Great Expectations* (1997). Over time, however, she has radically changed her repertoire of roles, appearing in comic adaptations like *Iron Man* (2008, 2010, 2013) and as a country singer in *Country Strong* (2010) in which she both acts and sings. In 2011, she also worked on Steven Soderbergh's epidemic thriller *Contagion*

"The heterogenous mixture, a rich and satisfying pudding, works really well, ... and changes from one mood to another with hardly any effort." *Sight and Sound*

BLADE

1998 – USA – 120 MIN. – HORROR FILM, ACTION FILM
DIRECTOR STEPHEN NORRINGTON (*1965)
SCREENPLAY DAVID S. GOYER, based on the comics of the same name
DIRECTOR OF PHOTOGRAPHY THEO VAN DE SANDE **EDITING** PAUL RUBELL **MUSIC** MARK ISHAM
PRODUCTION PETER FRANKFURT, WESLEY SNIPES, ROBERT ENGELMANN for AMEN RA FILM,
IMAGINARY FORCES (for NEW LINE CINEMA)
STARRING WESLEY SNIPES (Blade), STEPHEN DORFF (Deacon Frost), KRIS KRISTOFFERSON
(Whistler), N'BUSHE WRIGHT (Karen), DONAL LOGUE (Quinn), UDO KIER (Dragonetti),
TRACI LORDS (Racquel), ARLY JOVER (Mercury), KEVIN PATRICK WALLS (Krieger),
TIM GUINEE (Dr. Curtis Webb)

"There are worse things out there than vampires."

As parents have always known, discos are dangerous places. A young man lets himself be lured by a seductive young blonde (cameo appearance by ex-porn queen Traci Lords) into a secret dancing temple in the cold room at a local slaughterhouse. But this young techno party animal is in for a rude awakening: before he has a chance to wonder at the somber expressions of his fellow dancers, the sprinkler system turns the dance floor into a blood-bath. Our friend is surrounded by vampires. And things would get a lot worse were it not for the sudden appearance of a figure clad in black leather and a vampire-slayer's cap, who disperses the evil bloodsuckers with the help of a silver machete.

In fact, Blade (Wesley Snipes) is himself a vampire, but only just: his mother was bitten by a vampire shortly before he was born, and therefore her son became a "Daywalker." He is gifted with supernatural powers, but doesn't have to shun the light of day. And so, with the help of the aging vampire-hunter Whistler (Kris Kristofferson), Blade has declared war on his step-brothers and sisters. Whistler supplies Blade with the serum that suppresses his inborn thirst for blood, but which is gradually losing its effect. During a battle in a hospital, Blade saves the life of a young hematologist called Karen (N'Bushe Wright), who shows her gratitude by trying to develop a more effective serum.

Stephen Norrington is only marginally interested in the tragic dimension of the Blade figure from the '70s comic-strip original. Instead, the director stages his film version as a battle of the generations: Blade's archenemy Deacon Frost (Stephen Dorff), who is a transformed mortal himself, and therefore not a full-fledged member of the honorable batty brotherhood, rebels against the aristocracy of the hereditary bloodsuckers. These vampire elders, with their leader Dragonetti ruling from a long conference table, are like the board of directors of a large company. Referring to principles like rank and tradition, they close their eyes to the fact that their day is over. Frost is a revolutionary who has nothing less than the globalization of vampirism in mind, and with the help of an archaic demon he plans to transform the community of the undead into a kind of religious sect, to which human blood donors will convert of their own free will.

A generational conflict also lies at the root of the confrontation between Blade and Frost. Frost is a mixture between smart laptop-yuppie and a kind of horror-figure Robbie Williams, aptly described by one critic as a "Generation

3

WESLEY SNIPES Trained dancer Wesley Snipes (*1962) was discovered when he appeared in Michael Jackson's music video "Bad." After parts in two Spike Lee films, one of which was *Jungle Fever* (1991), Snipes has mainly appeared in action movies and thrillers, ranging from *Passenger 57* (1992) to *Game of Death* (2010). The *Blade* trilogy (1998, 2002, 2004) was incredibly successful for Snipes. His few excursions outside the action and thriller genres include the farce *To Wong Foo* (1995), in which he appears in drag, and the relationship drama *One Night Stand* (1997), which earned him Best Actor in Venice.

1 Crossing the line between life and death: Daywalker Blade (Wesley Snipes) struggles against his vampire legacy.

2 Army of darkness: although he is not born a vampire himself, Deacon Frost (Stephen Dorff, center) wants to destroy the rule of the vampire nobility with the help of his gang.

3 Lonely warrior: because his mother was killed by a vampire, Blade has dedicated his life to the fight against the undead.

4 After thousands of years of rule in the Underworld, the power of vampire supremo Dragonetti (Udo Kier) is under serious threat.

5 Aging hippie on a vampire hunt: Whistler (Kris Kristofferson) stands by Blade as a fatherly friend and medicine man.

6 Pretty playmate: Frost's girlfriend Racquel (Traci Lords) is in thrall to her lord and master.

4

"Blade is a vagrant between worlds, an avenging angel between day and night, van Helsing as an Afro-American superhero." *epd Film*

X Dracula." Above all, the conflict between the two outcast vampires is a cultural struggle between old-school rocker and pop star – between old-fashioned righteous anger and the cool calculations of a (blood-)hungry, charismatic climber. Wesley Snipes's biker getup is in tune with this contrast, as is the Blues and Country look of bard Kris Kristofferson, who appears as a kind of ex-hippie in his supporting role as Blade's fatherly friend and advisor, tripping out on bizarre designer drugs. The corrupt policeman who is a servant of the bloodsuckers and pays a visit to Karen in her apartment is drawn along similarly ironic lines. If we follow this line of interpretation, it is only natural to see the techno disco at the beginning of the movie as a kind of modern entrance to Hell, a sarcastic reference to the spirit of the times.

SH

5

6

BLACK CAT, WHITE CAT
CHAT NOIR, CHAT BLANC / CRNA MAČKLA, BELI MAČOR

1998 – GERMANY / FRANCE / YUGOSLAVIA – 130 MIN. – COMEDY

DIRECTOR EMIR KUSTURICA (*1955) **SCREENPLAY** GORDAN MIHIC
DIRECTOR OF PHOTOGRAPHY THIERRY ARBOGAST **EDITING** SVETOLIK ZAJC **MUSIC** NELLE KARAJLIC,
VOGISLAV ARALICA, DEJAN SPARAVALO **PRODUCTION** KARL BAUMGARTNER for CIBY 2000,
PANDORA FILM, KOMUNA, FRANCE 2 CINÉMA
STARRING BAJRAM SEVERDZAN (Matko Destanov), SRDAN TODOROVIC (Dadan),
BRANKA KATIC (Ida), FLORIJAN AJDINI (Zare Destanov), LJUBICA ADZOVIC (Sujka,
the grandmother), ZABIT MEMEDOV (Zarije Destanov), SABRI SULEJMANI (Grga Pitic),
JASAR DESTANI (Grga Veliki), ADNAN BEKIR (Grga Mali), STOJAN SOTIROV
(Customs official), PREDRAG PEPI LAKOVIC (Priest)
IFF VENICE 1998 SILVER LION for BEST DIRECTOR (Emir Kusturica)

"Love is still the most important thing!"

A Sinti settlement somewhere on the banks of the Danube. Matko (Bajram Severdzan) and his 17-year-old son Zare (Forijan Ajdini) bear up as best they can by trading on the black market. One day Matko decides to hold up a freight train that is loaded with fuel. He borrows the money to bribe the Bulgarian customs officer from an old godfather, whose gold teeth glitter as brightly as his mirror shades. When he lets Dadan (Srdan Todorovic) in on the raid, the gangster tricks him and Matko doesn't just lose the train, he loses the money too. Deep in the gangster's debt he has no other choice but to accept the suggestion that his son Zare marry Dadan's stunted sister, despite the fact that he is already in love with someone else. At the end however love triumphs and the unhappy wedding becomes an uproarious, joyful party where two grandfathers thought dead are resurrected, the bad guy winds up literally up to his neck in shit and two cats are the witnesses to the marriage.

Fairy tales, says Emir Kusturica, are the only way to express reality today. Politicians influence our day-to-day lives so much that reality seems to have become nothing more than a power game for the people in charge. "Real" reality, on the other hand, lies beyond our daily lives, in the realm of dreams and fairy tales. *Black Cat, White Cat* gives a visionary picture of this world, and it is anarchic, tough, and intensely physical, a world full of absurd situations and bizarre characters. We can't believe our Hollywood-trained eyes when a white goose is used to wipe a dirty body. But once we enter the world of the film there is no escape, and it draws us in like a vortex: we meet a hefty singer who can pull nails out of a beam with her behind, a pig that eats a small car bit by bit, a gangster who juggles with hand grenades, and a brass band who carry on playing even after they have all been tied to a tree.

After the controversy surrounding *Underground* (1995), it looked as if Emir Kusturica would never make another movie. French and German critics made such polemical attacks on his parable about the Yugoslavian civil war that he announced he was retiring from the film business for good. Luckily, his team were able to talk him into making a portrait of the musicians from *Underground* and this gradually developed into the idea for *Black Cat, White Cat*. Filming began in late summer 1996 in Slovenia and was finished two years later, due to permanently bad weather. This patience paid off; the light that floods the pictures glows as warmly as if the Danube were the Mediterranean.

The movie's energy comes from its vital creativity and its seemingly inexhaustible flow of ideas, but also from the optimism and love of the people that it demonstrates. However much Kusturica exaggerates his characters, he never makes them ridiculous but treats them with respect and affection. The director already made an earlier declaration of love for the Sinti and their way of life, also filmed mostly with amateur actors. But the melancholy that characterized *Time of the Gypsies* (*Dom za vesanje*, 1988) is blown away by the brass band. *Black Cat, White Cat* is a vibrant comedy on the joys of life and the power of love.   NM

"It's a mad scramble though the Felliniesque realm of Kusturica's imagination, and it proves nothing if not this much: give this man the Danube, Gypsy musicians and a camera, and you've got a party." *The New York Times*

1 The wild music, a combination of traditional Balkan sounds and modern beats, originates from Emir Kusturica's band The No Smoking Orchestra.

2 Branka Katic fizzes with pure energy as Ida. Wherever she whirls, the feathers fly.

3 The eternally broke Matko (Bajram Severdzan) borrows money from his godfather Grga (Jasar Destani).

4 Ida and Zare (Forijan Ajdini) are paired up and sold off by the old people. But they won't stand for that.

5 "Kiss me, stupid": Emir Kusturica quotes Billy Wilder and *Casablanca*.

6 Jasar Destani in his first cinema role. In real life, he works as a smelter in an iron factory.

EMIR KUSTURICA A poet of the cinema, Emir Kusturica loves to be provocative. His movies are like a rowdy carnival, populated by bizarre figures and earthy images. His magical dream worlds have their roots in the history and myths of his homeland. He was born in Sarajevo in 1954 and studied at the Film Academy in Prague. Since his debut *Do You Remember Dolly Bell?* (*Sjećaš li se Dolly Bell?*, 1981) he has won all the major European film awards, including the Golden Palm for *When Father Was Away on Business* (*Otac na službenom putu*, 1985) and the award for Best Director at Cannes for his great epic *Time of the Gypsies* (*Dom za vesanje*, 1988). Kusturica, who is constantly criticized for his controversial political views, dealt with the theme of the Balkan conflict in *Underground* (1995) and *Life is a Miracle* (*Zivot je cudo*, 2004). In 2008, he released a film about Argentinian football legend Diego Maradona: *Maradona by Kusturica*.

RUSHMORE

1998 – USA – 93 MIN. – COMEDY
REGIE WES ANDERSON (*1969)
SCREENPLAY WES ANDERSON, OWEN WILSON DIRECTOR OF PHOTOGRAPHY ROBERT D. YEOMAN
EDITING DAVID MORITZ MUSIC MARK MOTHERSBAUGH PRODUCTION BARRY MENDEL,
PAUL SCHIFF for AMERICAN EMPIRICAL PICTURES, TOUCHSTONE PICTURES
STARRING JASON SCHWARTZMAN (Max Fischer), BILL MURRAY (Herman Blume),
OLIVIA WILLIAMS (Rosemary Cross), SEYMOUR CASSEL (Bert Fischer),
BRIAN COX (Dr. Nelson Guggenheim), MASON GAMBLE (Dirk Calloway),
SARA TANAKA (Margaret Yang), STEPHEN MCCOLE (Magnus Buchan),
CONNIE NIELSEN (Mrs. Calloway), LUKE WILSON (Dr. Peter Flynn)

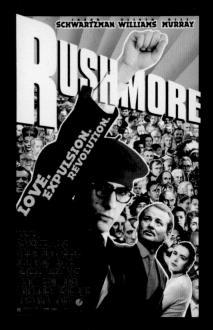

"I always wanted to be in one of your fuckin' plays."

One could take Max Fischer (Jason Schwartzman) for a dreamer like so many other young heroes with crazy ideas that overrun the American high-school genre. Naturally, Max too has a dream as is already given away by his odd appearance in an English school blazer: he would like nothing more than to stay at Rushmore for ever, for this wonderful private school is his life. He is, however, not one to idle away his time with fantasies and would much rather put them into action: he heads the debate team, the calligraphy club, the fencing team, the choir, the beekeeping society as well as many other projects – the majority he founded himself. His pièce de résistance is the theater group with their Hollywood-style adaptations of motion picture classics like Serpico (1973) or Apocalypse Now (1979). The special effects rival those of George Lucas – earplugs and protective eyewear are recommended.

Unfortunately, thanks to his diverse interests and various engagements, Max is the school's worst student – everyone has their own priorities. Naturally this is also true for his strictly forbidden love for the new elementary school teacher, Rosemary Cross (Olivia Williams), who notices, with increasing irritation, his creepy advances. Things take a turn for the worse as his new friend, the quirky entrepreneur Herman Blume (Bill

1   Group portrait with a melancholy figure: the eccentric entrepreneur Herman looks upon his own life with disgust – one of Bill Murray's most well-known roles.

2   Harvard or the Sorbonne? Max Fischer (Jason Schwartzman) the math wiz exists only in his imagination. In reality, he's the worst student at Rushmore.

3   The United Nations of Rushmore: there is no club or activity too obscure for Max Fischer to lead. His involvement far exceeds any curriculum.

Murray), begins to vie for Rosemary's affection as well. It's no longer about school. A few retaliatory campaigns and a truly dangerous later attack and things come to a head: Max has to leave Rushmore for good. His dream is over.

Rushmore is the first milestone in Wes Anderson's oeuvre, which uncannily resembles his protagonist's sublime activities. His creative impulse isn't concerned at all with reality. Just like Max, he attaches great importance to outward appearances without paying particular attention to how they are actually perceived. In follow-up films such as The Royal Tenenbaums

(2001) and The Life Aquatic with Steve Zissou (2004), he follows much the same pattern: Anderson creates utterly unique worlds full of arcane notions, the intrinsic melancholy of which is not accessible to everyone. Rather than real life, his films resemble the great human dramas that Max presents in his school plays.

Particularly in this type of production, everything has to be just right. Thus, Anderson offers a host of cultural references and a hand-picked soundtrack with rather unknown Britpop gems from the 1960s. Above all, he also casts actors who effortlessly bring depth to what could be very

OLIVIA WILLIAMS She's like the English teacher little boys dream of their entire lives. However, back in her native country, Olivia Williams went overlooked for quite a while. Her big break came when she got a call from Kevin Costner, who, apparently on a whim, cast her in his film The Postman (1997). At the time, Williams was already 29 years old. Prior to this, the actress, born in London in 1968, studied at Cambridge and acted at the Royal Shakespeare Company Theater. Costner's science fiction megaflop, only her second film role, brought the british talent to Hollywood. Her performance in Wes Anderson's Rushmore (1998), which is as intelligent as it is warm-hearted, effectively shows Williams as a teacher – and this wasn't to be her last role. She became even more widely known in her role as the wife of Bruce Willis's character Malcome Crowe in The Sixth Sense (1999). After that, she appeared once again in smaller roles in smaller films as well as in critically acclaimed, though only moderately successful, television series such as Miss Austen Regrets (2008) and Dollhouse (2008–10). The enchanting British coming-of-age drama An Education (2009) put her back on the map – a withdrawn teacher, she serves as moral compass for the young star Carey Mulligan. Now at the height of her powers, she was breathtaking in Roman Polanski's political drama The Ghost Writer (2010): Williams plays the equally cold and fascinating spouse of an ailing British prime minister, whom she supports by any means necessary – illegal or even immoral. Younger colleagues can learn a lot from Olivia Williams, who has always had more to offer than just her good-natured appearance.

4 Oedipal surrogate family: the love triangle with Herman and Miss Cross (Olivia Williams) creates unwelcome competition for Max.

5 Rushmore for ever: at the school where the tragiccomic hero sees his destiny, he portrays himself as an unrecognized genius.

6 Only authentic in a school uniform: actor Jason Schwartzman showed up to his audition with a self-made Rushmore emblem.

7 Gentle but assertive: as Miss Cross, Olivia Williams has to put an underaged admirer in his place.

8 Tit for tat: the competition between Max and Herman for Miss Cross's affections erupts in acts of senseless violence.

"All in all, *Rushmore* is a genre-defying marvel, switching between outrageous humour and genuine pathos at a moment's notice."

The Guardian

superficial: alongside the imperturbable looking Jason Schwartzman, discovered specially for this film, this pertains as well to Bill Murray.

Thanks to the sad role of Herman Blume, the comedian and actor enjoyed a comeback. Can you be mad at a man who, out of pure frustration, demolishes the bike of his 15-year-old rival? Blessed himself with two oafs for sons, Herman finds in Max not so much a surrogate son but rather an equal, someone he can talk to – someone who seems to have an even better handle on life than he does. Next to these two overgrown children, Olivia seems incredibly serious and mature. She would never allow herself to be kissed by a minor – unless, of course, he manages, with a lot of fake blood, to fake a serious injury.

With his impeccable comedic timing and a brilliant depth of focus, Anderson set a new bar with this film. But for which genre? In his perfect fictional worlds, the comedy and tragedy of human existence always go hand in hand. One can easily peg him as a traditionalist, who does nothing more than take ideas from classics such as *The Graduate* (1967) or *Harold und Maude* (1971) and repackage them for a modern audience. Like Max, however, he created this audience himself with an utterly unique sensibility – and, in doing so, inspired plenty of imitators. His cinematic worlds, whose protagonists seem slightly autistic, may seem strange. Nevertheless, they make you want to live in them for ever. Rushmore forever – what a dream.

PB

"*Rushmore* is an almost indefinable genre of its own. A comedy with a menacing edge? An ironic romance? Hard to call. Anderson, the director and co-writer, and Wilson, co-writer, have a vision like no one else's." *The Washington Post*

SAVING PRIVATE RYAN ♟♟♟♟♟

1998 – USA – 170 MIN. – WAR FILM
DIRECTOR STEVEN SPIELBERG (*1946)
SCREENPLAY ROBERT RODAT **DIRECTOR OF PHOTOGRAPHY** JANUSZ KAMINSKI **EDITING** MICHAEL KAHN
MUSIC JOHN WILLIAMS **PRODUCTION** STEVEN SPIELBERG, IAN BRUCE, MARK GORDON,
GARY LEVINSOHN for AMBLIN ENTERTAINMENT, DREAMWORKS SKG, MUTUAL FILM
COMPANY (for PARAMOUNT)
STARRING TOM HANKS (Captain Miller), TOM SIZEMORE (Sergeant Horvath), EDWARD BURNS
(Private Reiben), BARRY PEPPER (Private Jackson), ADAM GOLDBERG (Private Mellish),
VIN DIESEL (Private Caparzo), GIOVANNI RIBISI (Wade), JEREMY DAVIES
(Corporal Upham), MATT DAMON (Private Ryan), TED DANSON (Captain Hamill)
ACADEMY AWARDS 1999 OSCARS for BEST DIRECTOR (Steven Spielberg), BEST CINEMATOGRAPHY
(Janusz Kaminski), BEST FILM EDITING (Michael Kahn), BEST SOUND (Gary Rydstrom,
Gary Summers, Andy Nelson, Ronald Judkins), BEST SOUND EFFECTS EDITING
(Gary Rydstrom, Richard Hymns)

"What's the use in risking the lives of the eight of us to save one guy?"

With an abrupt, muffled crack, a bullet pierces a steel helmet. Boats landing on the beach are met by salvos of machine gunfire, soldiers run into a hail of bullets. Death and blood are everywhere. One soldier is hurled into the air, his thigh is blown off, another searches for his left hand. Steven Spielberg shows D-day, the landing of the allied forces on the French Atlantic coast on June 6, 1944, like something out of a horror movie that grabs the viewer with physical force. It lasts 25 almost unbearable minutes, before we cut to America, where military bureaucracy is dealing with the administration of the dead. Secretaries sit at desks and compose telegrams of condolence like a production line. Here people type, while in Europe they die. From afar the invasion is a strategic necessity, while on the beaches of Normandy, as one critic wrote, the participants experience it as a meaningless "chaos of noise, filth, blood, vomit and death." Immediately after this shocking opening, Spielberg establishes the contrast between military tactics and their practicalities, which result in nothing but undignified death.

A decision by the military leadership then introduces the actual theme of the film. During the Normandy landing three sons of the Ryan family in Iowa have died, while a fourth, James Ryan (Matt Damon), has been parachuted into France behind the German lines. To save mother Ryan from losing him as well, he must be sent home. The task of finding Ryan is given to Captain Miller (Tom Hanks), an experienced and reliable soldier, but a man badly affected by the burdens of the war as we see from his trembling hands. Together with a small group of soldiers – Mellish, a sniper (Adam Goldberg), Wade, a first-aider (Giovanni Ribisi), and Upham, an interpreter who has no experience of war (Jeremy Davies) – he sets off to find Ryan. He finds him, and he and his troops take part in a battle over a strategically important bridge. Only one of them survives, the solider who we see in the framework of the movie, set in our times.

War movies are fraught with problems. Should the horrors be presented realistically or metaphorically? Should a director show the action on the battlefield or should he describe its consequences for the survivors? Spielberg chose a realistic mode for the opening and final sequences of this movie. They mirror each other, although the final sequence is not quite as ferocious. He filmed the opening sequence with 3000 extras in 30 days on the Irish coast, and the intensity that resulted may not be unique in modern cinema, but is certainly a rare thing. The camera mingles with the soldiers, blood

1 He hardly talks about his life back home, and his men are not supposed to see his shaking hands. Captain Miller (Tom Hanks) doesn't doubt the sense of the war, but he does doubt whether he can survive it.

2 Miller and Sergeant Horvath (Tom Sizemore, left) have to lead their men straight towards the German positions.

and filth spurt onto the lens, and the sound cuts out when we see underwater pictures of sinking corpses. The viewer is directly involved in the events and there is no option to retreat into the position of an observer.

The middle part of the movie has a more distanced narrative perspective. During his search for Ryan, Miller is busy with the arithmetic of death. He has lost 94 men, he reckons, but has saved ten or twenty times as many. A gruesome sum, but one way for the soldiers to make their daily work of death more bearable. However, another calculation seems to contradict this

logic: risking the life of eight soldiers and Miller to save one life, that of Ryan. Is that morally justifiable? Aren't they just as human as he is? Is he worth more than they are?

The movie doesn't have an answer to that question, but it does raise the issue and the characters repeatedly turn it over in their minds. And the resulting tension shows us the grisly absurdity of war perhaps more effectively than any of the realistic action scenes can.

HJK

> # "I asked myself throughout, is this a mission of mercy or a mission of murder? But I can't answer the question. I don't think anyone can."
> Steven Spielberg in *Time Magazine*

3 The American military cemetery where the film begins.

4 "The film's persuasive power lies in the camera-work of Janusz Kaminski, which is reminiscent of the weekly news reports from that time."
epd Film

TOM HANKS The *New York Times* claimed that Hanks had never put his everyman qualities to better effect than in *Saving Private Ryan* (1998). Hanks (*1956) is this generation's James Stewart – the boy next door. Audiences identify with him as with no other actor, whether he is playing a burned-out, ex-baseball player in *A League of Their Own* (1992), a widowed single father in *Sleepless in Seattle* (1993), or a guy stranded in an airport in *Terminal* (2004). His gay lawyer with AIDS in *Philadelphia* (1993) was a sensitive and likeable person; he then became the quintessential American in the title role of *Forrest Gump* (1994), which takes us through three decades of history. Other historical roles include the astronaut Jim Lovell in *Apollo 13* (1995) and the 9/11 victim in *Extremely Loud & Incredibly Close* (2011). After Spencer Tracy in 1938 and 1939, Hanks was the first person to receive an Oscar for Best Leading Actor two years in a row: in 1994 for *Philadelphia* and in 1995 for *Forrest Gump*. He directed the musical comedy *That Thing You Do!* in 1996 and the tragicomedy *Larry Crowne* in 2011.

5　Master of death: sniper Jackson (Barry Pepper) on the lookout.

6　An allusion to the German film *Die Brücke* (*The Bridge*, 1959): after they have found Ryan, Miller and his men have to defend a bridge.

"It has its place in cinema history, due to the first 25 minutes. The picture it gives of this war is already as mythically transfigured as the violent event in its entirety, just as *Gone with the Wind* showed the numbers of wounded in the ruins of Atlanta."

Süddeutsche Zeitung

6

THE MATRIX ❦❦❦❦

999 – USA – 136 MIN. – SCIENCE FICTION

DIRECTOR ANDY WACHOWSKI (*1967), LARRY WACHOWSKI (*1965)
SCREENPLAY ANDY WACHOWSKI, LARRY WACHOWSKI DIRECTOR OF PHOTOGRAPHY BILL POPE
EDITING ZACH STAENBERG MUSIC DON DAVIS PRODUCTION JOEL SILVER, DAN CRACHIOLO
for SILVER PRODUCTIONS
STARRING KEANU REEVES (Neo), LAURENCE FISHBURNE (Morpheus), CARRIE ANNE MOSS
(Trinity), HUGO WEAVING (Agent Smith), GLORIA FOSTER (Oracle), JOE PANTOLIANO
(Cypher), MARCUS CHONG (Tank), JULIAN ARAHANGA (Apoc), MATT DORAN (Mouse),
BELINDA MCCLORY (Switch)
ACADEMY AWARDS 2000 OSCARS for BEST FILM EDITING (Zach Staenberg), BEST SOUND
EFFECTS EDITING (Dane A. Davis), BEST VISUAL EFFECTS (Steve Courtley, John Gaeta,
Janek Sirrs, Jon Thum), BEST SOUND (David E. Campbell, David Lee, John T. Reitz,
Gregg Rudloff)

ON MARCH 31ST THE FIGHT FOR THE FUTURE BEGINS.

"The Matrix is the world that has been pulled over your eyes to blind you from the truth."

A Cinderella story in a technological Wonderland: Thomas Anderson (Keanu Reeves) spends his days in a tiny office at a computer firm, doing his best to avoid working. At night, using the pseudonym "Neo," he hacks his way through the international data network. His boss's threats to kick him out are as much a part of the daily routine as dealing in illegal diskettes, which he keeps hidden inside a book titled *Simulacra and Simulation* – an early reference to the central theme of the film, which is the rift between reality and perception. Somewhere out in cyberspace Morpheus (Laurence Fishburne) is waiting for him, believing him to be the Savior, but Neo has not yet heard his call.

That call is a call to revolution, and for liberation from the machines. Morpheus is the leader of a rebellion whose sole aim is to free mankind from its undeserved bondage. In *The Matrix*, the human race has been enslaved by the artificial intelligence of its electronic apparatus, which derives its energy from human cells. People are lined up in endless rows, like units in a power station, and while their bodies are trapped in this giant battery, their minds roam free in a computer-generated parallel universe. This prison that gives

the illusion of freedom is the matrix of the title, and it has all the appearance of reality.

The movie initially inspired controversy on account of its cross-cultural plundering, but critics were united in the opinion that *The Matrix* would set stylistic trends. Techno discos, crumbling Victorian houses, abandoned subway stations, and wastelands of social housing – images of global turbo-capitalism alternating with pictures of postindustrial decay present a portrait of the postmodern world. *The Matrix* marks the spot where late capitalism tips over into the new economy, where the oversized production grounds of mono-industry make way for the revolutionary cells of the new market. In that new economy questions like the limits of our knowledge become increasingly pressing, and it is questions like those that are raised by *The Matrix*, with giddy twists and disorienting turns. Our world is revealed to be a façade and the real world looks more like the hippest and coolest music videos of the '90s. The monopoly on the interpretation of reality no longer belongs to the person who has the strongest arguments or the best evidence, it belongs instead to the person who's most good-looking. Style is reality

"Our main aim in *The Matrix* was to shoot an intellectual action movie. We like action movies, guns and kung fu, so we'd had enough of watching mass-produced action movies that didn't have any kind of intellectual content. We were determined to put as many ideas as possible into the film." Larry Wachowski in *American Cinematographer*

1 Trinity (Carrie Anne Moss) and the other rebels can only escape the illusory world of the Matrix using telephone lines.

2 Neo (Keanu Reeves) is the chosen one, who will inform the world about all the computer-generated scenery, that at least is the claim made by …

3 … Morpheus (Laurence Fishburne), leader of the rebels in the fight against the Agents.

and truth says the film, its greenish tint an imitation of the screen color of early computer monitors.

In Ovid's *Metamorphoses*, Morpheus is the son of Sleep, and the god of dreams. "Neo" is the Greek prefix for "new." Trinity (Carrie Ann Moss), the third protagonist, completes this pop-culture three-in-one as the Holy Spirit. In practically every scene and dialogue, *The Matrix* delights in pointing out parallels between ancient mythology and modern pop culture, piling up quotations from other films on top of references to philosophical disputes

before pulling them apart in the scenes that follow. Accusing this movie of not being serious is like expecting pop music to follow the rules of mathematical logic. The scene with the Oracle is especially brilliant: the Oracle is an old woman who bakes cookies and spouts platitudes, but her prophecies turn out to be true in the end. *The Matrix* makes ingenious use of anything that can serve as a stone in its mosaic: the world is a mine of these stones for our imagination.

MH

"On the visual front, it's been such a success that most subsequent action films include a passing genuflection to *The Matrix*. Which probably defines the genius of the Wachowski brothers: by sheer ingenuity in making new from old, they've become a point of reference." *Télérama*

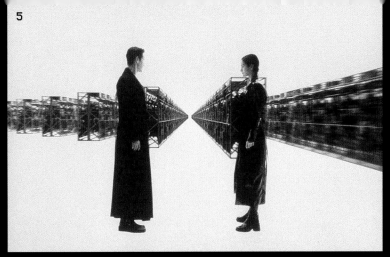

4   In skintight black leather, angel of death Trinity fights an agent.

5   Computer batteries generate the illusion of the world that we live in.

6   Next summer's fashion: *The Matrix* not only set standards in the domain of special effects, but even created a "look" which was taken up by films and music videos.

7   The rebel base is located on a neo-noir version of the legendary Nautilus submarine, which cruises through the interior of the Matrix.

"The Wachowskis clearly designed *The Matrix* as a comic book, before it became a screenplay, and many decisions taken 'because it's cooler' disregard the discipline that you would expect of a literary film." *Sight and Sound*

"MATRIX" EFFECTS The Wachowski brothers are great fans of "anime" (Japanese comics and animations) and Hong Kong action movies, a penchant evident in *The Matrix* (1999). The brothers brought in Hong Kong veteran Yuen Woo-Ping for the fight sequences, and Yuen went on to prove his talents again in Ang Lee's *Crouching Tiger, Hidden Dragon* (2000). Specialist John Gaeta was brought in for the computer animation. *The Matrix* made the "bullet time" effect famous: dozens of cameras were placed in a circle around Keanu Reeves and the film was shot simultaneously by all of them in extreme slow motion. This meant that the actor could then be frozen in one position and a camera shot simulated around him. The sequels *Matrix Reloaded* and *Matrix Revolutions* (both 2003) produced spectacular images. In Part 2, for instance, Neo is fighting Agent Smith, who has replicated himself a hundredfold. Real people were filmed fighting in this scene; afterward, their faces were digitally superimposed with Smith's.

8 Burn, baby, burn: mutiny on the rebels' ship.

9 Mind triumphing over matter: Neo and Smith (Hugo Weaving) defy the laws of gravity with perfect balance.

10 Morpheus and Agent Smith await two sequels which were filmed simultaneously and came out in theaters in 2003.

ALL ABOUT MY MOTHER ⚆
TODO SOBRE MI MADRE

1999 – SPAIN / FRANCE – 101 MIN. – MELODRAMA
DIRECTOR PEDRO ALMODÓVAR (*1951)
SCREENPLAY PEDRO ALMODÓVAR **DIRECTOR OF PHOTOGRAPHY** AFFONSO BEATO **EDITING** JOSÉ SALCEDO
MUSIC ALBERTO IGLESIAS **PRODUCTION** AGUSTIN ALMODÓVAR, CLAUDE BERRI for EL DESEO,
RENN PRODUCTIONS, FRANCE 2 CINÉMA
STARRING CECILIA ROTH (Manuela), ELOY AZORÍN (Estéban), MARISA PAREDES (Huma Rojo),
PENÉLOPE CRUZ (Sister Rosa), ANTONIA SAN JUAN (Agrado), CANDELA PEÑA (Nina),
ROSA MARÍA SARDÀ (Rosa's mother), FERNANDO FERNÁN GÓMEZ (Rosa's father),
TONI CANTÓ (Lola), CARLOS LOZANO (Mario)
IFF CANNES 1999 SILVER PALM for BEST DIRECTOR (Pedro Almodóvar)
ACADEMY AWARDS 2000 OSCAR for BEST FOREIGN LANGUAGE FILM

"The only genuine thing about me is my feelings."

The loss of a child is the worst thing that can happen to a mother. Manuela (Cecilia Roth) never mentioned the child's father, even when asked, but now that she is completely on her own she continues her son's search for his other parent. Bowed by suffering and yet filled with strength she is driven back deep into her own past, and she travels from Madrid to Barcelona, from her present existence back to an earlier one. The people she meets on this journey to the end of the night generally only appear on our screens as the bad crowd in television crime series, as pathetic informers or more likely as corpses. Here, transsexuals and junkie prostitutes, pregnant nuns, and grouchy divas are not only the main characters, but with all their failings and weaknesses, they also win our sympathy.

In her search for comfort, Manuela eventually finds the father of her dead son Estéban (Eloy Azorín), and he has now become a dark angel of death, a terminally ill transsexual who earns his living as a prostitute. Eighteen years ago when they were a couple he was also called Estéban, but now (s)he calls herself Lola (Toni Cantó). Although (s)he was once attractive, those days are long gone: Estéban the First no longer exists and Lola is not long for this world either. Nevertheless, at the end of the movie a third Estéban is born, giving us a utopian hope against all the odds.

The audience shares Manuela's perspective and the Spanish director guides us skillfully through the glittering microcosm of Barcelona's transsex-

ual scene. Almodóvar however has no intention of giving us a documentary, he does not claim to portray objective reality in an authentic manner, and neither is it his intention to teach us a lesson in pity. Instead he takes all the expressive means at the disposal of a melodrama to their extreme: tears, blood, blows, violence, fucking, birth, love, hate, life, and death. The plot may sound unlikely, but nothing seems artificial or false and that is the true miracle of this movie, an effect due in no small part to its fantastic actresses.

They all play actresses in the movie as well: Manuela does role plays with hospital employees to teach them how to deal with the families of deceased patients, and when Nina (Candela Peña), partner of the theater diva Huma (Marisa Paredes) can't go on stage because she's too doped up, Manuela takes her place. The faithful companion Agrado (Antonia San Juan) is perhaps the greatest actress in the true sense of the word; her body has been operated on innumerable times until it is nothing but artificial illusion. One of the best scenes is where she has to announce the cancellation of a play but manages to whip up the disappointed audience into storms of enthusiasm with an autobiographic monologue. This movie about mothers is also dedicated to all actresses who have ever played actresses.

At their best Almodóvar's men are senile like the father (Fernando Fernán Gómez) of AIDS sufferer Rosa (Penélope Cruz), but for the most part men are conspicuous by their absence. However, even in his short appearances

1 Women in the mirror: Marisa Paredes (with lip-pencil) and Cecilia Roth.

2 Three women, three different stories: Manuela (Cecilia Roth, left), whose son died, and Rosa (Penélope Cruz, right), whose son provides a glimmer of hope at the end of the film, on either side of Rosa's mother (Rosa María Sardà).

3 The actress Huma Rojo (Marisa Paredes), larger than life, looks through the railings at her fan Estéban (Eloy Azorín), who is soon to die.

4 Penélope Cruz, "shooting star" of Spanish cinema.

5 It's the "end of the line for desire" not only for the dreams of Almodóvar's heroines, but also as a play in the film.

the double father Estéban/Lola – who is in theory the villain of the piece – is given a dignity which no other character acquires in the course of the whole movie. Almodóvar respects every single human emotion, however bizarre his characters might appear. "The only genuine thing about me is my feelings," says Agrado, the faithful transsexual girlfriend in *All About My Mother*. This also applies to Almodóvar's movie, where feelings always remain genuine despite the visual artistry. And that's more than can be said of most films.   MH

"*All About My Mother* is all about art, women, people, life, and death, and must be one of the most intense films I've ever made." Pedro Almodóvar in *Cahiers du cinéma*

PEDRO ALMODÓVAR He went from being an icon of Spain's gay subculture to one of Europe's most important filmmakers: Pedro Almodóvar. In the process, his early provocative invectives at church and society in films like *Tie Me Up! Tie Me Down!* (*¡Átame!* 1990) gave way increasingly to greater depth and complexity in characterisation. In films like *Bad Education* (*La mala educación*, 2004) and *Broken Embraces* (*Los abrazos rotos*, 2009) he provided a far more substantial and highly personal confrontation with bourgeois society. However the razor-sharp satire and his unique melodramatic signature remained. Hollywood recognized his work as well, awarding the Oscar for Best Foreign Language film to *All About My Mother* (*Todo sobre mi madre*,1999) and another to *Talk to Her* (*Hable con ella*, 2002), this time for Best Original Screenplay.

EYES WIDE SHUT

1999 – USA – 159 MIN. – DRAMA, LITERATURE ADAPTATION
DIRECTOR STANLEY KUBRICK (1928–1999)
SCREENPLAY STANLEY KUBRICK, FREDERIC RAPHAEL, based on Arthur Schnitzler's *Dream Story* (*Traumnovelle*) DIRECTOR OF PHOTOGRAPHY LARRY SMITH EDITING NIGEL GALT
MUSIC JOCELYN POOK, GYÖRGY LIGETI, DMITRI SHOSTAKOVICH, CHRIS ISAAK
PRODUCTION STANLEY KUBRICK, JAN HARLAN for POLE STAR, HOBBY FILMS
(for WARNER BROS.)
STARRING TOM CRUISE (Dr. William Harford), NICOLE KIDMAN (Alice Harford),
MADISON EGINTON (Helena Harford), JACKIE SAWIRIS (Roz), SYDNEY POLLACK
(Viktor Ziegler), SKY DUMONT (Sandor Szavost), MARIE RICHARDSON (Marion),
TODD FIELD (Nick Nightingale), RADE SERBEDZIJA (Milich), LEELEE SOBIESKI
(Milich's daughter)

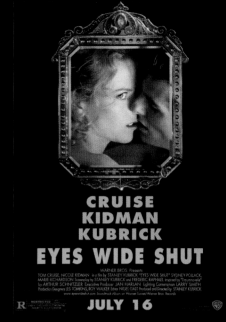

"May I ask why a beautiful woman who could have any man in this room wants to be married?"

Traditionally, Hollywood is only interested in marriage insofar as the customary kiss at the end of the movie provides the obligatory happy ending and hints at a future wedding, whose preparation has filled the preceding two hours. The marriage takes place during and after the credits and Hollywood remains in a state of infantile bachelordom. In mainstream films, married couples seldom appear in prominent roles; in Stanley Kubrick's *Eyes Wide Shut* by contrast, sexuality, faithfulness, and desire inside marriage are the main themes.

Eyes Wide Shut is admittedly not a Hollywood film in any conventional sense. It was made in England, but as Tom Cruise and Nicole Kidman played the main roles, the film qualified automatically for the premiere multiplex league. They play what they were real life, at least at the time the movie was made: a married couple. Bill Harford is a doctor, his wife Alice paints. Unambiguous advances are made to both of them – separately – at a party they go to together. Although they reject them, the possibility of unfaithfulness sparks off a crisis in their marriage.

Driven by his wife's confessions of her sexual fantasies about another man, Bill sets off aimlessly into the night and into the abyss of his subcon-

scious. His wanderings are punctuated by black-and-white images of Alice's imagined night of passion with a naval officer – or are we seeing her memories? Bill's sexual odyssey spins him around in a whirl of desirable women who for one reason or another are all forbidden: the daughter of a patient who has just died, a prostitute, the underage daughter of the owner of a costume shop, and the masked, naked beauty he met at an orgy that he should not have attended.

The model for *Eyes Wide Shut* is Arthur Schnitzler's *Dream Story*, which is set in Vienna at the turn of the 19th century. The movie is set in contemporary New York. It isn't a literary adaptation in the conventional sense, but an experiment that follows Schnitzler's model for long stretches and then deviates at important points. There was much critical debate about whether enough of the bourgeois ideal of marriage has survived the last hundred years to make Schnitzler's Freudian investigation of married morals still relevant today. Kubrick's opponents accused him of having an antiquated concept of society and morality, whereas others considered his movie a successful modernization, particularly as today's sexual behavior is still relatively conservative in spite of the sexual revolution.

2

1. In spite of the length of time taken to shoot *Eyes Wide Shut* Nicole Kidman and Tom Cruise were prepared to accept paychecks way below their usual income.

2. The portrayal of marital sexuality is a rarity in Hollywood.

3. The Harfords' marital crisis forces William, a successful doctor working on the Upper East Side, to take a long painful look inside himself.

4. Nicole Kidman was highly regarded as an actress well before her marriage to Cruise.

STANLEY KUBRICK Many English filmmakers move to Hollywood, but Stanley Kubrick did it the other way round. He moved to the UK after his experiences of the Hollywood system (*Spartacus*, 1960) and the financial and production problems with *Lolita* (1962). His largely independent productions in England showed his mastery of various genres and won him complete freedom and control over production, through films like *Dr. Strangelove* (1964), *2001: A Space Odyssey* (1968), and *A Clockwork Orange* (1971). Kubrick became a living legend, and withdrew from the public eye while continuing to make films at ever longer intervals: *Barry Lyndon* (1975), *The Shining* (1980), *Full Metal Jacket* (1987), and his final legacy, *Eyes Wide Shut* (1999) He passed on his project *A.I. Artificial Intelligence* to Steven Spielberg, who released the film in 2001, two years after Kubrick's death.

Many legends surround the story of the movie's production: instead of the nine months originally planned, Kubrick filmed in complete secrecy for 19 months in a studio near London. Stars such as Harvey Keitel and Jennifer Jason Leigh were swapped around and edited out, during or even after the filming. In the orgy scene, which is a cross between a Venetian carnival and a Baroque inquisition in Moorish halls, digital figures and objects were added in the US to obscure the audience's view of the proceedings to prevent the movie from ending up on the porn shelves in video shops. When Kubrick, control freak and grand master of PR, died a week after the film was finished, it was even claimed that his death was his ultimate, best-ever publicity stunt.

Even if Bill defends monogamy with rational arguments in his discussions with Alice, his behaviour betrays his forbidden desires. At what point does secret sexual desire break the vow of married faithfulness and where do reality and dreams converge? Paradoxically, the marriage partner is both beloved subject and desired object: Alice's self-confidence and freely admitted desire is as much a witness to the insufficiency of language as Bill's weak attempts to justify his behavior. Both are attracted to outsiders, but in the final instance, they remain faithful to each other.

MH

5 William Harford roams through Manhattan by night, a driven man – and "lucky," as the newspaper proclaims, he certainly is not.

6 Not long after *Eyes Wide Shut* was completed the press announced the separation of Cruise and Kidman after more than ten years – half an eternity for Hollywood.

7 For a long time Cruise, born in New York state in 1962, was considered to be a good-looking boy with no acting talent – but roles in *Eyes Wide Shut* and *Magnolia* (1999) won many critics over to his side.

8 Director Sydney Pollack played the part of roué Viktor Ziegler for his colleague and friend Kubrick.

"**There are many questions left unanswered in *Eyes Wide Shut*. However, these are questions that viewers themselves can answer. Everything is there.**"

Kubrick's brother-in-law Jan Harlan in
Stanley Kubrick: The Director as Architect

FIGHT CLUB

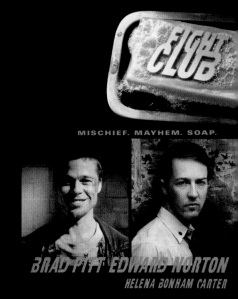

999 – USA – 139 MIN. – THRILLER

DIRECTOR DAVID FINCHER (*1963)

SCREENPLAY JIM UHLS, based on the novel of the same name by CHUCK PALAHNIUK

DIRECTOR OF PHOTOGRAPHY JEFF CRONENWETH EDITING JAMES HAYGOOD MUSIC DUST BROTHERS

PRODUCTION ART LINSON, CEAN CHAFFIN, ROSS GRAYSON BELL for LINSON FILMS for FOX 2000 PICTURES, REGENCY ENTERPRISES, TAURUS FILM)

STARRING BRAD PITT (Tyler Durden), EDWARD NORTON (Narrator), HELENA BONHAM-CARTER (Marla Singer), MEAT LOAF ADAY (Robert Paulsen), JARED LETO (Angel Face), ZACH GRENIER (Richard Chesler), RACHEL SINGER (Chloe), THOM GOSSOM JR. (Detective Stern), GEORGE MAGUIRE (Leader of "Remaining Men Together"), PAT MCNAMARA (Jacobs)

> *"Our generation has had no Great Depression, no Great War. Our war is a spiritual war. Our depression is our lives."*

Hollywood producers like to say of good scripts that they begin like an earthquake then slowly build up to a climax. *Fight Club* comes very close to that: in a furious opening sequence the camera races through the nerve system of a human body accompanied by the music of the Dust Brothers. It captures the tiny hairs and drops of sweat on the surface of the skin before finally focusing on a pistol between the teeth of the man whose body we have just seen, whose voice will guide us through the movie. The movie changes time and place many times at a furious speed, winding backwards and forwards until the story finally begins from the beginning.

He can't sleep. His doctor won't prescribe him anything for it. When you can't sleep, everything looks like the copy of a copy of a copy. The young narrator can only find peace by infiltrating self-help groups under false pretenses, so he fakes testicular cancer, tuberculosis, and incest. Only in the face

of the pain and fears of others can the anonymous narrator (Edward Norton) find himself – he can cry and sleep. An ambitious young yuppie, he starts doubting his career and lifestyle and ends up convinced that he is deeply dissatisfied. The catalyst he needs to help him to this realization and the trigger of the action of the movie is Tyler Durden. When his Ikea apartment is burnt out, he goes to stay with Tyler and so begins one of the most unusual male friendships in recent film history, and their relationship becomes the driving force behind the rest of the movie. With ostentatious coolness and almost pretentious nonchalance, Brad Pitt plays Durden as a demonic, seductive alternative to the narrator's permanent insecurity.

What do men do when they don't know what to do? They fight until they bleed. *Fight Club* doesn't actually offer any concrete solutions to society's ills but it draws a precise, comprehensive picture of social disaffection. It's a

3

"If the spirit has gone to sleep, the body has to take care of feeling alive. A fight is just the right atavistic ritual to remedy postmodern damage to civilization." *Der Spiegel*

BRAD PITT From pretty face to one of Hollywood's most famous stars, Brad Pitt was first introduced to the public in a Levi's commercial ("20th Century Boy"). Born in Oklahoma in 1963, Pitt began his rapid rise to stardom with a short but impressive appearance as the hitchhiker in *Thelma & Louise* (1991), where he gave Thelma an unforgettable sexual experience before running off with her savings. Pitt quickly shook off his image as the hunk with the six-pack and learned the craft of serious acting in melodramas like *Legends of the Fall* (1994) and *A River Runs Through It* (1992). He really found his forte when he began to work with director David Fincher, playing memorable characters in the thriller about a serial killer, *Se7en* (1995), in the satire on consumer society *Fight Club* (1999), and in the literary epic *The Curious Case of Benjamin Button* (2008). Time and again he has demonstrated his feel for touching, powerful characterizations as in *Moneyball* (2011), but he has equally indulged in deliciously outlandish roles like the fitness studio jackass in *Burn After Reading* (2008) and the gung-ho, Nazi-hating colonel in *Inglourious Basterds* (2009).

1   Masculinity in crisis: the anonymous narrator (Edward Norton) unexpectedly finds himself in the arms of Robert Paulsen (Meat Loaf Aday) again.

2   Who wouldn't want to be like Tyler Durden (Brad Pitt)? – Good-looking, charming, quick-witted, and uncompromising.

3   America's urban guerillas of the future? Brad Pitt's casual nonchalance meets Edward Norton's broken office worker existence.

4 "The internal monologue gives a kind of context and also humor. In the absence of this voice, the story is simply sad and ridiculous."
David Fincher

5 With the role of Marla Singer, Helena Bonham-Carter, who was born in England in 1966 and until now had usually favored harmless costume parts, opened up a whole new sphere of activity.

6 The narrator (Edward Norton) meets enigmatic femme fatale Marla Singer for the first time at a self-help group.

THE MESSENGER: THE STORY OF JOAN OF ARC

1999 – FRANCE / USA – 158 MIN. – HISTORICAL FILM, DRAMA
DIRECTOR LUC BESSON (*1959)
SCREENPLAY ANDREW BIRKIN, LUC BESSON DIRECTOR OF PHOTOGRAPHY THIERRY ARBOGAST
EDITNG SYLVIE LANDRA MUSIC ERIC SERRA PRODUCTION PATRICE LEDOUX for GAUMONT,
LEELOO PRODUCTIONS
STARRING MILLA JOVOVICH (Joan of Arc), JOHN MALKOVICH (Charles VII), FAYE DUNAWAY
(Yolande d'Aragon), DUSTIN HOFFMAN (Conscience), PASCAL GREGGORY (Duke of
Alençon), VINCENT CASSEL (Gilles de Rais), TCHEKY KARYO (Dunois), RICHARD RIDINGS
(La Hire), DESMOND HARRINGTON (Aulon), TIMOTHY WEST (Cauchon), JANE VALENTINE
(Joan as a child)

"Follow me!"

France in 1420. War has raged for decades and large stretches of the country are occupied by the English, but Jeanne (Jane Valentine) has a happy childhood in her home village of Domrémy. The devout girl goes to confession several times a day and tells the priest that God speaks to her. One day when Jeanne is playing in the fields she has a vision. When she comes to her senses, she finds a sword lying next to her in the grass. Excited, she runs home only to witness how the English burn the village down and rape and murder her sisters. We then skip forward nine years. The war is still raging, and Jeanne (Milla Jovovich), who is now a young woman, believes that she has discovered the meaning of her vision: God has chosen her to lead the French to victory against the English and help the Dauphin (John Malkovich) onto the throne of France. She is received at court and manages to convince the Dauphin of the truth of her mission. She rides to Orléans at the head of the army.

Luc Besson has always been a master of the big-budget spectacular, and his vision of Joan of Arc is very much a continuation of the style he used in *The Fifth Element* (1996), his previous film. There are few stories that have been filmed as often as the life of this French national heroine. Besson however is probably the first to concentrate almost exclusively on the fight at Orléans and on the action. The fighting takes up almost half of the movie, while her childhood, trial and sentencing are shown almost in passing. His Joan above all is a warrior, an amazon-like figure. Accordingly, the movie's most beautiful moments are when Milla Jovovich rides into battle with short hair and shining armor. Besson is in his element here.

However, when we compare this movie with earlier versions it becomes clear how unusual and even unsuitable all this action is in a story that is motivated above all by spiritual processes and by religious and moral issues. Jacques Rivette's *Jeanne la pucelle* (1994) for instance develops Joan's personality and story with incredible calm and power, but as a supporter of anti-intellectual cinema, Besson aims to do the exact opposite. He wants to grab spectators from the opening frame. His film has no time for development and

4

1   Sent by God to rid France of the English: top model Milla Jovovich is a Joan of Arc for the masses in the 1990s.

2   Spectacular cinema: Faye Dunaway in the role of Yolande d'Aragon in period costume with shaved brow.

3   As in classic adventure films, the old warhorses get the sympathy vote in the film (in the center: Tcheky Karyo).

4   Luc Besson in his element: almost half the film is dominated by tumultuous battle scenes.

5   Power crazy and cynical: Charles VII (John Malkovich) concocts his plots surrounded by his advisers.

"Is Joan a servant of God or a pill-popping freak who watches too much MTV?" *The Washington Post*

progression, but merely shows events. The camera is in permanent movement looking for brilliant images, while the elliptical narrative style means that there are no slow moments in the story. Besson externalizes everything, and we see both Joan's vision and her conscience. When she is plagued by doubt in prison, a dark man appears to her in a monk's habit (Dustin Hoffman) and confronts her with the contradictions of her existence. Joan's psychological makeup is also overly obvious and her behavior is reductively explained as a consequence of her traumatic childhood experience. Her story is simplified until it becomes little more than an artificial pictorial intoxication. Besson's attempt to create a contemporary Joan of Arc for the mass audiences of the '90s fails because the complexity of his chosen material contradicts

5

6

"The battle sequences are impressive – Besson
(The Fifth Element) has a thunderclap visual style.
But too much of the rest is the adventures of a
flighty action heroine."

San Francisco Examiner

7

6 Pillaging demons: Joan's transformation is triggered by a traumatic childhood experience.

7 Joan of Arc as an Amazon: Luc Besson turns the French national heroine into the champion of a jousting tournament. Whereas earlier films tried to explore the spiritual, moral, and religious dimension of the figure, Besson's version is above a visually dazzling spectacular showpiece.

JOAN OF ARC MOVIES Joan of Arc is a historical figure who was born in Domrémy in 1412 and died in Rouen in 1431. The story of France's liberator was first filmed in the earliest days of cinema history, and since then numerous great directors have tried their hand at the story. Carl Theodor Dreyer's famous silent film *La passion de Jeanne d'Arc* (1928) concentrated on her trial, as did Robert Bresson's *Le Procès de Jeanne d'Arc* (*The Trial of Joan of Arc*, 1962). Victor Fleming's *Joan of Arc* (1948) by contrast was nothing more than a star vehicle for Ingrid Bergman. In *Saint Joan* (1957), Otto Preminger investigated the story's moral dimensions. Finally, Jacques Rivette staged the life of *Jeanne la pucelle*, (*Joan the Maid*, 1994) using medieval books of hours before Luc Besson turned the devout virgin into an action heroine in *The Messenger: The Story of Joan of Arc*.

AMERICAN BEAUTY ♟♟♟♟♟

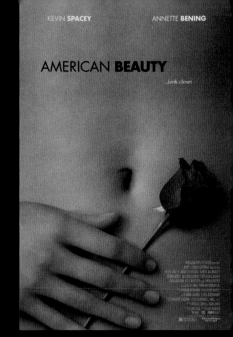

999 – USA – 121 MIN. – DRAMA

DIRECTOR SAM MENDES (*1965) SCREENPLAY ALAN BALL DIRECTOR OF PHOTOGRAPHY CONRAD L. HALL
EDITING TARIQ ANWAR, CHRISTOPHER GREENBURY MUSIC THOMAS NEWMAN
PRODUCTION BRUCE COHEN, DAN JINKS for DREAMWORKS SKG, JINKS/COHEN COMPANY
STARRING KEVIN SPACEY (Lester Burnham), ANNETTE BENING (Carolyn Burnham),
THORA BIRCH (Jane Burnham), WES BENTLEY (Ricky Fitts), MENA SUVARI
(Angela Hayes), PETER GALLAGHER (Buddy Kane), CHRIS COOPER (Colonel Frank Fitts),
ALLISON JANNEY (Barbara Fitts), SCOTT BAKULA (Jim Olmeyer), SAM ROBARDS
(Jim "JB" Berkley)
ACADEMY AWARDS 2000 OSCARS for BEST PICTURE, BEST ACTOR (Kevin Spacey),
BEST CINEMATOGRAPHY (Conrad L. Hall), BEST DIRECTOR (Sam Mendes), and
BEST ORIGINAL SCREENPLAY (Alan Ball)

"You have no idea what I'm talking about, I'm sure. But don't worry, you will someday."

In one year's time Lester Burnham (Kevin Spacey) will be dead: that much we learn right at the beginning of the movie. And he already knows this himself, for he's the one who tells his own story. A dead man speaks to us from off screen, and the strangest thing about it is his amused detachment. With a sweeping movement making the offscreen narration seem like a message of salvation, the camera moves down on the world from above and closes in on the dismal suburban street where Lester lives. We are introduced to the situation in which he finds himself: his marriage to Carolyn (Annette Bening) is over, and she considers him a failure, while his daughter Jane (Thora Birch) hates him for not being a role model. The only highpoint of Lester's sad daily routine is masturbating under the shower in the morning while his wife gathers roses in the garden to decorate the dinner table where they conduct their daily fights.

Family happiness, or whatever passed for it, only ever existed in the photos that Lester often looks at to remind himself of his past, and of the interest in life which he once had but which is now buried under the pressure of conformity. It is only when he falls in love with Angela (Mena Suvari), his daughter's Lolita-like friend, that he rediscovers his zest for life. This second spring changes Lester, but his wife Carolyn meanwhile is doing worse and worse as a property dealer. He reassesses his position and discovers old and forgotten strengths. She by contrast becomes inextricably entwined in the fatal cycle of routine and self-sacrifice. As Lester puts it, trying to live as though their life were a commercial nearly destroys them both. Outward conformity and prosperity results in inner impoverishment. The business mantras that Carolyn repeats over and over to herself to bolster her self-confidence sound increasingly ridiculous under the circumstances.

At this point, it becomes abundantly clear what we are intended to understand by "American Beauty." The title is not a reference to the seductive child-woman who helps Lester break out of the family prison – that would be too superficial. The subject of *American Beauty* is the question of the beauty of life itself. Mendes's movie is about whether or not it is possible to live a fulfilling life in a society where superficiality has become the norm. To put it in more philosophical terms, *American Beauty* uses the expressive means of drama and satire to go through all the possibilities for leading an honest life in a dishonest environment. Sadly this turns out to be impossible, or at least Lester's attempt ends in death.

It's a gem of a movie, thanks to Sam Mendes's careful use of film techniques. He never exposes his characters to ridicule and he protects them from cheap laughs by giving them time to develop. He also gives depth to their relationships and arranges them in dramatic constellations. Mendes's experience as a theater director shows in a number of carefully staged scenes whose strict form is well suited to the Burnham's oppressive and limited family life. Many scenes put us in mind of plays by Samuel Beckett, like the backyard sequence where Rick teaches Lester not to give in to circumstance. The symmetrical arrangements of characters around the table or the television are further reminders of family dramas on the stage.

2

3

4

1   A seductively beautiful image

2   Hollywood's new bright young things: saucy Angela
    (Mena Suvari)

3   … and sensitive Jane (Thora Birch).

4   Carolyn Burnham (Annette Bening) on the brink
    of madness.

5   Liberation from the familial cage brings happiness
    to Lester Burnham (Kevin Spacey).

"At first the film judges its characters harshly; then it goes to every effort to make them win back their rights." *Frankfurter Allgemeine Zeitung*

In an important subplot, Lester's daughter Jane falls in love with Rick, the boy next door, who is never seen without his video camera and films constantly, to "remind himself," as he says. He documents the world and discovers its beauty in grainy video pictures of dead animals and people. It is his father, the fascist ex-marine Colonel Frank Fitts – brilliantly acted by Chris Cooper – who in a moment of emotional turmoil shoots Lester Burnham and thereby fulfills the prophecy made at the beginning of the film. The hopeless struggle between internal and external beauty comes to a bloody end, but the issue remains open. The movie points to a vague possibility for reconciling these two opposites, but at the end this seems to have been an illusion. Despite our right to the "pursuit of happiness," material and spiritual wealth seem to be mutually exclusive, and the good life remains a promise of happiness which is yet to be fulfilled. With irony and humor, *American Beauty* shows that modern American society's mental state is by no means as rosy as the initiators of the Declaration of Independence would have hoped.

BR

KEVIN SPACEY Where would cinema be without Kevin Spacey? Born in 1959, this friendly, understated actor has played such complex and disturbing characters as John Doe, "The Man Without Qualities," in *Se7en* (1995), and sinister puppet master Roger "Verbal" Kint in *The Usual Suspects* (1995). Spacey is an enigmatic minimalist who needs only a few striking gestures to produce wonderful emotional cinema with cool irony: as Lester Burnham in *American Beauty* (1999), for instance. When he dies at the turning point of a story – as he does in *L.A. Confidential* (1997) – it's a great loss, both for us and for the movie. But there is much more to Spacey: as well as directing and starring in the biopic of musician Bobby Darin, *Beyond the Sea* (2004), he sang all the songs himself. He is also the artistic director of the Old Vic Theatre in London.

"When I made *American Beauty*, I wanted the film's vision to offer every spectator a very intimate experience. I hope it's a universal work, which helps one understand life that little bit better." Sam Mendes in *Le Figaro*

6 Grotesque victim of his own ideology: sinister neighbor Colonel Fitts (Chris Cooper) shortly before his surprise coming out.

7 Scenes from a marriage in ruins.

8 Wes Bentley is very convincing as Ricky Fitts, the introverted young man from next door.

9 Jane is fascinated by Ricky's puzzling hobby.

10 Life's true beauty can only be appreciated in a video image.

10

THE BLAIR WITCH PROJECT

In October of 1994
three student filmmakers disappeared
in the woods near Burkittsville Maryland
while shooting a documentary
A year later their footage was found

1999 – USA – 87 MIN. 1999 – USA – 87 MIN. – HORROR FILM
DIRECTOR DANIEL MYRICK (*1964), EDUARDO SANCHEZ (*1969)
SCREENPLAY DANIEL MYRICK, EDUARDO SANCHEZ **DIRECTOR OF PHOTOGRAPHY** NEAL FREDERICKS
EDITING DANIEL MYRICK, EDUARDO SÁNCHEZ **MUSIC** TONY CORA **PRODUCTION** GREGG HALE,
ROBIN COWIE, MICHAEL MONELLO for HAXAN FILMS, ARTISAN ENTERTAINMENT
STARRING HEATHER DONAHUE (Heather), MICHAEL WILLIAMS (Michael), JOSHUA LEONARD
(Joshua), BOB GRIFFIN (Fisherman), JIM KING (Interview partner), SANDRA SANCHEZ
(Waitress), ED SWANSON (Fisherman with glasses), PATRICIA DECOU (Mary Brown),
MARK MASON (Man with the yellow hat), JACKIE HALLEX

THE BLAIR WITCH PROJECT

"It's very hard to get lost in America these days and even harder to stay lost."

We know the story from the brothers Grimm: young people get lost in the woods and struggle with a witch. In the contemporary adaptation *The Blair Witch Project* there is however no tempting gingerbread and the witch doesn't get pushed into the oven – instead film students Heather (Heather Donahue), Michael (Michael Williams), and Joshua (Joshua Leonard) set off into the woods in Maryland with their camera to investigate stories of a witch, and they come to a sticky end. First the three youngsters ask people in the village of Blair about the stories, then they go off into the woods to look. It soon becomes ominously clear that they are being watched and they realize too late that they are lost.

The Blair Witch Project cost only a fraction of the cost of a normal Hollywood production. The plot is driven by the movie's own frugal production conditions. A horror movie disguised as a documentary, it begins with a text insert saying that in October 1994 three film students disappeared in the woods near Burkittsville, Maryland, while making a documentary film and that their film material was found a year later. This material is what we are about to see. Unlike Danish Dogme films such as *The Celebration* (*Festen*, 1998), which base their stark simplicity on a pseudo-religious creed and a wish to take cinema back to its basics, in this case the movie's lack of technical sophistication is an integral part of its storyline.

Physical movement always has a psychological dimension in cinema: as the three students move further and further away from a normal investigative outing, they penetrate deeper and deeper into the woods and become more and more convinced that they are hopelessly lost. The nearer they get to the witch's house, the closer they are to the darkness within themselves. The would-be filmmakers become increasingly tense. They neither look nor act like future stars, but more like we would imagine ordinary film students; they are not particularly attractive, they're not necessarily very nice, and they're ultimately a bit nerdy. This makes it all the more believable that we are seeing the material from their filming expedition: wobbly and unfocused images of a journey with no return, to which the pictures are the only witnesses. Their journey through the woods of Maryland is also an excursion into American history. This wild countryside on the East Coast was where the first settlers arrived, and it was here that James Fenimore Cooper's last Mohican roamed and hunted. It is a sad reflection on today's civilization that the descendants of this pioneering generation are destroyed by their forefathers' legends. City dwellers in the wilderness are mostly their own worst enemies, and they fall victim to their own fears rather than to the hostile environment. Trapped in a situation that seems increasingly hopeless, the three students mercilessly document each other's despair and psychic disintegration.

Its innovative marketing aside, the movie still basically functions as a relatively old-fashioned horror film. The three students tramp up hill and down dale, and live in terror of what they might find in front of their tent in the morning. But there is actually nothing to be seen – we can't make out anything for sure in the partly blackened pictures and the fear only exists where it is at its worst: in our own heads.

MH

"*Blair* is the clearest example of a new phenomenon: the film's success was driven not by a conventional publicity campaign, but by a web site combined with word of mouth." *Süddeutsche Zeitung*

MARKETING *The Blair Witch Project* cost 35,000 dollars and in the USA alone the movie made 140 million – profit margins which most investors can only dream of. The movie first attracted attention in January 1999 at the Sundance Festival, which is the El Dorado for US independent film. Artisan, a small distribution company, secured the distribution rights to *BWP* and began an unrivaled marketing campaign. Week after week the Internet site www.blairwitch.com published new tidbits on the background to the mythology of the Blair Witch. When the movie was released in June 1999 only 27 copies were made, although this number was gradually increased. As copies were kept short, cinema screenings sold out in a few places and the word on the street spread. This is quite unlike the usual Hollywood practice where the market is flooded with as many copies as possible.

1 Face to face with terror – the observer is stuck there with his own fear.

2 Michael (Michael Williams) and Joshua (Joshua Leonard) in the face of horror, which is always located somewhere near the camera.

3 Securing evidence of an expedition into the heart of darkness.

4 Seemingly realistic images of a fictional story.

THE INSIDER

999 – USA – 157 MIN. – THRILLER

DIRECTOR MICHAEL MANN (*1943)
SCREENPLAY ERIC ROTH, MICHAEL MANN, based on the article "THE MAN WHO KNEW TOO MUCH" by MARIE BRENNER in *VANITY FAIR*, MAY 1996 DIRECTOR OF PHOTOGRAPHY DANTE SPINOTTI
EDITING WILLIAM GOLDENBERG, DAVID ROSENBLOOM, PAUL RUBELL
MUSIC PIETER BOURKE, LISA GERRARD, GRAEME REVELL PRODUCTION PIETER JAN BRUGGE, MICHAEL MANN, MICHAEL WAXMAN for BLUE LIGHT PRODUCTIONS, FORWARD PASS, KAITZ PRODUCTIONS, MANN/ROTH PRODUCTIONS, TOUCHSTONE PICTURES
STARRING AL PACINO (Lowell Bergman), RUSSELL CROWE (Jeffrey Wigand), CHRISTOPHER PLUMMER (Mike Wallace), DIANE VENORA (Liane Wigand), PHILIP BAKER HALL (Don Hewitt), LINDSAY CROUSE (Sharon Tiller), DEBI MAZAR (Debbie De Luca), STEPHEN TOBOLOWSKY (Eric Kluster), COLM FEORE (Richard Scruggs), GINA GERSHON (Helen Caperelli), MICHAEL GAMBON (Thomas Sandefur), RIP TORN (John Scanlon)

"What the hell do you expect? Grace and consistency?"

Jeffrey Wigand (Russell Crowe) is what is known as an insider: as a former employee of the cigarette manufacturer Brown & Williamson, he has information about the dangerous additives in tobacco, which increase addiction and cause cancer. This should be enough to finish off the tobacco lobby, who stand accused of endangering public health. But things turn out a little differently. When this loyal and conscientious scientist tells his boss that he is worried about the possible dangers of a flavor enhancer, he is immediately fired. His redundancy money is at stake and with it his family's hard-earned prosperity. The firm tries to force him to sign a contract promising to say nothing about his work, but Jeffrey refuses and then the psychological terror against him and his family begins. Threatening, stony-faced musclemen in big white limousines observe his every movement, nocturnal visitors to the backyard disturb the children, and his wife receives terrifying death threats by e-mail. With breathtaking speed and drastic changes of perspective, Dante Spinotti's camera shows how Jeffrey Wigand's world breaks down practically overnight. There are unfocused close-ups, hectic swings, daring camera angles, and quick cuts combined with slow motion as the camera captures Jeffrey's persecution complex and his psychological collapse. The pictures seem to fall apart, just like Jeffrey's life. His wife can't

take it any longer and leaves him. In desperation, Jeffrey finally turns to Lowell Bergman (Al Pacino), who is the producer of *60 Minutes*, a famous television news show. The movie changes its narrative perspective at this point. *The Insider* shows Bergman as a forthright, persuasive man from the very beginning. His negotiating skills even get him an interview with the Islamic Hezbollah leader. This episode foreshadows Wigand's case, showing the tobacco industry to be a criminal organization and its bosses and leaders to be shameless criminals who think nothing of presenting their appalling deeds as promises of happiness. This is where *The Insider* comes to its real theme, which is the difficulty of being successful, upright, and truthful as an individual in a land where every aspect of life is ruled by a conglomerate of industrial, legal, and media cartels. The insider Jeffrey Wigand becomes an outsider. The tobacco industry puts private detectives on his trail, the media are only interested in him as a headline that increases circulation, the legal system uses the "Wigand case" to increase its own importance, and all of them profit from him financially. Even the influence of the few upright people in the corrupt system disappears before our very eyes. Lowell Bergman is sent on holiday when the managers of CBS stop the broadcast of an interview with Wigand because it might endanger the channel's lucrative sale to a subsidiary

3

"You have to speak Pacino's language. Before and after the take. 'Cos he always comes up and asks what I thought of the take, what we might do differently. Then it's really important to find the right words. Anyone who thinks Pacino is a 'method actor' will realize that's all nonsense. Pacino is a graduate of the Pacino School of Acting." Michael Mann in *Süddeutsche Zeitung*

1 Humiliated but not completely crushed, in the end Jeffrey Wigand (Russell Crowe) loses everything – except his beliefs.

2 Al Pacino is outstanding as crafty media action man Lowell Bergman.

3 Lowell Bergman is unflinching in the battle against the tobacco industry's machinations.

4 The revelations in the media catapult Jeffrey Wigand and the tobacco mafia into an existential crisis.

company of the tobacco firm. But Bergman doesn't let them pull the wool over his eyes and his morals are not for sale. He knows only too well that truth is what the public think is true. He goes to work incognito to find out the truth about the machinations of the tobacco companies and bring them to the public's attention, while also hoping to find some kind of justice for Jeffrey. But in the end even he fails, and he gets out of the whole dishonest business.

Michael Mann and Dante Spinotti had worked together since *Red Dragon* (1986, video title *Manhunter*). The distinguishing characteristics of their work, as they demonstrated most perfectly in *Heat* (1995), are supercool sets and highly mobile camera techniques. *Heat* has an extraordinary lyrical quality in the poetic sheen of its wild shootouts, and every shot and cut in *The Insider* is saturated with the same style. The cinemascope format means that the movie takes the audience to the very limits of what cinema can offer. The flood of pictures however never overwhelms the plot and characters, and *The Insider* takes time to develop various different plot strands and believable psychological profiles for its main characters. Although the movie is dominated by an atmosphere of permanent menace, this is a thriller without a single death. And when it stops being a psychological thriller and becomes a media and legal drama, it still doesn't break step. Two and a half hours fly by. *The Insider* only comes to a halt when Bergman Lowell is finally forced to give up.

BR

MICHAEL MANN Michael Mann's understated aestheticism was groundbreaking for the cinema of the '90s. After attending the London International Film School, Mann (*1943) began to make a name for himself in the mid-'60s as a director of commercials and documentaries. Back in the USA, he wrote for TV cop series *Starsky & Hutch* before making his impressive cinema debut with *Thief* (1981). Years before Jonathan Demme, he brought Hannibal Lecter to the screen in *Manhunter* (1986, original title: *Red Dragon*). He left a lasting legacy for the gangster movie genre with *Heat* (1995), in which he brought together superstars Al Pacino and Robert De Niro; with the superb assassin drama *Collateral* (2004) starring Tom Cruise; and with *Public Enemies* (2009), his biopic about the bank robber John Dillinger. Things had come full circle to an extent in 2006 when he directed *Miami Vice* with Colin Farrell and Jamie Foxx; as its producer, he had made a significant contribution to developing the pioneering neon aesthetic of the eponymous

5 In the end even alcohol is no help anymore.

6 News makers are powerful but isolated: anchorman
Mike Wallace (Christopher Plummer).

7 The news is always a compromise between quota
requirements and the truth.

"Since *Miami Vice* Mann has loved great turbulent drama beneath a flat, cool surface."
epd Film

THE STRAIGHT STORY

the Straight story

An eloquently simple,
deeply emotional movie.

999 – USA / FRANCE – 112 MIN. – ROAD MOVIE
DIRECTOR DAVID LYNCH (*1946)
SCREENPLAY JOHN ROACH, MARY SWEENEY DIRECTOR OF PHOTOGRAPHY FREDDIE FRANCIS
EDITING MARY SWEENEY MUSIC ANGELO BADALAMENTI PRODUCTION NEAL EDELSTEIN,
ALAIN SARDE, MARY SWEENEY for ASYMMETRICAL PRODUCTIONS, CIBY 2000,
LE STUDIO CANAL+, LES FILMS ALAIN SARDE, THE PICTURE FACTORY,
THE STRAIGHT STORY INC.
STARRING RICHARD FARNSWORTH (Alvin Straight), SISSY SPACEK (Rose Straight),
EVERETT MCGILL (Tom), JOHN FARLEY (Thorvald Olsen), KEVIN P. FARLEY (Harold Olsen),
HARRY DEAN STANTON (Lyle Straight), JANE GALLOWAY HEITZ (Dorothy),
JENNIFER EDWARDS–HUGHES (Brenda), JOSEPH A. CARPENTER (Bud),
DONALD WIEGGERT (Sig)

"I've got to make this trip on my own."

Alvin Straight (Richard Farnsworth) is an aging patriarch. He lives in the American outback together with his seemingly retarded daughter, who has lost the custody of her children. Alvin is a good man, honest and polite, full of good advice, and ready to help wherever he can. Alvin has a brother living at the other end of the Midwest. He hasn't spoken to his brother for quite a while, as their relationship went sour after an old argument. When his brother Lyle suffers a stroke, Alvin decides that he wants to see Lyle one more time. And so he climbs onto the uncomfortable seat of his mini tractor (complete with trailer) and heads for Mt. Zion, Wisconsin. He is a penitent on a pilgrimage, at the end of which lies forgiveness.

The Straight Story forms a kind of counterpart to Lynch's previous film Lost Highway (1997). While the first film delved alarmingly into the spiritual depths of its central figure, making the images themselves into expressions of psychological disturbance, The Straight Story, at least when viewed super-ficially, seems to be a parable of loneliness and slowness. The Straight Story is told in extended passages of sparse dialogue, and bright, quiet pictures. Cameraman Freddie Francis's opulent landscape shots evoke a peaceful atmosphere tinged with pathos – an atmosphere that spills over into the lives of the human figures in it. Alvin meets only humane and helpful people along his torturous route. When he finally arrives at his destination, Lyle is already doing much better, as though Alvin Straight's bone-headed determination had miraculously healed the rift between the two brothers. And even though they exchange very few words, their brotherhood is reestablished. This at least is the story on the surface – a story based on a true incident, which Lynch retells with the appropriate directness and simplicity. Yet from another point of view, the thoughtful, sentimental "straight story" is a front for another story which is part of the theme that Lynch has been exploring since Blue Velvet (1986): the secret torments that people harbor, and the abyss that lies just below

"With a minimum of external effects Lynch has achieved a maximum of human emotion. The simple story that he tells is ultimately about the dignity of the protagonists." *Frankfurter Allgemeine Zeitung*

1   The journey on the highway to happiness is long and arduous.

2   Daring to make a fresh start at the end of his life: Alvin Straight (Richard Farnsworth) blazes a trail.

3   Life has left visible traces of its passage.

4   Comical family idyll in the countryside: father and daughter (Sissy Spacek as Rose Straight).

5   Alvin Straight: never wavering and keeping straight on ahead …

6   … even in the face of dangerous competition out on the road.

7   Imperturbable and out in front: the slowest sets the pace.

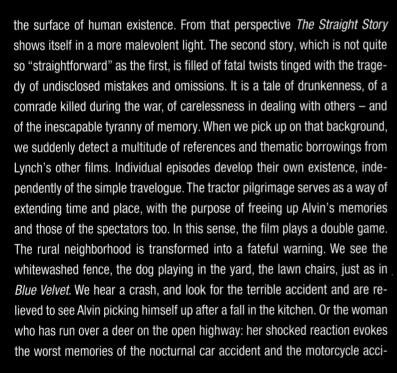

the surface of human existence. From that perspective *The Straight Story* shows itself in a more malevolent light. The second story, which is not quite so "straightforward" as the first, is filled of fatal twists tinged with the tragedy of undisclosed mistakes and omissions. It is a tale of drunkenness, of a comrade killed during the war, of carelessness in dealing with others – and of the inescapable tyranny of memory. When we pick up on that background, we suddenly detect a multitude of references and thematic borrowings from Lynch's other films. Individual episodes develop their own existence, independently of the simple travelogue. The tractor pilgrimage serves as a way of extending time and place, with the purpose of freeing up Alvin's memories and those of the spectators too. In this sense, the film plays a double game. The rural neighborhood is transformed into a fateful warning. We see the whitewashed fence, the dog playing in the yard, the lawn chairs, just as in *Blue Velvet*. We hear a crash, and look for the terrible accident and are relieved to see Alvin picking himself up after a fall in the kitchen. Or the woman who has run over a deer on the open highway: her shocked reaction evokes the worst memories of the nocturnal car accident and the motorcycle acci-

dent in *Wild at Heart* (1990). Like *Wild at Heart* and, most recently, *Lost Highway*, *The Straight Story* is a radical new take on the road movie genre. Not only does it treat the central transportation motif ironically, with the almost laughable garden tractor, but the insufferable slowness of Alvin's progress turns the trip itself into an endless Calvary in an infinite wilderness. Lynch obsessively repeats and develops his own motifs and themes, going over them time and again, and constantly revealing fresh facets.

Alvin is oppressed by his memories, and the passage of time is not enough to heal his wounded soul. It is as impossible to erase the ugly truths of his memories as it is to portray them adequately. They lie beyond the beauty of the landscape, the grace of old age, or the monumental calm of the rural idyll. Ultimately it is the restrained acting of the main character that draws our attention to the story below the surface. Richard Farnsworth, unforgettable as Alvin, once worked as a stunt man with the Marx Brothers. He was terminally ill with cancer when making this film, and he put an end to his own life a few weeks after his 80th birthday.

BR

FILM QUOTATION Quotation actually means the word-for-word transposition of one text passage into another text for purposes of reference. Filmmakers too have always made frequent use of quotation or cross-reference from other films. The golden age of film quotation arrived with the French Nouvelle Vague of the '60s, when quotation established itself as an art form in cinema historiography. There has been a renewed interest in the technique since the '80s. The current high point in the use of film quotation is unquestionably Quentin Tarantino's *Pulp Fiction* (1994) which consists almost exclusively of references to other films and genres. David Lynch is one of the subtlest masters of the quotation technique.

NOTTING HILL

1999 – GREAT BRITAIN – 124 MIN. – ROMANTIC COMEDY
DIRECTOR ROGER MICHELL (*1956)
SCREENPLAY RICHARD CURTIS DIRECTOR OF PHOTOGRAPHY MICHAEL COULTER EDITING NICK MOORE
MUSIC TREVOR JONES PRODUCTION DUNCAN KENWORTHY for NOTTING HILL PRODUCTIONS,
WORKING TITLE
STARRING JULIA ROBERTS (Anna Scott), HUGH GRANT (William Thacker), RHYS IFANS
(Spike), GINA MCKEE (Bella), HUGH BONNEVILLE (Bernie), EMMA CHAMBERS (Honey),
TIM MCINNERNY (Max), JAMES DREYFUS (Martin)

"Rita Hayworth used to say: 'They go to bed with Gilda; they wake up with me.'"

What happens when you fall in love with a well-known actress without even realizing that she is famous? Right! You're just as clumsy as you would be trying to approach any other woman. William Thacker (Hugh Grant), a bookshop owner who is as nice as he is unsuccessful, plays this part with bravura.

Movie star Anna Scott (Julia Roberts) comes to London for the premiere of her new film and spends some free time incognito in the picturesque district of Notting Hill. Here, seemingly miles away from the influence of the gossiping press, she is not immediately recognized. An amorous adventure begins when she comes into William Thacker's bookshop looking for travel books, and William promptly spills orange juice all over her.

The main character in this romantic comedy gets his name from the English writer William Thackeray, whose panoramic society novels investigated human weakness with sympathy and understanding. He deconstructed the idea of the hero and criticized bourgeois values like property and status. Like Thackeray's works, Notting Hill is based around an impossible love story between the rich and the poor, between the unsuccessful William and the successful Anna, between the stiff Englishman and the beautiful, vibrant American. They keep in touch and Anna sees a chance to break out of her golden cage. For her, taking part in the life of ordinary people means

winning back a part of her own life that she badly misses. William loves Anna's carefree beauty. The world of success and riches means nothing to him.

They flirt one moonlit night, climbing over the fence into a park to sit on an ancient bench. However, when Anna's boyfriend arrives in London from the US, their relationship comes to a swift, if temporary end.

When Anna has to flee from her own past – naked photos of her have turned up in the press – she turns up unexpectedly at William's flat to hide. The next morning, hordes of paparazzi besiege the house, and she is furious and leaves him. William's flatmate Spike let the cat out of the bag in the pub the night before after a couple of beers. The two are separated once more and this time it no longer looks like things will end happily. The efforts of William's friends to introduce him to other women can't make him forget his unhappiness. The passing of time is shown in poetic pictures: while William strolls through Notting Hill market, the four seasons leave their mark on the setting within one single shot. His longing for Anna is finally fulfilled when she comes back to London for another film premiere.

Notting Hill is an old-fashioned movie in the best sense of the word. Alongside the two successful stars of the genre who act perfectly and with

"Of course, the character of Anna Scott is drawn up so that she remains a fairy-tale princess until the very end. Otherwise, the film would have got too complicated and wouldn't have been a romantic love story."

Frankfurter Allgemeine Zeitung

HUGH GRANT Voted one of the "100 Sexiest Stars in Film History" in 1995 by *Empire Magazine*, Hugh Grant is a multitalented actor who has been very successful on stage and television, and even more so in the movies. Born in London in 1960, the Oxford graduate's distinguishing characteristics are his boyish, sensitive, intelligent, if often sleepy-eyed, good looks. He began playing romantic heroes in film versions of literary classics, such as the adaptation of E. M. Forster's novel *Maurice* (1987). He then switched increasingly to romantic comedies, including *Four Weddings and a Funeral* (1993), *Notting Hill* (1999), and *Did You Hear About the Morgans?* (2009).

1 Two people who were made for each other: bookseller William Thacker and Hollywood actress Anna Scott (Hugh Grant and Julia Roberts).

2 Bookworm as lady-killer: William Thacker in his shop.

3 Incognito: media star Anna Scott is always on the run.

4 Spike (Rhys Ifans), William's flatmate, throws a temporary spanner in the works.

out affectation are some offbeat figures who could only exist in England. Spike, William's flatmate, counterbalances the two main figures in an amusing manner with his advice and his pithy comments, his lanky figure, and his scruffy hippie appearance. But *Notting Hill* has some critical undertones too. It takes more than one sideswipe at the mass media, contrasting Anna's terrible treatment in the papers with the respectful admiration of the people on the street. Yet it's thanks to the media that the two lovers find each other again: at the last moment William manages to get into a press conference and mix with the reporters. He asks Anna in an understated, charming manner whether she intends to return to the USA. The ruse succeeds, and Anna promises to stay "forever."

BR

THE LIMEY

1999 – USA – 90 MIN. – GANGSTER FILM, NEO FILM NOIR
DIRECTOR STEVEN SODERBERGH (*1963)
SCREENPLAY LEM DOBBS DIRECTOR OF PHOTOGRAPHY EDWARD LACHMAN EDITING SARAH FLACK
MUSIC CLIFF MARTINEZ PRODUCTION JOHN HARDY, SCOTT KRAMER for ARTISAN
ENTERTAINMENT
STARRING TERENCE STAMP (Wilson), LESLEY ANN WARREN (Elaine), LUIS GUZMÁN (Ed),
BARRY NEWMAN (Avery), JOE DALLESANDRO (Uncle John), NICKY KATT (Stacy),
PETER FONDA (Terry Valentine), AMELIA HEINLE (Adhara), MELISSA GEORGE (Jennifer),
MATTHEW KIMBROUGH (Tom)

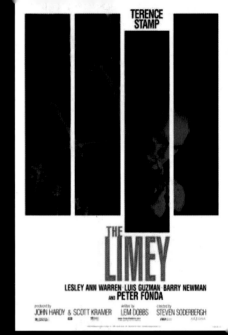

"Do you understand half the shit he says? – No, but I know what he means."

The English are not fond of talking. Americans, on the other hand, most definitely are. In his film *The Limey*, American cinema prodigy Steven Soderbergh concentrates on showing rather than saying. A newspaper clipping with the information that a woman has been killed on the Mulholland Highway, a photograph of the young woman, a man sitting pensively in an airplane: images take the place of words in setting up the story. The name of the man in the airplane is Wilson (Terence Stamp), and he is investigating the mysterious circumstances surrounding the car accident in which his daughter Jenny died. As in the best examples of film noir, Wilson has already reached a kind of ending as the story begins. The airplane scene takes place after the mystery has been solved and Wilson has finished his savage vendetta against his daughter's killers. He is on his way home, returning to his private life in England. He didn't kill media promoter Terry Valentine (Peter Fonda) who had been having an affair with his daughter. Instead, he forced him to talk, and, in a strange sense, saw his own mirror image. Jenny, he learned, was killed accidentally in a fistfight. She loved Valentine and she was trying to stop him

committing more crimes by betraying him to the police. When she was a child, she had once threatened to do the same to her criminal father. Now, all Wilson has left are his memories. Silent, blue-toned images of his daughter playing on the beach are shown again and again. A flash of light dances over her features. There is poetry in this repose, a stillness that contrasts with the other hectic and agitated images of the film. Wilson starts to be extremely depressed in the face of his failure and his loss. In casting Terence Stamp, Soderbergh made a first-class choice. The British actor's stony-faced style seems the perfect medium for expressing both the brutal and the tragic sides of Wilson's character. The director plays with this interaction between emotion and cold detachment: in one scene, Wilson enters a warehouse, and a handheld camera follows him in. His questions are followed by a fistfight, and Wilson is brutally beaten and thrown out. He picks himself up and goes back in, but this time the camera stays outside. Shots are fired. The camera films calmly from a safe distance. There are flashes of light and screams, and one man escapes from the warehouse and runs past the camera. Wilson returns

3

1 With story features and iron determination Wilson (Terence Stamp) tracks down his daughter's murderers.

2 Organized crime lives high above the roofs of the metropolis: Peter Fonda plays music producer Terry Valentine.

Agitated, the camera picks up and closes in on him. He calls: "Tell him, I'm coming." Soderbergh's sequencing of shots disrupts the chronology of events and their chain of causality. The spectators only discover the plot connections bit by bit, as they gradually piece together the story. Often they have to rely on assumptions. This process of mystification is intensified by the separation of action and sound: a figure is shown, we hear him talking, but his lips are not moving. Image and tone are not synchronized again until the next shot. In addition, Soderbergh integrates images from a totally different film. Scenes from Ken Loach's debut movie *Poor Cow* (1967) – also starring Terence Stamp – are incorporated as flashbacks into Wilson's happier past. In fact The Limey is also a homage. Parts of it look exactly like Jean-Luc

Godard's first film *À bout de souffle* (*Breathless*, 1959), thanks to the hand-held cameras, the jump cuts, and the seemingly improvised gangster story. But Wilson is quite different to Michel Poiccard, the small-time crook played by Jean-Paul Belmondo in the Godard film. Wilson is a professional, an expert criminal who is taking care of business, and nothing can stand in his way. Terry Valentine in his white suit and Wilson in black are like two sides of the same coin, each the embodying a different lifestyle, one American and the other English. And yet they have much more in common than they would care to admit. For that reason, although Terry has Wilson's daughter quite literally on his conscience, Wilson lets him live.

BF

"Soderbergh's style evokes the memory of John Boorman's *Point Blank*, which in its time was misunderstood because of its similarly complex narrative style and which also dealt with revenge taken by a determined loner." *epd Film*

JUMP CUT A jump cut is an abrupt transition between shots. It may involve continuous motion being interrupted by the removal of certain film material, or a static scene being disrupted by rapidly shifting points of focus. By fragmenting temporal and spatial continuity the director can actively steer the viewer's attention. Jump cutting is used extensively by Jean-Luc Godard in *À bout de souffle* (*Breathless*, 1959) as a move away from conventional "continuity editing" and a way of drawing the attention of the spectators to the structural aspect of film. It can also be used as a technical means of placing the viewer at the center of the dramatic action, as for example, in Steven Spielberg's *Jaws* (1975).

3 The smart ruler of the underworld.   **4** Beauty, elegance, and crime make an unholy trinity.   **5** Gangsters together: the showdown leads to self-knowledge.

BEING JOHN MALKOVICH

1999 – USA – 112 MIN. – COMEDY
DIRECTOR SPIKE JONZE (*1969)
SCREENPLAY CHARLIE KAUFMAN DIRECTOR OF PHOTOGRAPHY LANCE ACORD EDITING ERIC ZUMBRUNNEN
MUSIC CARTER BURWELL, BÉLA BARTÓK PRODUCTION STEVE GOLIN, VINCENT LANDAY,
SANDY STERN, MICHAEL STIPE for GRAMERCY PICTURES, PROPAGANDA FILMS,
SINGLE CELL PICTURES
STARRING JOHN MALKOVICH (John Horatio Malkovich), JOHN CUSACK (Craig Schwartz),
CAMERON DIAZ (Lotte Schwartz), NED BELLAMY (Derek Mantini), ORSON BEAN
(Dr. Lester), CATHERINE KEENER (Maxine), MARY KAY PLACE (Floris), K. K. DODDS
(Wendy), REGINALD C. HAYES (Don), BYRNE PIVEN (Captain Mertin)

"I think, I feel, I suffer."

To be famous and desired. To be inside someone else, to see what he sees, to feel what he feels. To be a star, to enjoy his privileges, and to bathe in his success, and yet remain incognito – that would be the perfect material for a fairy tale, a play, or a movie. Well clear the stage and raise the curtain, because the play's called *Being John Malkovich*.

Struggling puppeteer Craig Schwartz (John Cusack) could use more public and financial success for his virtuoso marionette theater. The lonely "Dance of Despair" of his wooden hero, an expression of Craig's own mental state, is performed with astonishing perfection and intensity, but the public prefers something bigger. To get into television and become famous you need gigantic puppets, the sort that you would have to manipulate from the side of a bridge. This is the starting point for newcomer Spike Jonze's bizarre film comedy. The frustrated Craig is forced to work as a filing clerk for the Lester Corporation, where he meets and falls for the fetching Maxine.

vehicle for the self-centered preoccupations of all three becomes John Malkovich, who plays himself. This trick allows for a side story about the identity of actors and the problems they have giving expression, face, and body to countless different characters without losing themselves in the process.

The main story is dedicated to the kafkaesque idea that by crawling through a dwarf-sized door in the wall of floor 7 ½ of an office building, it is possible to enter into the head of John Malkovich and take part in his life. Based on this unusual and arresting idea, *Being John Malkovich* becomes an ironic illustration of the theory that we only see ourselves through the eyes of others. A convoluted amorous quadrangle develops. John Cusack and Cameron Diaz play the young couple whose relationship falls apart after Craig's discovery. At first they take turns sliding through the dark corridor beyond the small door that leads into the skull of John Malkovich. He is

1 The anguish of not being master in your own house: John Malkovich.

2 The light at the end of the tunnel is called John Malkovich.

3 Queue here for bliss.

"Hollywood hasn't dared to entrust itself so casually to an absurd initial idea for many years." *Frankfurter Allgemeine Zeitung*

part is not averse to Maxine's advances. Together, they stage their sexual adventure with the help of John Malkovich's body, cuckolding Craig at the same time. In contrast to her character in Tom DeCillo's media satire *Living in Oblivion* (1995, a film whose high spirits are shared by *Being John Malkovich*) Catherine Keener's portrayal of the clever Maxine is coldly erotic. Thanks to her business sense the hole in the wall leading to John Malkovich's brain becomes a source of income, and the secret passage becomes an insider attraction for anyone willing to pay money to have a prominent identity for a change, even if it's only for 15 minutes. That's the length of the visits, and afterwards visitors find themselves miles away lying in the dirt beside the New Jersey turnpike. When Malkovich finally discovers the unscrupulous business, it's already too late. His ego is no longer master in its

own abode. Craig has taken possession of his mind, and Maxine changes her loyalties to Craig alias Malkovich, from whom she is expecting a child. Craig has finally made it: he's transformed Malkovich into a living puppet and he basks in the brilliance of his success. As if the story were not already full of supernatural situations, it then transforms into a tale of migrating souls like *Cocoon* (1985) where the undead are forced to change their host bodies from time to time. After Maxine's outrageous kidnap attempt, Craig leaves the body of John Malkovich to make room for the spirit of Captain Merten, the builder of the office building with the seventh-and-a-half floor. Craig's attempt to achieve happiness by exploiting John Malkovich's fame turns out to be an illusion of the mind.

BR

"It is precisely the vanity, which Malkovich portrays with remarkable self-irony and without exaggeration so that it always seems authentic, that makes many scenes so funny." *Frankfurter Allgemeine Zeitung*

FILMS ABOUT FILMMAKING Cinema has always been preoccupied with its own processes: from scriptwriting (*Sunset Boulevard*, Billy Wilder, 1950) to camerawork (*The Camera Man*, Buster Keaton, 1928), to directing (*8½*, Federico Fellini, 1963), acting (*Chaplin*, Richard Attenborough, 1992), and location shooting (*Living in Oblivion*, Tom DiCillo, 1995). But the movie business does more than just examine the jobs in the production process. In remakes and filmic references, directors consistently return to images created by other filmmakers, and thus construct their own history. Quentin Tarantino has proved a past master of self-referential cinema with movies from *Pulp Fiction* (1994) and *Kill Bill* (2003, 2004) to *Inglourious Basterds* (2009).

4   Puppeteer Craig Schwartz (John Cusack) as a fake Mephistopheles.

5   Cameron Diaz in the role of the wife Lotte Schwartz discovers that she is in love with Maxine.

6   The shock of realization: I am not myself.

7   Unscrupulous femme fatale Maxine (Catherine Keener) turns everybody's head.

MAGNOLIA

1999 – USA – 188 MIN. – DRAMA, EPISODIC FILM
DIRECTOR PAUL THOMAS ANDERSON (*1970)
SCREENPLAY PAUL THOMAS ANDERSON DIRECTOR OF PHOTOGRAPHY ROBERT ELSWIT
EDITING DYLAN TICHENOR MUSIC JON BRION, AIMEE MANN PRODUCTION PAUL THOMAS
ANDERSON, JOANNE SELLAR for GHOULARDI FILM COMPANY, NEW LINE CINEMA,
THE MAGNOLIA PROJECT
STARRING JOHN C. REILLY (Jim Kurring), TOM CRUISE (Frank T. J. Mackey),
JULIANNE MOORE (Linda Partridge), PHILIP BAKER HALL (Jimmy Gator),
JEREMY BLACKMAN (Stanley Spector), PHILIP SEYMOUR HOFFMAN (Phil Parma),
WILLIAM H. MACY (Quiz Kid Donnie Smith), MELORA WALTERS (Claudia Wilson Gator),
JASON ROBARDS (Earl Partridge)
IFF BERLIN 2000 GOLDEN BEAR

"It would seem that we're through with the past, but it's not through with us."

According to Quentin Tarantino, the plot of *Pulp Fiction* (1994) is three stories about a story. Shortly before that, the film virtuoso Robert Altman gave the episodic movie new elegance with *Short Cuts* (1993), where many short stories revolve around a center, overlap, move away from each other again, and form new combinations. Although director Paul Thomas Anderson originally tried to play down the link, *Magnolia* can definitely be seen in relation to these earlier movies. The denial was probably just the reaction of a promising young filmmaker who wanted audiences to take a second look at his *Boogie Nights* (1997).

At the center of the tragicomedy *Magnolia* is Big Earl Partridge (Jason Robards), a TV tycoon of the worst kind. He lies dying, a wilting magnolia. Earl is the key figure, the man behind the scenes and the origin of all evils. His name alone is a program for the movie ... Earl is the only figure who always stays in the same place, unable to move from his deathbed. When the camera looks down on him from above and the mighty fanfare from Richard Strauss's *Also sprach Zarathustra* sounds, it's not just an ironic reference to

his once all-powerful influence, but also to the end of Stanley Kubrick's *2001 – A Space Odyssey* (1968). There we see the astronaut David Bowman as an old man alone on a big bed, shortly before the next evolutionary leap transforms him into the famous fetus from the final shot of 2001 and the cycle of human development moves onto a higher plane. Earl's end also signifies new beginnings, but before that can come about all the suffering that he has brought into the world must be dealt with. And that is no easy task.

With great humor and sympathy, *Magnolia* tells the stories of all the people on whose lives he has had such a lasting influence. First of all comes Earl's son Frank (Tom Cruise) who trains frustrated men to become super-macho in his "Seduce and Destroy" seminars. He got this motto from his father, who destroyed his wife with his complete lack of consideration. Now, shortly before his death, the shallow patriarch searches for his lost son, who he had abandoned as a teenager when his mother fell ill with cancer. When the two come together at the end, their broken relationship is shown in all its misery. Earl's young wife Linda (Julianne Moore) only married him for his

1

2

"Almost exactly in the middle is *Magnolia* – which lasts for three hours and isn't a second too long – so close to its characters that we can almost feel their breath."

Frankfurter Allgemeine Zeitung

1 Prodigal son (Tom Cruise) and hated father (Jason Robards).	**2** Relationship at an end: scenes from a marriage on its deathbed. Julianne Moore in the role of Linda Partridge.	**3** The incarnation of law and order: good-natured police officer Jim Kurring (John C. Reilly).

4 Claudia (Melora Walters), abused by her own father and addicted to drugs, provides an optimistic ending to the film.

5 Phil (Philip Seymour Hoffman), the carer of ailing patriarch Earl, demonstrates patience and sensitivity.

6 Confessions under duress: homosexual Donnie (William H. Macy) becomes the victim of his inferiority complex.

money. She realizes the shallowness of her own character and starts to go through a crisis of identity. Quiz master Jimmy Gator (Philip Baker Hall) presents the bizarre show "What Do Kids Know?" for Big Earl Partridge TV Productions, where three children compete against three adults answering general knowledge questions. Jimmy has absorbed his boss's way of thinking to such a degree that his extramarital affairs even include his daughter Claudia, who is now a cocaine addict and funds her habit with occasional prostitution. When the neighbors complain about her loud music, she gets a visit from a policeman who promptly falls in love with her, and even greater confusion ensues. Finally, there are the two child prodigies who have become famous through the quiz show. Former child star Donnie now tries vainly to chat up a good-looking barman and Stanley wets his pants at the show's decisive moment, as the production team's strict rules don't allow him to go to the lavatory before the broadcast.

The movie's interpersonal conflicts run along the fault lines between parents and children and men and women. All these relationships have been ruined by an inability to build up and maintain friendships, and by the impossibility of any real communication. *Magnolia* is an affectionate but cynical critique of the medium of television, and all the people in the movie seem to be trying to emulate its clichés. Behind everything is the television magnate Earl. The characters' lives are nothing more than television made flesh, absurd TV drama on the wrong side of the screen.

The movie begins with a macabre, satirical undertone and it becomes increasingly sarcastic and even cynical. An amused, concise voice-over at the beginning talks about the absurdity of life and denies the existence of coincidence, and the film goes on to prove that thesis. Although at first the episodes appear to be a transitory collection of unconnected events, a dense network of links gradually appears. The movie draws the audience into a whirl of

PAUL THOMAS ANDERSON Paul Thomas Anderson (*1970) left the New York Film Academy after only two days, to get back to the practical work he was familiar with from TV and video production. He developed his short film *Cigarettes & Coffee* (1993) into his first feature, the gambling drama *Hard Eight* (1996). After *Boogie Nights* (1997) and *Magnolia* (1999), he was seen as a great directorial talent on account of his innovative and complex plots and characters. His next films – the bittersweet romcom *Punch-Drunk Love* (2002) and a powerful saga about an oil prospector, *There Will Be Blood* (2007) – failed to live up to his masterpiece, *Magnolia*.

7 The strain of the TV quiz is written all over the face of young genius Stanley (Jeremy Blackman).

8 Donnie runs into more and more trouble.

9 Learning from children: a hard task even for MC Jimmy Gator (Philip Baker Hall).

failed relationships and unfulfilled yearnings for freedom, love, and mutual respect. This descent influences the movie's images, and their rhythm becomes slower and their colors darker, and spectators start to feel that the downward spiral could go on forever. But *Magnolia* is anything but a pessimistic movie: shortly before the final catastrophe, all the figures suddenly begin to sing the same song wherever they happen to be. After the initial surprise, this absurd directorial idea turns out to be a wonderful trick, which counteracts the seemingly inevitable end with offbeat humor in a manner not dis-

similar to the song at the end of *Monty Python's Life of Brian* (1979). When it rains frogs at the very end, spectators heave a sigh of relief along with the characters in the movie. This surreal event makes it clear that anything is possible in this movie. We may not be able to believe our eyes, but "it did happen" as the text under the pictures tells us. The event shakes the characters out of their lethargy and reminds them of the incredible opportunities that life can offer. And a small smile into the camera in the final shot holds the key to the way out of this crisis whose name is life.   BR

"*Magnolia* takes a long run-up, then jumps and lands in the middle of our present. It is the first film of the new millennium." *Frankfurter Allgemeine Zeitung*

"The film pauses for a moment: suicides forget to press the trigger, addicts forget their fix, and those in pain their pain. Then the play is over, the world appears fresh once more, the dead are buried and the living are given a second chance." *Süddeutsche Zeitung*

10 Tom Cruise in the unusual role of a repulsive advocate of machismo.

11 Victim of self-delusion: Julianne Moore is a convincing Beauty and the Beast.

SLEEPY HOLLOW ⚱

1999 – USA – 105 MIN. – HORROR FILM, CRIME FILM, LITERATURE ADAPTATION
DIRECTOR TIM BURTON (*1958)
SCREENPLAY ANDREW KEVIN WALKER, based on the novel *THE LEGEND OF SLEEPY HOLLOW*
by WASHINGTON IRVING DIRECTOR OF PHOTOGRAPHY EMMANUEL LUBEZKI EDITING CHRIS LEBENZON,
JOEL NEGRON MUSIC DANNY ELFMAN PRODUCTION SCOTT RUDIN, ADAM SCHROEDER,
FRANCIS FORD COPPOLA for PARAMOUNT PICTURES, MANDALAY PICTURES
STARRING JOHNNY DEPP (Constable Ichabod Crane), CHRISTINA RICCI (Katrina Anne Van
Tassel), MIRANDA RICHARDSON (Lady Mary Van Tassel), MICHAEL GAMBON (Baltus Van
Tassel), CASPER VAN DIEN (Brom Van Brunt), JEFFREY JONES (Reverend Steenwyck),
CHRISTOPHER LEE (Magistrate), MARC PICKERING (Masbath), CHRISTOPHER WALKEN
(The Hessian Horseman)
ACADEMY AWARDS 2000 OSCAR for BEST ART DIRECTION–SET DECORATION (Rick Heinrichs,
Peter Young)

"Truth is appearance, but appearance isn't always truth."

This truism, first expressed by Jean-Luc Godard, is exploited by filmmakers every second. And it is only because audiences know the principle so well that they are entertained by the film industry's more ghastly and peculiar offerings. Even if it means watching a film in which 18 people are beheaded by a headless, black-clad, and merciless horseman. For that's what we get in the cheerful grisliness that is Tim Burton's *Sleepy Hollow*. The fact that Washington Irving's short story *The Legend of Sleepy Hollow* (1820) is widely known and has served as the basis for a number of films, might also play a role, and it makes some, if not all of the story, a lot easier to swallow.

Luckily, spectators have an ally in Ichabod Crane, the main character in this gothic mystery-horror. The year is 1799. Armed with the scientific instru-

ments of the Enlightenment, Constable Crane (Johnny Depp) is sent to Sleepy Hollow, a small Dutch settlement not far from New York City, to investigate a series of mysterious murders. All of the victims have been beheaded. The villagers don't take to Crane's modern methods, and in fact his outlandish instruments and feeble attempts at logical argumentation are of little use. Things take a new turn when he has a personal encounter with the feared horseman, who is the ghost of a soldier punished for his bloody involvement in the American War of Independence by being beheaded with his own sword. This terrifying meeting leaves a deep mark on Crane and his enlightened worldview threatens to crumble, and for a while it seems that age-old superstitions and the archaic powers of a bygone age have caught up with him. But the Enlightenment is not so easily defeated, and he takes up the challenge

"*Sleepy Hollow* is a masterpiece of visual and emotional atmosphere, Burton's best film to date." *epd Film*

of understanding the strange phenomena. Following this salutary shock to his system, the fearless criminologist Crane becomes a perfect Sherlock Holmes figure. His Dr. Watson is the young Masbath (Marc Pickering), who lost his own father in the battle with the horseman. Unearthing some hidden facts, Masbath helps Crane find his way back onto the right track. What he finds is a web of intrigue and conspiracy woven by the two most influential families in town, the Van Tassels and the Van Garretts, together with the Mayor, Brom Van Brunt, and the Reverend Steenwyck. It all revolves around property and inheritance. It seems that the horseman is operating at the behest of one of these parties, and his victims are not chosen at random at all. Yet in the end,

it turns out that it is not Crane's prime suspect Baltus Van Tassel (Michael Gambon) who is at the bottom of the uncanny attacks, but his second wife (Miranda Richardson), stepmother to the beautiful Katrina Van Tassel (Christina Ricci). Using the skull of the dead soldier, she conjures up his ghost to carry out her revenge for past injustices.

With consummate visual precision, this story about the conflict between the Enlightenment values and Romantic beliefs leads us to a blackened windmill. In fact, as well as reminding us of *Frankenstein* (1931) it's also a replica of a windmill from a 1937 Disney animation entitled *The Old Mill* (Burton worked for quite a while as an animation artist with Disney. He also has a

"Fairy tales are overwhelming. And in any case there is no safer medium than the cinema." Tim Burton in *steady cam*

1 Echoes of Caspar David Friedrich: gothic romanticism to die for. Johnny Depp in the part of Constable Ichabod Crane.

2 Seductress or witch? Katrina (Christina Ricci) hides a dark secret.

3 It's not just superstition: love too makes you blind.

4 The tools of the Enlightenment are powerless in Sleepy Hollow.

5 Demonic eroticism and deadly passion: stepmother Lady Mary (Miranda Richardson).

6 Fearless and determined, Ichabod gets to the mill.

weakness for the horror films produced by the British Hammer Studios, as well as B movies, which are low-budget features made in the 1950s. These two film traditions combine in the windmill scene and in the carriage chase that follows it. *Sleepy Hollow* has sets rich in detail and looks quite unreal, filmed as it is in dark, blue-tinted images that are a suitably threatening realization of Andrew Kevin Walker's script. Walker previously wrote the script for the sinister thriller *Se7en* (1995), but it is the uncredited influence of Tom Stoppard, screenplay writer of *Brazil* (1985), that gives the film its ironic perspective, adding a strangely humorous tone to what would otherwise be a straightforward tale of terror. Gothic horror and enlightened laughter combine – and the truth lies somewhere in between.

BR

"Burton, who never willingly speaks about his models, for the set and costumes unmistakably took a look at the work of one of America's most unusual painters, Albert Pinkham Ryder (1847–1917), who was known as the 'Painter of Dreams.'" *steady cam*

HAMMER FILM STUDIOS Founded in 1948 by Will Hammer and Sir John Carreras, Hammer Studios was the biggest financial success in the history of British film studios. Their first hits came in 1956 with a series of low-budget horror film productions. Later, they also made costume dramas, science fiction, and psychological thrillers, but the horror genre remained at the center of their output. The films served to make the graphic portrayal of violence acceptable, and, thanks to Technicolor and morally unhampered depictions, breathed new life into classic horror figures like Dracula, Frankenstein, and the Werewolf. Major stars who worked there include Peter Cushing and Christopher Lee, and directors like Joseph Losey also worked for a time at Hammer Studios.

STAR WARS: EPISODE I – THE PHANTOM MENACE

1999 – USA – 133 MIN. – SCIENCE FICTION, ADVENTURE FILM
DIRECTOR GEORGE LUCAS (*1944)
SCREENPLAY GEORGE LUCAS **DIRECTOR OF PHOTOGRAPHY** DAVID TATTERSALL
EDITING BEN BURTT, PAUL MARTIN SMITH **MUSIC** JOHN WILLIAMS
PRODUCTION RICK MCCALLUM for LUCASFILM LTD.
STARRING LIAM NEESON (Qui-Gon Jinn), EWAN MCGREGOR (Obi-Wan Kenobi), NATALIE PORTMAN (Queen Amidala / Padmé Naberrie), JAKE LLOYD (Anakin Skywalker), SAMUEL L. JACKSON (Mace Windu), TERENCE STAMP (Chancellor Finis Valorum), PERNILLA AUGUST (Shmi Skywalker), FRANK OZ (Yoda), IAN MCDIARMID (Senator Palpatine), OLIVER FORD DAVIES (Sio Bibble), AHMED BEST (Jar Jar Binks)

"There's always a bigger fish."

The empire strikes back: for many years now, computers have had dramatic authority and even acted as narrators in movies. The *Star Wars* trilogy changed the design of computer games in the '70s and '80s, and now computers influence contemporary film. Technology freak George Lucas made sure of that by founding his own special effects company. Smash hits at the box office like the *Toy Story* films (1995, 1999, 2010) are impressive examples of the potential that still waits to be released. Lucas himself prophesized in an interview that there would be a boom in monumental films, thanks to the virtually unlimited visual potential of computer technology and its comparatively low-budget costs.

For the time being, however, Lucas himself is concentrating on old stories, and filling in the background to the phenomenally successful *Star Wars* trilogy (1977, 1980, and 1983). *Episode I – The Phantom Menace* predates the adventures of the Skywalkers – Darth Vader and Luke, Obi-Wan Kenobi, the

Jedi knights, the Princess, R2D2, C3PO, and all the popular figures that populate the fairy-tale world. Jedi knight Qui-Gon (Liam Neeson) and his pupil Obi-Wan Kenobi (Ewan McGregor) are fighting against a double-dealing trading empire that has taken over the small planet of Naboo and is trying to get rid of its occupants. Good struggles against evil, and lightsabers battle against droids, fighting robots, and the dark side of the Force, which is plotting to do away with the good Queen Amidala (Natalie Portman). During their crusade, the knights land on the planet Tatooine, where they find little Anakin Skywalker (Jake Lloyd), who is living with his mother in serfdom to a scrap metal merchant called Watto. The boy has extraordinary powers and this is how the story of Anakin Skywalker, later Darth Vader, begins. George Lucas enriches his movie with references to the most famous monumental action films in the history of the cinema, including the *Ben Hur* movies (1907, 1925, and 1959). In the podracing sequences, which won an MTV Movie Award,

1   The powers of darkness are fiendishly good fighters.

2   The monks of the future spread the light by the sword: Ewan McGregor as Obi-Wan Kenobi.

3   Striking similarities: reality and make-believe become indistinguishable thanks to lavish special effects. Natalie Portman as Queen Amidala.

"The flawlessness with which these figures are put next to real actors is supremely impressive, in fact the technical flawlessness is possibly the most impressive

Stars Wars brings together the historical film model and computer-generated pictures of the digital age as the ancient charioteers are transformed into joystick acrobats on two huge turbines. But the technology does have its pitfalls: the excellent cast of the movie demonstrate the downside to computerized realism, and how difficult it is for actors to work in a totally digitalized environment. *Star Wars* is an indication that technological changes will require the same kind of quantum leap for acting as the transition from silent film to the talkies.

Star Wars however is not just a computerized fairy tale for game-addicted console freaks, it's also a nostalgia trip for all those grown up fans of the original trilogy. The result is perfect family cinema with great entertainment value. The sets effortlessly combine the architecture of ancient temples with futuristic touches from *Metropolis*, old-fashioned blend-ins with modern morphing effects and battle scenes in the open field with Asian martial arts sword fighting. In keeping with the rules of the genre good wins at the end in spite of the death of the Jedi Qui-Gon, and the evil trading empire finally bows down to the good queen. The evil that has been sown will not grow until later. Episode II – *Attack of the Clones* (2002) and Episode III – *Revenge of the Sith* (2005) tell the story of how the innocent Anakin Skywalker becomes – or rather is turned into – the evil Darth Vader.   BR

5

"The film is a riot of signs and symbols that you can put together and interpret as you will."

epd Film

4 Holy Family iconography: fatherly Jedi knight Qui-Gon Jinn (Liam Neeson) takes the child with special powers away from his Marian mother.

5 Wisdom is helpless in the face of evil: Samuel L. Jackson as Mace Windu.

6 The computer game is harsh reality here: Anakin Skywalker (Jake Lloyd) on the starting line of the pod race.

GEORGE LUCAS AND INDUSTRIAL LIGHT AND MAGIC Industrial Light and Magic (ILM) was the special effects firm founded by George Lucas in 1975 for his *Star Wars* movie. The aim was to work with young artists to develop revolutionary and innovative methods for the computer simulation of spaceship movement in fight scenes, making them look as realistic as possible. The runaway success of *Star Wars* was the reward for all Lucas's groundbreaking work. ILM went on to become the top company for computer-generated special effects. As well as visual effects, ILM also developed the cinema sound standard THX to bring even greater perfection to the movie-going experience. THX regulates the acoustics according to the conditions in an individual cinema (e.g. size of screen, viewing angle, air-conditioning noise, equipment components). Modern special effects from *Raiders of the Lost Ark* (1981) and *Harry Potter and the Philosopher's Stone* (2001) to *Super 8* (2011) would be unthinkable without Lucas's pioneering work.

7 Stunning animation ensures that the artificial figure of JarJar Binks looks as if he's organic.

8 Computer-generated warrior ballet.

9 This is how rulers of the future look: the corpulent King Jabba.

"Digital realism is an American speciality; they invest huge sums of money in the design of complete film illusions such as *Toy Story 2* or *Star Wars: Episode I.*"

epd Film

CROUCHING TIGER, HIDDEN DRAGON ♟♟♟♟

WO HU ZANG LONG

2000 – CHINA / HONG KONG / TAIWAN / USA – 120 MIN. – MARTIAL ARTS FILM, FANTASY
DIRECTOR ANG LEE (*1954)
SCREENPLAY JAMES SCHAMUS, WANG HUI LING, TSAI KUO JUNG, based on a novel by
WANG DU LU **DIRECTOR OF PHOTOGRAPHY** PETER PAU **EDITING** TIM SQUYRES **MUSIC** DUN TAN
PRODUCTION BILL KONG, HSU LI KONG, ANG LEE for UNITED CHINA VISION, SONY,
COLUMBIA, GOOD MACHINE, EDKO FILMS
STARRING CHOW YUN-FAT (Li Mu Bai), MICHELLE YEOH (Yu Shu Lien), ZHANG ZIYI
(Jiao Long Yu / Jen), CHANG CHEN (Xiao Hu Luo / Lo), LUNG SIHUNG (Sir Te),
CHENG PEI-PEI (Jade Fox), LI FAZENG (Yu), GAO XIAN (Bo), HAI YAN (Madam Yu),
WANG DEMING (Tsai)
ACADEMY AWARDS 2001 OSCARS for BEST FOREIGN LANGUAGE FILM, BEST CINEMATOGRAPHY
(Peter Pau), BEST MUSIC (Tan Dun), BEST ART DIRECTION (Tim Yip)

"Sharpness is a state of mind."

Crouching Tiger, Hidden Dragon is in every sense a fairy tale, while still remaining a classic martial arts film. This is no contradiction, the martial arts film genre is a perfect medium for telling fairy tales and has never been afraid of the extreme exaggeration that is necessary to film the fantastic. In *Crouching Tiger, Hidden Dragon*, the world of the fairy tale is already evoked by the setting: the synthesized studio shots, the fantastic landscapes shot on location in the People's Republic of China, and the original costumes and architecture. The historic reconstruction of an idyllic past goes hand in hand with its stylization. Into this opulent scenario steps Wudang master Li Mu Bai (Chow Yun-Fat). Wudang is a style of swordsmanship that teaches self-negation and internal strength. Sharp wits become the practitioner's greatest weapon. Li Mu Bai wishes to turn his back on his earlier life as a swordsman, in search of greater enlightenment, and therefore entrusts his fabled sword "Green Destiny" to the keeping of the state administrator in Peking. The sword is delivered by his female colleague Yu Shu Lien (Michelle Yeoh), who is bound to him in a sort of Platonic imprisonment through a secret bond of unspoken love. Jen (Zhang Ziyi), the daughter of an aristocratic family, also

lives in the city but is trapped in the gilded cage of her social circumstances. She is being forced into an arranged marriage. Jen has a servant and companion who is interested in far more than her socially appropriate upbringing. She is in fact the witch Jade Fox, wanted by the police for the murder of Li Mu Bai's teacher. Not only does she assist the beautiful Jen in maintaining her flawless looks and behavior, she also secretly trains her in various martial arts. Jen much prefers adventure to the dreariness of her sheltered life in the city. A lengthy flashback relates how she fell in love with the desert bandit Lo following his assault on her caravan. In spite of his wild appearance, Lo is a warm-hearted person. As a pair, they counterbalance Li Mu Bai and Yu Shu Lien. Although their youth makes it easier for them to ignore social constraints, their love is also destined for an unhappy end.

But before the film leads us into this web of relationships, a crime occurs: the priceless sword is stolen. A furious chase ensues, but the masked thief just manages to escape. The film's repeated chase scenes, where the participants follow each other over rooftops, through alleyways, and even over treetops may at first appear absurd, but are in fact an integral part of

Chinese folk mythology. By collaborating with the same team that choreographed the fight scenes in *The Matrix* (1999), Ang Lee reaches new heights of intercultural film style in *Crouching Tiger, Hidden Dragon*. The stolen sword acts as a kind of MacGuffin, carrying the story forward without playing an important role in its outcome. Even before all the relationships in the film are clearly established, transformations begin. During the chase and fight scenes they are literally set in motion. At times, the camera work reduces the action into dancing graphic patterns. Where the human eye can only discern lines of motion – in the rapid oscillation between long and short-range shots – the fight scenes nonetheless remain carefully controlled. They are a reflection of the same ethic of discipline and self-control that governs social behavior in the film. The art of fighting is also a social art.

"A faithful heart makes wishes come true."

Ang Lee's *Crouching Tiger, Hidden Dragon* is a remarkable martial arts film. While respecting the conventions of the genre, it is also a fascinating vehicle for the portrayal of tragic-romantic love stories in a poetic setting. The movie owes its persuasiveness to the manner in which Ang Lee extends the boundaries of the genre without betraying its innate virtues. As in his other films – especially *Eat Drink Man Woman* (1994), *The Wedding Banquet* (1993), *Sense and Sensibility* (1995), *The Ice Storm* (1997), and *Ride with the Devil*

1 Fairylike grace and unbridled energy are not mutually exclusive: beautiful and willful Jen (Zhang Ziyi) casts her spell over the film.

2 The sword of power is reason, and nobody knows this better than the monk Li Mu Bai (Chow Yun-Fat).

3 Love beyond death: earthly barriers are no obstacle. Michelle Yeoh in the role of Hu Shu Lien.

"Sword and saber shiver and redound like lovers in this portrait of contrasted temperaments locked in battle. This is a whirligig of literal revenges, slings and arrows ... Ang Lee enters the ranks of his past masters." *Libération*

(1999), the film whose production practically coincided with *Crouching Tiger, Hidden Dragon*, Lee's strength lies in the careful balance between the powerful visual images and the mastery of epic storytelling. This reflects Lee's equal experience of western and eastern culture. *Crouching Tiger, Hidden Dragon* has reflective moments where it devotes itself to its protagonists' personal concerns, but then it erupts into phases of extreme action, before settling effortlessly back into contemplative situations. The film never loses its rhythm, and great attention is paid to every detail.

Crouching Tiger, Hidden Dragon combines images of the director's youth in Taiwan with a story from the fourth book of a pentology by Du Lu Wang. The novel is a product of East Asian popular literature comparable with the penny romance, featuring stereotyped heroes and predictable love stories. Ang Lee adapts this cultural tradition with great skill. In his version, virtues like bravery, friendship, and honor turn out to be impossible ideals. He does not reject them, but takes leave of them with melancholy regret and not before he has pointed a way out of the resulting emptiness.

In contrast to the value system of a male-dominated society, the film emphasizes womanly virtues. In an irony typical of Ang Lee's films, the fate of the male protagonist lies in the hands of three women who are all struggling for independence from the patriarchal norm. Finally, *Crouching Tiger, Hidden Dragon* is an ideal film realization of the principle of Yin and Yang: contemplative stillness and furious action, peaceful dialogue and sword battles, the cramped city and the wide-open Chinese landscapes. The balanced harmony of its composition makes *Crouching Tiger, Hidden Dragon* a fairy tale constructed on an epic scale.

BR

"The choreography was new to me. It had its roots in the Peking Opera, and they are completely different from the Western method of producing action scenes."

Ang Lee in *epd Film*

4   At the moment of maximum concentration, body and soul fuse together.

5   Jen's desire for a life full of adventure and love is being fulfilled, but not quite as she imagines.

6 In the fantasy world of *Crouching Tiger, Hidden Dragon* the normal laws of physics don't apply.

7 During the fight, the rival women's bodies hover and fly through space with no apparent effort.

8 Brigand Lo (Chang Chen) makes a good haul.

MARTIAL ARTS FILMS Generally, martial arts films feature oriental combat sports and their accompanying philosophical traditions. The plots normally revolve around a hero figure whose sense of loyalty and justice free him from moral scruples in meting out vengeance to evildoers. In the martial arts film, which developed into a mass product in Hong Kong cinema, psychological complexity and development are less important than artistically translating spiritual states into choreographed body moves, bringing a subtle metaphorical dimension to the movement's dynamics. In the early '70s, the martial arts film found its way into the American action movie by way of Hong Kong cinema. Since then, martial arts movies have also influenced films like *The Matrix* (1999) and *Kill Bill* (2003, 2004). Along with global star Bruce Lee in the '70s and Jackie Chan and Jet Li, directors like John Woo and Tsui Hark have made martial arts acceptable within the action movie genre, giving it a whole new dimension.

BEFORE NIGHT FALLS

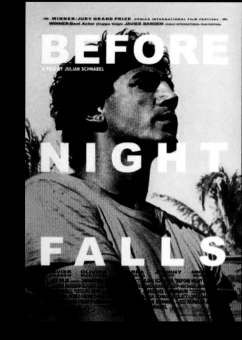

2000 – USA – 133 MIN. DRAMA, BIOPIC
DIRECTOR JULIAN SCHNABEL (*1951)
SCREENPLAY CUNNINGHAM O'KEEFE, LÁZARO GÓMEZ CARRILES, JULIAN SCHNABEL based on the autobiography by REINALDO ARENAS **DIRECTOR OF PHOTOGRAPHY** XAVIER PÉREZ GROBET
EDITING MICHAEL BERENBAUM **MUSIC** CARTER BURWELL, LAURIE ANDERSON, LOU REED
PRODUCTION JON KILIK for EL MAR PICTURES / GRANDVIEW PICTURES
STARRING JAVIER BARDEM (Reinaldo Arenas), OLIVIER MARTINEZ (Lázaro Gómez Carriles), ANDREA DI STEFANO (Pepe Malas), JOHNNY DEPP (Bon Bon / Lieutenant Victor), MICHAEL WINCOTT (Herberto Zorilla Ochoa), OLATZ LOPEZ GARMENDIA (Reinaldo's mother), SEBASTIAN SILVA (Reinaldo's father), GIOVANNI FLORIDO (young Reinaldo), PEDRO ARMENDÁRIZ JR. (Reinaldo's grandfather), LOLÓ NAVARRO (Reinaldo's grandmother)
IFF VENICE 2000 SPECIAL GRAND JURY PRIZE (JULIAN SCHNABEL), BEST ACTOR (JAVIER BARDEM)

"Beauty is the enemy. Artists are escapists, artists are counterrevolutionary."

Cuba, before the Revolution, somewhere in the countryside. Reinaldo, a boy without a father, grows up in poverty. At an early age, he carves poems into the bark of trees. When his poetic talent comes to the attention of a schoolteacher, his reward is a slap on the head from his grandfather. When the Revolution breaks out, Reinaldo, now a teenager, joins the rebel forces. He marches victoriously into Havana alongside Fidel Castro and Che Guevara. The years that follow are full of new liberties. As an adult, Reinaldo (Javier Bardem) discovers his homosexuality and lives it openly with his friends and lovers. He also makes a literary breakthrough and has his first book published. Before long however times change, and Castro's regime becomes increasingly mistrustful of independent artists and gays. Persecution begins and show trials are held. Reinaldo's years of suffering begin when he is arrested and imprisoned on flimsy evidence.

Before Night Falls is New York painter Julian Schnabel's second film, and like his debut film Basquiat (1996), this too, is a portrait of an artist. And in both cases the movies tell the deeply tragic life story of an outsider. Schnabel unrolls the pattern of an artist's life for whom truth, art, and beauty are inseparably linked and for whom failure is almost inevitable, given his unwillingness to compromise. The film is based on the autobiography of Cuban writer Reinaldo Arenas, which he wrote in exile in New York before committing suicide in 1990 while suffering from AIDS. Schnabel keeps the subjective perspective of the literary model without allowing the spoken word to intrude into the foreground of the movie. Even when Javier Bardem declaims some of Arenas's texts off camera, the real emphasis of the film remains on the images. Schnabel uses them to follow the emotions and imaginative leaps of the writer.

2

"This is a film which makes you want to know everything about its subject, to hear his voice again from a printed page. Extraordinary." *The Observer*

1 The sadistic prison governor: Johnny Depp proves twice over his preference for unusual roles in Julian Schnabel's movie.

2 Javier Bardem (right), who usually takes macho roles, shows his feminine side as Reinaldo Arenas.

3 Reinaldo (Javier Bardem, front left) enjoys unheard-of liberties in the immediate aftermath of the Revolution.

4 A blond angel: Johnny Depp (right) in his second brief part as Bon Bon, the beautiful transvestite.

5 Barely recognizable: an offbeat cameo appearance by Sean Penn (left) as a Cuban farmer.

3

4

5

The virtuoso camera movements and the slow rhythm of the images, perfectly harmonized with Carter Burwell's music, make *Before Night Falls* a poetic masterpiece in which Arenas's life and work seem to flow into each other. Although depicted with a certain reserve, Arenas's homosexuality is all-pervasive in Schnabel's extremely sensual movie.

But above all, *Before Night Falls* is Javier Bardem's film. He won the Best Actor award at the Venice Film Festival for his brilliant achievement and was nominated for both an Oscar and a Golden Globe. Bardem had long been a star in his native Spain and became known internationally for his part in Pedro Almodóvar's *Live Flesh* (*Carne trémula*, 1997). His previous roles had all been emphatically masculine, but in *Before Night Falls* he gives a finely nuanced performance of the homosexual writer, which is far removed from any of the usual gay clichés. He shows all the facets of Reinaldo's character, his initial timidity, his curiosity and joie de vivre, but also his toughness and his suffering. Johnny Depp's short but spectacular double appearance seems like an incarnation of the homosexual writer's feverish imagination: as the beautiful transvestite Bon Bon and the sadistic prison guard he plays two extremes of gay fantasy.

Schnabel's movie is also a statement about the widespread Cuba euphoria of today. Although it is in no way to be understood as a political pamphlet against the socialist state, *Before Night Falls* clearly shows the shadowy sides of Castro's regime, which some fail to see behind the whirl of music and folklore. The movie also reveals that it was equally impossible for Arenas to find a home in the USA of the '80s.

The movie's colors are never so stunning as in the sequences which show the writer's childhood, and never so gray and bleak as in the pictures of New York where Arenas, without health insurance and suffering from AIDS, puts a bitter end to his life with the help of sleeping tablets and a plastic bag printed with the words: "I love NY."

JH

OFF CAMERA "Off camera" is the area outside the picture that the audience is aware of but remains hidden to their view. Through noises or movements out of the picture or into the picture or through the gestures of the actors, off camera can play an important part in the action of a movie. For example, the dangers lurking for the hero off camera in thrillers are a simple, effective, and frequently used way of creating tension.

ERIN BROCKOVICH 🏆

2000 – USA – 131 MIN. – DRAMA
DIRECTOR STEVEN SODERBERGH (*1963)
SCREENPLAY SUSANNAH GRANT **DIRECTOR OF PHOTOGRAPHY** EDWARD LACHMAN **EDITING** ANNE V. COATES
MUSIC THOMAS NEWMAN **PRODUCTION** DANNY DEVITO, MICHAEL SHAMBERG, STACEY SHER,
GAIL LYON for JERSEY FILMS, COLUMBIA PICTURES, UNIVERSAL PICTURES
STARRING JULIA ROBERTS (Erin Brockovich), ALBERT FINNEY (Ed Masry), AARON ECKHART
(George), MARG HELGENBERGER (Donna Jensen), CHERRY JONES (Pamela Duncan),
DAWN DIDAWICK (Rosalind), DAVID BRISBIN (Dr. Jaffe), VALENTE RODRIGUEZ (Donald),
CONCHATA FERRELL (Brenda), ERIN BROCKOVICH-ELLIS (Waitress)
ACADEMY AWARDS 2001 OSCAR for BEST ACTRESS (Julia Roberts)

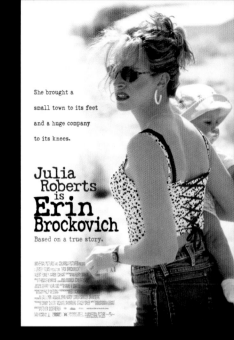

"For the first time in my life, I got people respecting me ..."

A failed job interview, a car accident, an orthopedic cushion round the pretty neck, high heels and short skirts, broke, unemployed, and a single mother – Erin Brockovich (Julia Roberts) is a modern woman alright.

Steven Soderbergh's movie tells a real-life incident from the life of lawyer's assistant Erin Brockovich. He comes to the point swiftly and directly. No false sentiment, no glamorous superwoman, but an emancipated, self-confident and attractive woman who understands how to assert herself – not with her elbows, rather with her powers of persuasion and by having the better argument. This is how she gets her job at the firm of defense lawyer Ed Masry (Albert Finney), who wasn't able to get her the compensation she desperately needed following her car accident. The overwhelmed lawyer can't resist and employs Erin on the spot out of sympathy, admiration, and a vestige of social conscience.

More or less by chance Erin ends up working on the Jensens' case, representing a family who have received an offer from a company that own a nearby factory and want to buy up their house and land. There seems to be an ulterior motive however, for the Jensens are seriously ill. What makes Erin suspicious is that for years the doctor who treats the Jensens has been in the pay of Pacific Gas & Electric, the company who also want to buy their house. During her research she finds documents from the local waterworks which record a high concentration of deadly poisonous hexavalent chromium that has never been officially monitored. She stumbles on an environmental scandal of enormous proportions. More and more people who live or lived near the factory and have become ill start to get in touch with her. A factory employee finally admits that the poisonous substance contaminates the water due to slipshod factory standards. A magistrate rules that the plaintiffs are right to

sue the company and a first partial success is scored. However, Erin's own family suffer because of her commitment to helping other people. George (Aaron Eckhart), the biker from next door, who under his macho exterior and initial difficulties turns out to be a highly sensitive replacement father for Erin's kids, eventually gives up and leaves the family.

But Erin is not to be stopped. When the case becomes too big and risky for the little lawyer's office, Ed Masry turns to a bigger legal firm. Erin feels she has been passed over, and things become critical. She knows and sympathizes with the affected families and their problems and this clashes with the new partner's cool, academic approach. However, only after Erin manages to get incriminating material from an informer is there a swift and financially lucrative compromise in favor of the injured parties.

"… please, don't ask me to give it up."

A plot summary alone cannot convey how unconventional Soderbergh's use of the real-life material is in comparison with other recent disclosure movies. *Erin Brockovich* contains echoes of Soderbergh's highly successful debut movie, *Sex, Lies, and Videotape* (1989), without losing the benefits of later film experiments like *Out of Sight* (1998). Light handheld camera sequences show how Erin's world falls apart and lend emotional depth to the pictures.

Some of them have an improvised feel that reminds us of French cinema. Picture montages that work like jump cuts and the light narrative touch are inevitable reminders of Godard's Nouvelle Vague classic *Breathless* (*À bout de souffle*, 1959). These moments alternate with more conventional, straight shots in which the movie takes time for the characters and their relationships to develop. The unobtrusive yet dramatic use of colors plays an important role. The camera accompanies the characters and empathizes with them, and the result is a movie that reveals small-scale, hidden human dramas and tragedies. Sensationalism never gets the upper hand over the precise observation of human life endangered by big industry and corporate law. If there is such a thing as a humanistic narrative style, then Soderbergh is one of its masters and *Erin Brockovich* is a prototype.

The movie owes much to Julia Roberts's acting. Although she is cast against her usual image, she performs magnificently. Seldom in contemporary cinema has an actress embodied emancipation so simply and yet so convincingly. In full knowledge of her social position, Erin always tries to get the best for her family in every situation. There is an almost comic side to her attempts to make society do what she wants rather than vice versa. In spite of what she knows of her own value on the merciless American job market, Erin winds up neither victim nor heroine, which makes her all the more sympathetic. Her separation from George is presented unpretentiously and realistically, and is one of the things which makes the movie so believable. There is no sentimental tragedy; Erin and George realize that their ways of life are too different when Erin begins to prioritize her job, and their separation is a

***Erin Brockovich* is the first of Soderbergh's films to draw its being from the rousing description of a person rather than from the buildup of a conflict."** *epd Film*

1   We love her like this: Julia Roberts in the role of the punchy Erin Brockovich.

2   Erin's main concern is for her children.

3   Happy family beyond any clichés.

4   Erin becomes right-hand man to lawyer Ed Masry (Albert Finney).

5   An unusual role for Harley-Davidson afficionado George (Aaron Eckhart).

6 The difficulties of her objective force Erin to adopt extreme measures.

7 George rises to the task of being a substitute father with style.

8 Committed information-seeker and family woman: Erin makes it her job to ensure a better future for small defenseless citizens.

"Erin may be a hero, but she's definitely no angel." *Sight and Sound*

JULIA ROBERTS Julia Roberts (*1967) became world famous overnight in 1990 with *Pretty Woman*, which brought her an Oscar nomination. The downside of this great success, however, was that she became typecast as the all-American beauty in romantic comedies. She managed to transform her image with her Oscar-winning role in *Erin Brockovich* (2000). She has since starred in increasingly challenging roles, as well as light entertainment movies such as the spy spoof *Confessions of a Dangerous Mind* (2002), relationship drama *Closer* (2004), and political satire *Charlie Wilson's War* (2007).

rational solution to the crisis. This realistic, honest, calm presentation isn't scandalous, but it is sensational; it causes the deep grief that inspires Erin to carry on. Instead of being followed by rage and aggression, as in mainstream cinema, in Soderbergh's film grief is followed by optimism in a synergetic process. Humor, which forms a link between the two, makes Erin and her boss an extraordinarily successful team. Cheekiness and wit are the best weapons against the adversities of everyday life. Erin's recipe for success is to show her teeth, smiling and undaunted. That gives us hope, and gives hope to the families that she is trying to help. In the end, truth lies in compromise, not in a drastic head-to-head. Simplicity instead of exaggeration, and a sense of proportion rather than heroism. This is the difference between *Erin Brockovich* and other films with similar themes like *Silkwood* (1983) with Meryl Streep in the leading female role. *The Insider* (1999), made shortly before *Erin Brockovich*, is a hint that a new trend in disclosure dramas is developing – although *The Insider* depends more on highly developed aesthetics than on sensitive understatement.

BR

WHAT LIES BENEATH

2000 – USA –129 MIN. – THRILLER
DIRECTOR ROBERT ZEMECKIS (*1952)
SCREENPLAY CLARK GREGG, based on a story by CLARK GREGG, SARAH KERNOCHAN
DIRECTOR OF PHOTOGRAPHY DON BURGESS **EDITING** ARTHUR SCHMIDT **MUSIC** ALAN SILVESTRI
PRODUCTION JOAN BRADSHAW, MARK JOHNSON, CHERYLANNE MARTIN for 20TH CENTURY
FOX, DREAMWORKS SKG, IMAGE MOVERS
STARRING HARRISON FORD (Norman Spencer), MICHELLE PFEIFFER (Claire Spencer),
DIANA SCARWID (Jody), MIRANDA OTTO (Mary Feur), JAMES REMAR (Warren Feur),
JOE MORTON (Dr. Drayton), AMBER VALLETTA (Madison Elizabeth Frank), VICTORIA
BIDEWELL (Beatrice), KATHARINE TOWNE (Caitlin Spencer), ELLIOTT GORETSKY (Teddy)

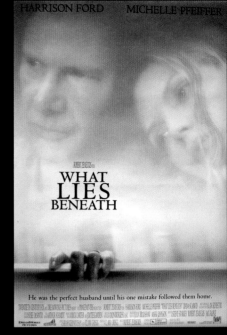

"Well, I'm seeing ghosts in the bathtub, aren't I?"

Claire and Norman Spencer (Michelle Pfeiffer, Harrison Ford) have a happy marriage. Actually it's a bit too happy for a couple "in the prime of life." It's only when daughter Caitlin (Katharine Towne) moves out to go to college that the situation changes. Like a good mother Claire misses her daughter and cries over the family photo album. Strange things start to happen in the neighborhood. Like L. B. Jeffries in Hitchcock's *Rear Window* (1954), Claire begins to suspect that the neighbor has murdered his wife – until suddenly the woman unexpectedly reappears. This part of the film seems to be a red herring, but in fact it's a hint at what is to come.

Robert Zemeckis's film not only borrows from Hitchcock, but also from horror classics like Roman Polanski's *Rosemary's Baby* (1968) and Stanley Kubrick's *The Shining* (1980). It gives us other clues apart from this first plot strand: doors open by themselves, a computer is switched on by a ghostly hand, and mysterious messages appear on the monitor, the bathtub con-

stantly fills with water, a picture showing Claire together with her husband falls off the wall again and again, and a mysterious key is found in a hole in the ground. The movements of these inanimate objects turn *What Lies Beneath* from family romance to melodrama, with aspects of the thriller and the ghost film thrown in for good measure. Clearly, a sinister secret is waiting to be discovered. Claire seems to lose her powers of perception and logic and begins to see paranoid hallucinations.

What she sees may or may not be real: the movie leaves that open. A short report on the back of the picture which falls down so many times tells of the disappearance of a young student. The ghost continues its determined efforts along conventional lines that still however have the power to shock. Claire sees a face in the reflective surface of the lake in front of the house, in the water in the bathtub, or in the bathroom mirror. The face gets clearer every time. Finally Claire is sure that it is Madison Elizabeth Frank, a student

"This film is like a belated gift in honor of Alfred Hitchcock's 100th birthday, giving the viewer a constant impression of déjà-vu."

epd Film

from the newspaper article who disappeared without a trace. The ghost is real and calling on a psychiatrist won't solve the problem. Things really get going after a spiritualist meeting, and Claire discovers the truth about her own past. A year previously she lost her memory in a car accident, and in a souvenir shop called "The Sleeping Dog" she discovers the key to the student's fate which is closely connected to her own.

Suddenly we realize that under the surface of the Spencers' wholesome world there is a hidden abyss very much in the Hitchcock tradition. Claire is not the caring, attractive mother she seems, nor is Norman Spencer merely a charming and successful scientist. In fact their marriage is on the rocks, Claire is a selfish monster and Norman is the cynical killer of the vanished student whose ghost is now seeking revenge. Moreover,

1   Claire (Michelle Pfeiffer) shortly before the bleakest moments in her marriage …

2   … to shady scientist Norman Spencer (Harrison Ford).

3   The view from the window onto the yard turns the neighbor into a monster.

4   Insight is a weak and treacherous light.

5   Risen from the watery grave of her own amnesia.

RED HERRING   A red herring is a distraction or deviation built into a story line to lead the main figure and the audience to particular conclusions that then turn out to be completely irrelevant to the rest of the plot. A red herring is a way of creating tension by giving the audience the chance to form false hypotheses and therefore a false sense of security. According to how much attention the movie gives the red herring motif, the audience are surprised, shaken, and annoyed by the early resolution and unexpected development. At the same time this shock or thrill intensifies the audience's emotional involvement. The art of playing with audience expectations was developed to perfection by Alfred Hitchcock, particularly in *Psycho* (1960).

---

the final shot of the seemingly never-ending showdown shows that Claire and Madison Elizabeth Frank are sisters "in spirit" in their relationship with Norman.

As well as the virtuoso music and film quotations (from the bathtub scene in *Fatal Attraction* [1987] and from Henri-Georges Clouzot's classic *Les Diaboliques* [*Diabolique*, 1955]), the film's central motif is the idea of the surface, under which nothing is quite as it seems. From the very beginning we can't quite trust our eyes, as the whole situation seems too perfect. Reflective surfaces then bring the truth to light.

Robert Zemeckis set out to make a perfect Hitchcock thriller, and he brought it off with incredible precision. But the movie does far more than rely on Hitch. Claire's paranoia reminds us of Rosemary Woodhouse in *Rosemary's*

Baby, and the transformation of Claire's face in the bath water is a quotation from the bathroom sequence with the young/old woman in *The Shining*. Claire's desperate escape from her bloodthirsty husband Norman at the end of the movie is also a quotation from that same film. Last, but not least, the underwater scenes remind us of Charles Laughton's *The Night of the Hunter* (1955). *What Lies Beneath* unmasks people as completely voyeuristic creatures in a Hitchcockian manner and is also a brilliant social satire as well as a thriller. Like his great role model, Zemeckis lays great emphasis on elegant visuals. In the course of the film the pictures become darker and darker and the camera follows the development of the story. To show "what lies beneath," it starts at eye level and moves gradually downwards.

GLADIATOR 𝍖𝍖𝍖𝍖𝍖

2000 – USA – 155 MIN. – MONUMENTAL FILM, HISTORICAL FILM, ACTION FILM
DIRECTOR RIDLEY SCOTT (*1937)
SCREENPLAY DAVID FRANZONI, JOHN LOGAN, WILLIAM NICHOLSON
DIRECTOR OF PHOTOGRAPHY JOHN MATHIESON EDITING PIETRO SCALIA MUSIC HANS ZIMMER,
LISA GERRARD, KLAUS BADELT PRODUCTION DOUGLAS WICK, DAVID FRANZONI,
BRANKO LUSTIG, STEVEN SPIELBERG for UNIVERSAL, DREAMWORKS SKG
STARRING RUSSELL CROWE (Maximus), JOAQUIN PHOENIX (Commodus), CONNIE NIELSEN
(Lucilla), RICHARD HARRIS (Marcus Aurelius), OLIVER REED (Proximo), DEREK JACOBI
(Gracchus), RALF MOELLER (Hagen), SPENCER TREAT CLARK (Lucius Verus),
DAVID HEMMINGS (Cassius), TOMMY FLANAGAN (Cicero)
ACADEMY AWARDS 2001 OSCARS for BEST FILM, BEST ACTOR (Russell Crowe),
BEST VISUAL EFFECTS (John Nelson, Neil Corbould, Tim Burke, Rob Harvey),
BEST SOUND (Ken Weston, Scott Millan, Bob Beemer), BEST COSTUMES (Janty Yates)

"In the end, we're all dead men."

Germania, Anno Domini 180. A hand sweeps through a golden yellow corn-field and gently touches the waving ears of corn – a dream-like image, a pre-monition of death. The dreamer is a general: Maximus (Russell Crowe), the greatest, undefeated in battle, beloved of the Roman people and by his mentor Marcus Aurelius (Richard Harris), Caesar of the Roman Empire. The movie contrasts this peaceful mental image with the bloody reality of battle that the warrior Maximus conducts with cold precision. The portrayal of battle at the beginning of the movie reminds us of the fighting scenes in John Boorman's *Excalibur* (1981).

Maximus's strategic intelligence, modesty, and unconditional loyalty make him Marcus Aurelius's favorite candidate to be his successor. With Maximus's help, he wants to purify the political center of his global empire of corruption, return to the virtues of old and give the senate in Rome more dem-ocratic powers. However, his jealous and power-hungry son Commodus (Joaquin Phoenix) is standing in his way. He realizes what his father is plan-

ning to do, so he murders him and becomes heir to the throne, and has Maximus thrown out of the army. To eliminate the popular hero for once and for all, Commodus orders that he be executed. However, Maximus manages to escape and he returns to the Roman province of Spain that is his native land, where he finds his family dead, murdered on Commodus's orders. His will to live sapped, Maximus is captured by a slave trader and sold to a glad-iator school.

His strategic intelligence and his experience of fighting mean that he soon becomes a successful gladiator. His new profession eventually takes him back to Rome, where he quickly becomes popular for his spectacular fighting, and eventually he attracts the attention of Commodus himself. In the meantime, Commodus's sister Lucilla (Connie Nielsen) and the democratically minded Senator Gracchus (Derek Jacobi) plan an intrigue against the emperor in which Maximus also becomes involved. Maximus's popularity forces Commodus to descend into the public arena to fight him in single combat

1

2

To be sure he will win, Commodus inflicts a serious wound on his opponent Maximus before the fight in the corridors of the Colosseum. In the final single combat both are killed and Commodus's sister Lucilla charges Gracchus with the running of the empire. The film moves into almost monochrome, bluish dream pictures that take up the motifs of the opening sequence and provide a frame. They tell of the end of Maximus's dream, the fulfillment of his longing for peaceful family life. A hand reaches for a gate, strokes through the ears of a cornfield, and wife and son welcome the warrior home.

Gladiator is a typical example of Ridley Scott's preference for imperfect heroes and huge extravagant sets, as in *Blade Runner* (1982) and *Alien* (1979). *Gladiator* marks the arrival of the computer-generated image in Scott's films. His approach to the venerable genre of the historical epic is surprisingly varied: he uses genre patterns from the Western for the revenge motif and from martial arts films for the gladiators' fights. He also uses dramatic methods from the action movie, and finally gives us a melodramatic ending that adds variety adds to the entertainment. Although many of the movie's conflicts are not actually resolved, *Gladiator* is visually overwhelming. Scott isn't always too particular with historical truth, but his dizzyingly sensual compositions, the fantastic editing, the excellent music of Hollywood's star composer Hans Zimmer, and the brilliant acting – particularly from Joaquin Phoenix as the incestuous, evil Commodus – make *Gladiator* an exciting and impressive historical movie.

BR

1 Nothing is impossible in Ancient Rome: virtuous tribune Maximus (Russell Crowe) is forced to become a gladiator…

2 … if the capricious Emperor Commodus (Joaquin Phoenix) so dictates.

3 Life and death decisions are made without reflection in the Emperor's box.

4 Losers become heroes in the magnificent battle scenes in the Colosseum.

5 Folk hero Maximus shortly before the fatal climax to his gladiatorial career.

RUSSELL CROWE Russell Crowe was born in New Zealand in 1964. His role as the violent, gruff policeman Bud White in Curtis Hanson's *L.A. Confidential* (1997) introduced him to a wider audience in America and beyond. A one-time child star in TV productions, he had stopped acting for a long time, but returned to the scene with great success in 1992 with a role in the Australian skinhead drama *Romper Stomper*. Having proved that he could also handle character roles convincingly in Michael Mann's whistleblower drama *The Insider* (1999), where he played a tobacco industry maverick, his performance as Maximus in *Gladiator* (2000) earned him an Oscar. Since then he seems to be working his way through every movie genre, always in thrilling roles: adventure (*Master and Commander*, 2003), comedy (*A Good Year*, 2006), gangster movie (*American Gangster*, 2007), Western (*3:10 To Yuma*, 2007), and investigative journalism (*State of Play*, 2009).

O BROTHER, WHERE ART THOU?

2000 – GREAT BRITAIN / USA / FRANCE – 106 MIN. – COMEDY
DIRECTOR JOEL COEN (*1954)
SCREENPLAY ETHAN COEN, JOEL COEN **DIRECTOR OF PHOTOGRAPHY** ROGER DEAKINS **EDITING** TRICIA COOKE,
ETHAN COEN, JOEL COEN (as RODERICK JAYNES) **MUSIC** T-BONE BURNETT
PRODUCTION ETHAN COEN for BUENA VISTA PICTURES, STUDIO CANAL,
TOUCHSTONE PICTURES, UNIVERSAL, WORKING TITLE FILMS
STARRING GEORGE CLOONEY (Ulysses Everett McGill), JOHN TURTURRO (Pete), TIM BLAKE
NELSON (Delmar), JOHN GOODMAN (Big Dan Teague), HOLLY HUNTER (Penny Wharvey),
CHRIS THOMAS KING (Tommy Johnson), MICHAEL BADALUCCO (George "Babyface"
Nelson), WAYNE DUVALL (Homer Stokes), RAY MCKINNON (Vernon T. Waldrip),
DANIEL VON BARGEN (Sheriff Cooley)

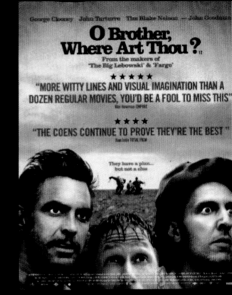

"We're in a tight spot!"

Joel and Ethan Coen have perfected the art of lovingly disemboweling well-known stories and stereotypes of cinema history. From the cinema in their heads they make wonderful movies about the things that they love, like the cinema itself and the stories to which it owes its existence. It was therefore only to be expected that sooner or later they would use the one story that is considered to be the root of all others – Homer's *Odyssey*. It is equally unsurprising that their adaptation is not a film of the epic but their own unique translation of the tale into cinematic pop culture. That said, it's still a remarkable achievement in the way it blends the ancient material with film myths of the '30s and contemporary country and pop music to form a densely textured fabric of quotation and allusion.

The story is a variation on its classical model. The vain and arrogant Ulysses (George Clooney) is stuck in prison, and he hints at a hidden sum of 1.2 million dollars to persuade his fellow prisoners Pete (John Turturro) and Delmar (Tim Blake Nelson) to escape with him. They're in a bit of a hurry as within three days the loot from a bank raid has to be dug up before the area where it is hidden is flooded. However, the real truth of the matter is that Ulysses wants to hit the road home as quickly as possible for the simple reason that his wife (Holly Hunter) is threatening to marry another man. A wonderfully funny odyssey through the south of the US ensues, along the banks of the Mississippi.

The three convicts are chained to each other and, as in the individual episodes of Homer's epic, they meet a hybrid figure from Greek mythology at every station of their escape or characters from the early era of the talkies. The borders between the two become blurred: first they meet a venerable soothsayer by the name of Homer who predicts that they will find treasure, then the one-eyed Cyclops figure Big Dan Teague who sells Bibles but turns out to be a no-good Ku Klux Klan member, then three seductive and cunning sirens washing their laundry who whisk Pete back into prison, and finally Ulysses's unfaithful wife, who even has the same name as the wife in Homer's epic, Penelope (alias Penny). During their escape they also make the acquaintance of a blues guitar player who has sold his soul to the devil, record a country song at a radio station with a blind manager under the band name The Soggy Bottom Boys (which then becomes a smash hit), and involuntarily become accomplices of the gangster George "Babyface" Nelson who gives them the loot from his bank raid. They have serious problems with slimy provincial politicians and a series of other bizarre companions.

As well as the typically caricatured and exaggerated characters, *O Brother, Where Art Thou?* includes the Coen brothers' characteristic stylized postcard pictures of idyllic, almost kitsch landscapes. The backdrop of the southern states is made up of an abundance of clichéd motifs such as enormous cornfields, never-ending railroads, boggy swamps, and antique

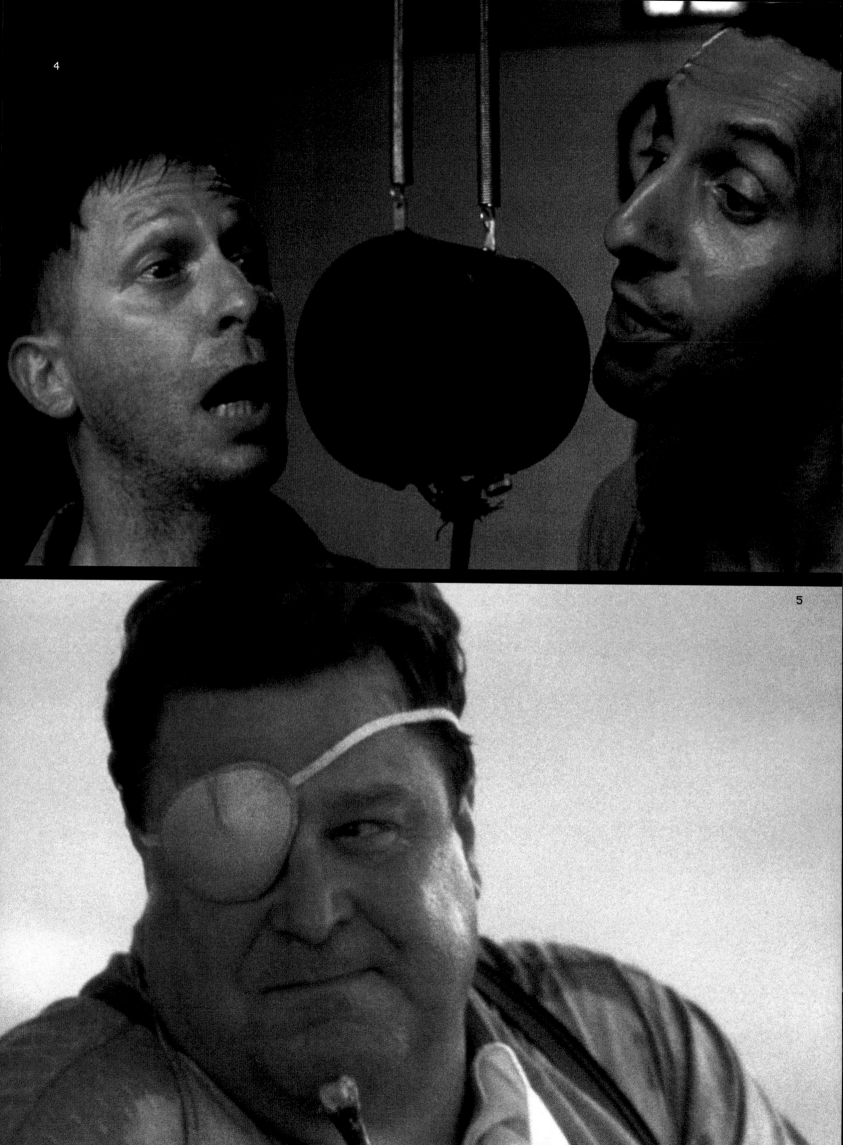

1 Ulysses, Pete, and Delmar: George Clooney, John Turturro, and Tim Blake Nelson (right to left) provide impressive evidence of their comic talent in *O Brother, Where Art Thou?*

2 In classic Laurel and Hardy style the three jailbirds are overpowered by a child.

3 Just like a sentimental painting: the exaggerated pose of a saved man.

4 Popular melodies by mistake: while on the run they produce songs that go straight to people's hearts.

5 The one-eyed Bible-seller reveals himself to be an unholy patron: John Goodman as Big Dan Teague.

6 Taking a roundabout route to their goal: the three jailbirds are linked by more than just their treasure hunt.

"The Coen brothers seem to have understood. In their films they help stupidity to improve its reputation. In *O Brother, Where Art Thou?* for example, there is nothing at all between the ears of the three jail-breakers Ulysses, Pete and Delmar. And it is only because they never stop to think that they survived their long voyage across the Mississippi." *Süddeutsche Zeitung*

cars. The synthetic atmosphere comes from the computer process used to digitally adapt the colors of the movie. Its soundtrack was completed before the film itself and is an irresistible compendium of American folk music. Inspired by Blues, Gospel, and Country, the movie is also part of a musical tradition where the music is ever-present. There are references and allusions aplenty. In *Miller's Crossing* (1990), *Barton Fink* (1991), *The Hudsucker Proxy* (1994), and all their other productions, the Coen brothers have always found inspiration inside the tradition of the movies. *O Brother, Where Art Thou?* is a homage to the director Preston Sturges, from whose comedy *Sullivan's Travels* (1941) it takes its curious title. Tired of the monotony of

shallow entertainment movies, the director John L. Sullivan sets out in Sturges's film to let society's underdogs, those at whom the popular movies are aimed, have their say. The title of the movie he plans to make is *O Brother, Where Art Thou?*

Because of the Coen brothers' love of parody there is always the danger that they might pull away the ground from under their own feet at some point, and there's a hint of the self-portrait about the ending, when the three convicts are about to be hanged and their absurd journey seems to have come to a close. But a flood wave saves them from that gruesome fate, and we are rewarded with a happy ending after all. BR

7   She has no sympathy for the way her husband's life is going: Ulysses's wife Penny (Holly Hunter) is already looking elsewhere.

8   The song of the sirens: undreamed-of prospects open up in the middle of the forest.

9   Ulysses the vain: George Clooney uses a hairnet and pomade for his role.

"The Coens love to butter up the screen with beautiful images, but when they have to they use dynamite." *Frankfurter Allgemeine Zeitung*

GEORGE CLOONEY From heartthrob Dr. Ross in the successful television hospital series *ER* to respected film actor, producer, and director: George Clooney (*1961) has had a pretty unique career. After his breakthrough in the weird horror movie *From Dusk till Dawn* (1996), he appeared regularly in the movies of his friend Steven Soderbergh (e.g. *Out of Sight*, 1998) and those of the Coen brothers. His filmography also features the gentle tragicomedy about a businessman, *Up in the Air*, as well as the madcap war satire, *The Men Who Stare at Goats* (both 2009). His directorial debut came in 2002 in the form of *Confessions of a Dangerous Mind*. His fourth film as director was the highly acclaimed political drama *The Ides of March* (2011).

MISSION: IMPOSSIBLE 2

2000 – USA – 123 MIN. – ACTION FILM, THRILLER
DIRECTOR JOHN WOO (*1946)
SCREENPLAY RONALD D. MOORE DIRECTOR OF PHOTOGRAPHY JEFFREY L. KIMBALL
EDITING STEVEN KEMPER, CHRISTIAN WAGNER MUSIC TORI AMOS (title song),
LALO SCHIFRIN (theme), HANS ZIMMER PRODUCTION TERENCE CHANG, TOM CRUISE,
MICHAEL DOVEN, PAUL HITCHCOCK, AMY STEVENS, PAULA WAGNER NAME for
CRUISE-WAGNER PRODUCTIONS, PARAMOUNT PICTURES
STARRING TOM CRUISE (Ethan Hunt), DOUGRAY SCOTT (Sean Ambrose), THANDIE NEWTON
(Nyah Nordoff-Hall), VING RHAMES (Luther Stickell), BRENDAN GLEESON (John McCloy),
DOMINIC PURCELL (Ulrich), RADE SERBEDZIJA (Dr. Nekhorvich), RICHARD ROXBURGH
(Hugh Stamp), JOHN POLSON (Billy Baird), WILLIAM MAPOTHER (Wallis)

"Every search for a hero must begin with something which every hero requires, a villain."

Chimera is a deadly disease. It is caused by an extremely dangerous virus created in a high-tech geneticists' laboratory belonging to McCloy, a pharmaceutics tycoon who wants to earn lots of money with the antidote. What would happen if it fell into the hands of unscrupulous criminals doesn't bear thinking about. At the very beginning of the movie, professional gangsters steal the briefcase containing the antidote Bellerophon in a spectacular airplane hijack. Using an astonishingly convincing disguise, they manage to surprise both passengers and crew, but they don't manage to steal the virus itself. The scientist Dr. Nekhorvich who dies in the plane crash was carrying it in his own body. When the kidnappers discover this, they try to sell the stolen antidote back to McCloy.

Ethan Hunt (Tom Cruise) is the hero who is assigned the recovery of the virus and its antidote by the head of the Secret Service – an impossible mission. Hunt is a James Bond figure who, like his role model, is given an enchanting female companion, Nyah (Thandie Newton). She is to play the decoy, but after a passionate affair under the Spanish sun they fall in love. The baddie, Sean Ambrose (Dougray Scott), is not just a former Secret Service colleague turned terrorist, but also happens to be Nyah's ex-boyfriend. The impossible mission is complicated by a love triangle.

Mission: Impossible 2 is the sequel to *Mission: Impossible* (1996) by Brian De Palma, and both are a continuation of the '60s TV series of the same name. Typically for its genre, *Mission: Impossible 2* is not concerned with

plausibility, logic, or seriousness but is ready to use any kind of movement which furthers its plot. In John Woo, the producers found a master choreographer for the action scenes. Woo had previously given a new lease of life to Hong Kong action films with classics like *A Better Tomorrow* (1985), *The Killer* (1989), *Bullet in the Head* (1990), and *Hard-Boiled* (1992). Woo's camera and montage techniques lend an incomparable lightness to the movie's action sequences.

Woo found his creative inspiration for *MI-2* in the Spanish Flamenco tradition. In the car duel between Ethan and Nyah the partners circle and woo each other, and the flamenco motif becomes a matter of passion and death. It is also mirrored in the structure of the plot; the two sides circle each other, and the aim of the dance is not only to carry out the assignment but also to

win the heroine's favor. The circling helicopter, the continual video surveillance, the mutual deception, the waiting, the faked attack, the hesitation, and the furious finale all add up to a deadly flamenco dance which is passionate and precise, and inscribed in the cinematic structure of the movie itself. The movie is characterized by distinctive Woo features like slow motion, shootouts slowed to deadly ballets, ascending white doves, masquerades, and games of identity. In *Face/Off* (1997), Woo gave this combination of images an almost mystical dimension. But *Mission: Impossible 2* is much more than a martial arts movie, and the motorbike duel in the showdown at the end of the film turns into a joust where two knights aim their steeds at one another.

Woo also permits himself a few ironic asides where his producers and the main character Tom Cruise are concerned. Sean Ambrose, who used to

3

1 For Ethan Hunt (Tom Cruise) no mission is impossible.

2 A razor-sharp scrape past death and it's straight back into the fray: Hunt won't be intimidated.

3 Echoes of the Terminator: the agent once again just manages to escape a blazing inferno.

4 Good mates: superstars Tom Cruise and Ving Rhames playing Luther Stickell.

"Like all Woo films, *Mission: Impossible 2* concludes with an extended action sequence of almost hallucinatory intensity." *Sight and Sound*

double for Ethan when they still worked together, says "You know, the hardest part about playing you is grinning like an idiot every 15 bloody minutes!" At the very end, order is restored in the manner of the best Westerns in a man to man shootout. After all the martial furor, Woo once again uses contemplative slow motion pictures – a welcome moment of calm.

BR

4

"Dougray Scott meets her with a purposeful gleaming in his eye, and as the scarf around her neck is about to slip away, he reaches out and catches it. You can argue that this is clichéd symbolism – Beauty captured by the Beast – but at least it's wonderfully executed." *Sight and Sound*

6

5 Hunt's attention is fixed not only on his mission…

6 … but also on the enigmatic Nyah (Thandie Newton), who has to act as bait.

JOHN WOO One of the main characteristics of cinema in the '90s was the use of the human body as a narrative object. The impetus came from Asian cinema, which has always used the body as the weapon of the spirit. In 1992, body cinema virtuoso John Woo moved to Hollywood and breathed new life into the action movie, firstly with *Hard Target* (1993) and even more so with *Face/Off* (1997). In gripping gangster ballads, leading the way with the Hong Kong production *A Better Tomorrow* (1986), Woo experimented with the cinematic possibilities of breaking down fast movements into their component parts with the help of editing and slow motion effects. The abstract nature of movement is the distinguishing feature of his body cinema philosophy, as developed in the '90s. In the most intense moments of his films, which are often balletic shootouts, Woo's broken heroes float through the air as if totally divorced from their surroundings. Woo's influence is also evident in Hollywood productions like *The Matrix* (1999).

DANCER IN THE DARK

2000 – DENMARK / GERMANY / NETHERLANDS / USA / GREAT BRITAIN / FRANCE /
SWEDEN / FINLAND / ICELAND / NORWAY – 140 MIN. – MUSICAL, MELODRAMA

DIRECTOR LARS VON TRIER (*1956)
SCREENPLAY LARS VON TRIER DIRECTOR OF PHOTOGRAPHY ROBBY MÜLLER EDITING FRANÇOIS GÉDIGIER,
MOLLY MARLENE STENSGAARD MUSIC BJÖRK PRODUCTION VIBEKE WINDELØV for ARTE
FRANCE CINÉMA, BLIND SPOT PICTURES, CINEMATOGRAPH, DANISH FILM INSTITUTE,
DINOVI PICTURES, FILM I VÄST, FRANCE 3 CINÉMA, GOOD MACHINE, ICELANDIC FILM
CORPORATION, LIBERATOR PRODUCTIONS, PAIN UNLIMITED, SWEDISH FILM INSTITUTE,
TRUST FILM, WHAT ELSE?, ZENTROPA ENTERTAINMENTS
STARRING BJÖRK (Selma Yeskova), CATHERINE DENEUVE (Kathy), DAVID MORSE (Bill),
PETER STORMARE (Jeff), UDO KIER (Dr. Porkorny), JOEL GREY (Oldrich Novy),
CARA SEYMOUR (Linda Houston), VLADICA KOSTIC (Gene Yeskova),
JEAN-MARC BARR (Norman)
IFF CANNES 2000 GOLDEN PALM, BEST ACTRESS (Björk)

"Because in a musical nothing dreadful ever happens."

A musical that ends with an execution – that could only work in European cinema. In Hollywood musicals, like those the main character Selma dreams about in *Dancer in the Dark*, nothing like that ever happens. In the tragedy by Danish director Lars von Trier two very different stories of music and violence collide with unrelenting narrative rigor and forceful images. Robby Müller's handheld camera images are uncompromising: they are faded and pale and seem improvised, like the life of the protagonist. Selma is a Czech immigrant who lives with her son Gene in a small trailer. She works in a factory at a metal press to earn the money she needs for an eye operation for her son. She tells the others however that she sends the money to her father in the Czech Republic.

Icelandic pop icon Björk plays the naive Selma, whose daydreams are integrated into the movie as musical sequences. The wan colors of everyday life are transformed into multicolored pictures, and there is dancing, laughter and singing. The rhythm of Selma's surroundings sets the beat for the songs and Selma stars in the dance sequences. Björk's singing is the same as it always is; her energetic voice booms out, only to sound fragile and childish a moment after. Selma's fantasies are illusions of a better life like in the film models from Hollywood's dream factories, perfect illusions to which she clings. The truth however is that Selma is an ordinary worker, who struggles to bring up her own son and dedicates the little free time she has to an amateur theater group. Selma's sight however is gradually failing as well and when she is no longer capable of working the metal press she is fired. Then her landlord and neighbor Bill steals her savings when she refuses to lend him money to finance his wife's extravagant lifestyle. Selma goes to see him to demand her money back. There is fighting, a shot is fired

3

1 An unusual pair: Icelandic pop star Björk as Selma Yeskova, and French grande dame of the cinema Catherine Deneuve as factory worker Kathy.

2 Innocent, childlike, and doomed: Selma is going incurably blind.

3 For Jeff (Peter Stormare), Selma remains unattainable.

> "'Björk cannot act, she can only feel,' Lars von Trier is supposed to have said after shooting the film. That may well be true, and it makes this film quite unique. The intense dedication and dedicated intensity with which she throws herself into her part – these are things she will not be able to give to another director a second time." *Süddeutsche Zeitung*

and hits Bill. This is followed by a longing for atonement completely in keeping with the Christian tradition of sacrifice. Bill becomes a penitent sinner, who can't however get the confession over his lips. To avoid being exposed in front of his wife, he begs Selma to solve his money and debt problems by killing him.

Lars von Trier's film constantly return to motifs of guilt and atonement, for which sight is the main metaphor. Bill's forbidden, greedy gaze makes him guilty while Selma's loss of sight by contrast calls forth her innocent musical fantasies. At the same time the movie thematizes sight on a visual level. It is difficult to watch because the pictures wander restlessly from one motif to another, although they are deprived of life, of color. Only in Selma's dreams do the pictures become colorful and lively, and only when she sings does the

improvised feel of the handheld camera give way to the glossy look of the musical montage as we know it from Busby Berkeley musicals like *42nd Street* (1933), *Gold Diggers of 1935* (1935), or *Broadway Serenade* (1939). As in Berkeley's films, the choreography in *Dancer in the Dark* is enhanced with careful editing, which replaces the camera as narrative authority during the musical scenes. The contrast between the rough pictures of miserable reality in which Selma fights for her life and the life of her son and the detailed musical dream sequences make the drama of Selma's life seem even more disastrous. When Selma is finally caught after she has killed Bill, the tragedy of her real life begins to seep into her fantasies as well. She is sentenced to death. She doesn't want new investigations that might lead to a pardon when she discovers that they would use up all the money she has saved for her son.

4 Music dispels the worries of everyday life.

5 Choreography as a study of movement: Von Trier uses phase sequence photography of the dancing in a visual experiment.

MUSICALS The advent of the talkie or sound movie produced the musical genre in the late '20s. The success of films like *The Broadway Melody* (1929), which were initially more akin to filmed dance performances, marked the beginning of a boom. In the '30s, former army drill officer Busby Berkeley had a lasting influence on the genre by replacing individual dances with technically and formally perfect routines. At the same time, the genre began to produce its own stars, with Fred Astaire and Ginger Rogers blazing the trail. From the '40s onward, the various style elements began to coalesce, to form the modern musical in which both dreams and reality suspend the rules of everyday life. The end of the studio system in Hollywood signaled the decline of the musical, although the early/mid-'60s saw a revival with films such as *West Side Story* (1961) and *The Sound of Music* (1965). And the genre is alive and kicking once again. The proof – films like the double Oscar-winning *Moulin Rouge!* (2001), sixfold Oscar winner *Chicago* (2002), and box-office smash *Mamma Mia!* (2008).

She chooses death to give her son sight, which means life. And just as her musical fantasies become more and more a part of the real events, the film itself becomes a melodramatic vortex. It drags viewers irresistibly into the shattering scene at the end of the movie when Selma is hanged, but continues singing. She falls through a trapdoor in the floor into a kind of stage room where the spectators see her swinging dead from the end of the rope. The curtain falls swiftly, the movie has reached its tragic climax at the moment where musical and drama meet. Selma's last song is interrupted by violent death. BR

5

SPACE COWBOYS

CLINT EASTWOOD TOMMY LEE JONES
DONALD SUTHERLAND JAMES GARNER

2000 – USA – 130 MIN. – DRAMA
DIRECTOR CLINT EASTWOOD (*1930)
SCREENPLAY KEN KAUFMAN, HOWARD KLAUSNER DIRECTOR OF PHOTOGRAPHY JACK N. GREEN
EDITING JOEL COX MUSIC CLINT EASTWOOD, LENNIE NIEHAUS PRODUCTION CLINT EASTWOOD,
ANDREW LAZAR for CLIPSAL FILMS, MAD CHANCE, THE MALPASO COMPANY,
VILLAGE ROADSHOW PRODUCTIONS
STARRING CLINT EASTWOOD (Frank Corvin), TOMMY LEE JONES (Hawk Hawkins),
DONALD SUTHERLAND (Jerry O'Neill), JAMES GARNER (Tank Sullivan), JAMES
CROMWELL (Bob Gerson), MARCIA GAY HARDEN (Sara Holland), WILLIAM DEVANE
(Eugene Davis), LOREN DEAN (Ethan Glance), COURTNEY B. VANCE (Roger Hines),
RADE SERBEDZIJA (General Vostow)

"Boys will be boys."

Clint Eastwood's space comedy *Space Cowboys* begins like the early careers of its now greying main characters: in black and white. In a flashback to the year 1958 we see young air force hotshots from Team Daedalus. They break all the existing height and speed records, crash prototype airplanes worth millions of dollars into the desert sand, and dream of burning their wings as they all want to be the first person to fly to the moon. They are all heartbroken when NASA is founded and sends a chimpanzee to the moon instead of one of them.

Forty years later, the Cold War is long over. A Russian communication satellite has become defective and as its failure is likely to cause a civil war in the former Soviet states, NASA manager Bob Gerson (James Cromwell) offers to help the Russians. Oddly enough the Russian satellite was made according to the same specifications as the American Skylab model, which

Frank Corvin (Clint Eastwood), a former member of Team Daedalus, designed in 1969. No one else knows now how to deal with the old-fashioned Skylab technology, so Team Daedalus is reactivated to repair this Russian hulk from the satellite Stone Age.

The team meet up again for the first time in decades. Tank Sullivan (James Garner) has swapped his officer's bars for the pulpit of a Baptist church; the engineer Jerry O'Neill (Donald Sutherland) designs roller coasters and pursues young women; Hawk Hawkins (Tommy Lee Jones) shows amateur pilots what a double loop-the-loop is.

Clint Eastwood, 1930 vintage, has aged gracefully as an actor, and as a director he gives his characters the same dignity. Even during the NASA aptitude tests, when they have to let their trousers down, they cut as dashing a figure as their age will allow. For 30 days they struggle with modern

1

2

"No actor, with the possible exception of Paul Newman, has aged better on film than Eastwood, who turned 70 in May and whose lined and weathered face makes Mt. Rushmore look like the Pillsbury Doughboy." *Los Angeles Times*

3

4

5

technology and their failing physical strength, until at last they are sent up into space to repair the satellite, which turns out to be a deadly relic of the Cold War.

Ken Kaufman and Howard Klausner wrote the screenplay to *Space Cowboys* inspired by John Glenn, who carried out his last space shuttle mission at the age of 77. The predictable story with its conventional conflicts – the ancient rivalry between the pilots Corvin and Hawkins, the tension between the young and the old astronauts, the way the old confront death and disease – is enlivened with some witty dialogue. It's a screenplay that is caught between comedy and drama, but above it's a showpiece for its loveable and charismatic aging actors.

Clint Eastwood allows plenty of time for the plot to develop. The reunion of the old comrades and their preparations for takeoff take up two-thirds of the film. Only then are the dreams of the four men realized.

Eastwood was almost certainly attracted to this movie by the idea of letting four old war horses fight one last battle. *Space Cowboys* is a space age Western, and Westerns were the genre that made Clint Eastwood a Hollywood icon.   APO

1   A fine view: astronaut Frank Corvin (Clint Eastwood) looks at the blue planet.

2   A task that only experienced hands can do: Corvin and his team are in outer space to repair a Russian satellite.

3   Tank Sullivan (James Garner) is a member of the team of astronauts.

4   Jogging for their trip into space. As well as Frank and Tank, Hawk Hawkins (Tommy Lee Jones) and Jerry O'Neill (Donald Sutherland) are also part of the team.

5   The flight into space requires highly specific preparation. The team in training.

HIGH FIDELITY

2000 – USA – 113 MIN. – COMEDY, MUSIC FILM
DIRECTOR STEPHEN FREARS (*1941)
SCREENPLAY D. V. DEVINCENTIS, STEVE PINK, SCOTT ROSENBERG, JOHN CUSACK, based
on the novel of the same name by NICK HORNBY **DIRECTOR OF PHOTOGRAPHY** SEAMUS MCGARVEY
EDITING MICK AUDSLEY **MUSIC** HOWARD SHORE **PRODUCTION** TIM BEVAN, RUDD SIMMONS for
DOGSTAR FILMS, NEW CRIME PRODUCTIONS, TOUCHSTONE PICTURES, WORKING
TITLE FILMS
STARRING JOHN CUSACK (Rob Gordon), IBEN HJEJLE (Laura), TODD LOUISO (Dick),
JACK BLACK (Barry), LISA BONET (Marie DeSalle), CATHERINE ZETA-JONES
(Charlie Nicholson), JOAN CUSACK (Liz), TIM ROBBINS (Ian Raymond), LILI TAYLOR
(Sarah), NATASHA GREGSON WAGNER (Caroline)

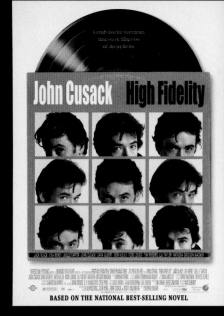

BASED ON THE NATIONAL BEST-SELLING NOVEL

"Do I listen to pop music because I'm miserable? Or am I miserable because I listen to pop music?"

Life is like an LP record: one groove sums up all its aspects, however various they may be. On average it only contains one hit – but precisely because of this it is worth buying, at least for the connoisseur. Rob (John Cusack) is a connoisseur, as well as a music fetishist and a failed Casanova. Together with his friends Barry (Jack Black) and Dick (Todd Louiso) he runs a record shop where time seems to stand still. A niche that is also a hideaway, they gather there to indulge their little quirks and judge the rest of the world by their own taste in music. They are stuck in a phase sometime at the end of the '80s when choosing between the analog vinyl of the good old LP record and the digitally reworked plastic of the unfeeling CD was still a matter of faith … From a distance, that sort of passion now seems comic and absurd, but watching the film, we are all reminded of a phase in our own lives despite ourselves. Unobtrusive colors and spare furniture makes this pseudo-exis-

tentialism visible to outsiders and are as necessary as printed T-shirts which express the wearer's current mental state.

Following the logic of the music market, unhappy Rob, hyperactive Barry, and shy Dick put their faith in a ranking system by which all human experience can be evaluated: the universal principle of the "Top 5." It simplifies many things but also makes others more difficult. The "Top 5" is the lowest common denominator in the specialist discussions of these three students of pop, but it is also the basis for Rob's monologue on his failed relationships. Apart from his mother, up till now five women have influenced his life. *High Fidelity* tells us in flashbacks how they managed to get onto Rob's personal "Top 5" relationship list. Each one has their own good and bad points but, like on an LP, only one turns out to be a top hit: Laura, convincingly played by Iben Hjejle. Rob is the movie's all-knowing, repressed

1 Good vibrations: music makes it possible to get close to someone. Rob Gordon (John Cusack) and his girlfriend Laura (Iben Hjejle).

2 Experts together: Rob and his friend Dick (Todd Louiso).

3 Embarrassing confessions: Rob and Liz (Joan Cusack).

4 Barry (Jack Black) isn't the sharpest tool in the box.

5 Sparkling eyes and a smile to die for: only Laura can save Rob.

"With Rob, Frears manages to create the Woody Allen effect to a certain extent: he's annoying from time to time, but we like him." *epd Film*

macho narrator, and he comments with intensely black smugness on the qualities of his exes. Like Jeff Daniels in Woody Allen's *The Purple Rose of Cairo* (1985), Rob steps out of the fictive story, looks straight into the camera and directs his monologue at the audience. This involuntary conspiracy has some extremely funny moments. John Cusack's combination of innocence and mischief remind us of the unnerving and pleading eyes of comedian Oliver Hardy, pushed into "another fine mess" thanks to his partner Stan Laurel. Like his model Hardy, Rob takes on the role of victim, although he sometimes ignores the fact that he is not entirely innocent in the calamities that befall him. We learn for instance from a conversation between Laura and her friend Liz that Rob has been unfaithful, that she had an abortion because he was having an affair, and that he hasn't paid back the money that he owes her.

Fortunately, Rob is able to escape from this largely self-induced misery in music. Stephen Frears's movie follows Nick Hornby's novel with black humor and gentle irony. Hornby describes that time in the life of growing men when the divide between pop culture and philosophy seems to be bridged. Pop songs become vessels of almost supernatural wisdom which can help with the trials and tribulations of life. This vinyl philosophizing however is incomprehensible to Rob's potential partners. His escape into music isn't just a way of escaping from his failures, but also an activity that turns him into an extremely lonely man, and soon Laura has had enough and leaves him. He tries his luck with the singer Marie DeSalle (Lisa Bonet) but the brief affair only salves his battered ego and is little more than a one-night stand. He wants more. In desperation, he follows some advice from Bruce Springsteen and visits each of his past girlfriends, whose attraction, like an out-dated hit, has greatly worn off. They are all now either ill or married. Inevitably, Rob returns to Laura. In the meantime his friends have been successful: Dick falls in love with a customer and Barry finally finds a band.

In the end music brings everything together again, and the relationships between women and men take on the form of a musical composition, an idea also used in the poetic images of Alain Resnais's wonderful *Same Old Song* (*On connaît la chanson*, 1997). Three singles who only find harmony when they play together: the LP turns out to be a good metaphor for life after all.

BR

VOICE-OVER The voice of a narrator who is not visible in the movie is known as a voice-over. In documentary films, the voice-over mostly comments on the pictures while voices in a feature film take on the narrative of the movie's plot. Here the voice-over comments on actions or explains the context, it prepares future events or explains connections to events which are not shown in the movie. As opposed to continual editing, the voice-over emphasizes the narrative structure of a feature film. Both documentary films and film noir make frequent use of this technique, but comedies often use it as well.

TRAFFIC 𝗜𝗜𝗜𝗜

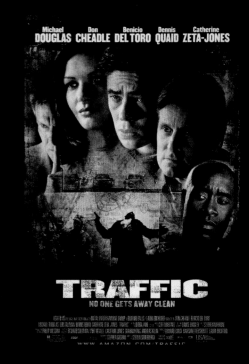

2000 – USA / GERMANY – 143 MIN. – CRIME FILM, POLITICAL THRILLER
DIRECTOR STEVEN SODERBERGH (*1963)
SCREENPLAY STEPHEN GAGHAN, based on the TV series *TRAFFIC* by SIMON MOORE
DIRECTOR OF PHOTOGRAPHY PETER ANDREWS (aka Steven Soderbergh) EDITING STEPHEN MIRRIONE
MUSIC CLIFF MARTINEZ PRODUCTION LAURA BICKFORD, MARSHALL HERSKOVITZ,
EDWARD ZWICK for INITIAL ENTERTAINMENT GROUP, BEDFORD FALLS PRODUCTIONS,
SPLENDID MEDIEN AG, USA FILMS
STARRING MICHAEL DOUGLAS (Robert Wakefield), DON CHEADLE (Montel Gordon),
BENICIO DEL TORO (Javier Rodriguez), LUIS GUZMÁN (Ray Castro), DENNIS QUAID
(Arnie Metzger), CATHERINE ZETA-JONES (Helena Ayala), ERIKA CHRISTENSEN
(Caroline Wakefield), STEVEN BAUER (Carlos Ayala), MIGUEL FERRER (Eduardo Ruiz)
ACADEMY AWARDS 2001 OSCARS for BEST SUPPORTING ACTOR (Benicio Del Toro),
BEST DIRECTOR (Steven Soderbergh), BEST FILM EDITING (Stephen Mirrione),
BEST ADAPTED SCREENPLAY (Stephen Gaghan)
IFF BERLIN 2001 SILVER BEAR for BEST ACTOR (Benicio Del Toro)

"How can one fight a war when the enemy is your own family?"

The sun shines mercilessly on Mexico. The heat is so terrible that on the American border even the landscape itself seems tanned. Mexico, land of the lawless and refuge of so many movie villains, is more a metaphor than a real place, and here, it's the home of drug dealing. The USA has great difficulty controlling the southern border, and the Mexican and the American police forces are powerless to stem the tide of drugs which floods through the border into the country. The borderlands are as unwelcoming as they are unreal, and yet it is here that a great crime is taking place. Javier Rodriguez (Benicio Del Toro) is from the Mexican drug squad and he has contacts who give him information about illegal drug deals. Unfortunately his hands are tied, because his boss, General Salazar, is himself a member of the rival drug cartel in the border town Tijuana. All that Rodriguez dreams of are floodlights for the stadium so that the town's children can play baseball there after dark.

On the other side of the border in the USA a judge named Robert Hudson Wakefield (Michael Douglas) is made America's drug commissioner, while his daughter Caroline (Erika Christensen) is taking the first steps towards drug addiction.

Carlos Ayala (Steven Bauer) is the subject of ongoing investigations on both sides of the border. He gets drugs into America and organizes their distribution. Carlos is arrested, but his wife Helena (Catherine Zeta-Jones) takes his place and carries on the business with a firm hand – for the good of her children, as she says. All she wants is to never have to go back to the gutter that she came from.

These three interwoven stories all deal with the same themes: the tense relationship between the private and public spheres and the difficult relationship between family and politics. They are also about the responsibility of one generation for the next. The problem is that the drug business has

1 Concerned for her own family: Helena Ayala (Catherine Zeta-Jones) as mother-to-be and syndicate boss.

2 Embarrassing questions: attorney Arnie Metzger (Dennis Quaid) and the drug dealer's wife. Should you ply an illegal trade in order to be able to support your own family? Helena knows her answer.

3 Drug commissioner Robert Wakefield (Michael Douglas) is having trouble explaining: what good are the law and justice, if their weapons aren't up to the job?

"One of the main themes is certainly greed. That's a human emotion that I don't understand. I have experienced it often enough, but I don't understand it."

Steven Soderbergh in *Frankfurter Allgemeine Zeitung*

long since conquered private spheres that cannot be controlled by politics, while politicians are still trying to mechanically control the country's borders.

Traffic tells of a lack of responsibility, of a lack of perspective, and of a problem that could destroy the foundations of society. Traffic isn't about illegal border crossings between Mexico and the USA, nor is it about the hopelessness of fighting against drugs in just one place. The border is merely an image and a surface, for the real transgressions and catastrophes are happening elsewhere. They take place in the private sphere, in the family, and in the lives of children who are sacrificed for profit margins. Behind the official façade of pretty promises and efforts, the root of the problem lies in broken families.

Steven Soderbergh, who manages the camera himself under a pseudonym, dissects this surface with cinematic means, and penetrates to the core of the problem with great care and intensity. Places are marked out with exaggerated color and light, with Mexico overexposed with a yellow filter and the USA shown in a cold blue light. Smooth surfaces are destroyed by the use of grainy film and the handheld camera sometimes gets unbearably close to the action, leaving the audience nowhere left to hide. The various plot strands separate and then combine, breaking up the chronology with abrupt changes of theme and scene. Single episodes are often only linked by very small details and it is impossible to identify who the main characters are or to unravel the various story lines. What remains is a disturbing picture of ruined youth, exemplified in the story of the addict Caroline. Eventually the

"Soderbergh places before our eyes a scourge that imperils the entire human race ... And since the work is, in purely cinematic terms, a miracle of imagination and variety, this production marks an epoch in both the seventh art and the history of our time." *Le Figaro*

roblem rises to the surface and returns to its origin. The perfect surface of he Wakefield's family life is corroded and its certainties begin to crumble. Wakefield holds his first press conference as drug commissioner, and, earching desperately for the right words, he admits that he can't support the government's official policies. Meanwhile, on the other side of the border, avier Rodriguez has worked wonders: the children of Tijuana are finally able o play baseball in the floodlights. Seeing the family as part of the public

sphere and behaving responsibly in small matters is the answer that *Traffic* offers, which may not sound original but is extremely convincing in the context of the film. Thanks to Soderbergh's cinematic vision, the movie is not sensationalist but quietly self-confident and artistic. As Jean-Luc Godard said, it's not enough to make political films – films must also be made political. Steven Soderbergh manages to do that in *Traffic*.

BR

BENICIO DEL TORO Benicio Del Toro was born in 1967. After Peter Weir's *Fearless* (1993), his next, more prominent role was as gangster Fred Fenster in *The Usual Suspects* (1995). As well as roles in Abel Ferrara's *The Funeral* (1996) and *Basquiat* (1996), he was extremely successful in the high-pitched comedy *Fear and Loathing in Las Vegas* (1998). Del Toro's distinguishing features are his slurred, husky voice and cold, reserved minimalism, punctuated by explosive emotional outbursts. His best roles to date have been in *Traffic* (2000) (for which he won an Oscar) and the political biopic *Che* (2008, also directed by Steven Soderbergh) which earned him an award at Cannes.

4 Children on the road to ruin: Caroline Wakefield (Erika Christensen) and her boyfriend.

5 His dejection knows no bounds: police officer Javier Rodriguez (Benicio Del Toro) in his almost hopeless mission against drug dealing.

ALMOST FAMOUS

2000 – USA – 123 MIN.– MUSIC FILM, DRAMA
DIRECTOR CAMERON CROWE (*1957)
SCREENPLAY CAMERON CROWE **DIRECTOR OF PHOTOGRAPHY** JOHN TOLL **EDITING** JOE HUTSHING,
SAAR KLEIN **MUSIC** NANCY WILSON, diverse rock songs **PRODUCTION** CAMERON CROWE,
IAN BRYCE, LISA STEWART for VINYL FILMS
STARRING PATRICK FUGIT (William Miller), BILLY CRUDUP (Russell Hammond),
FRANCES MCDORMAND (Elaine Miller), KATE HUDSON (Penny Lane), JASON LEE
(Jeff Bebe), PHILIP SEYMOUR HOFFMAN (Lester Bangs), ANNA PAQUIN (Polexia),
FAIRUZA BALK (Sapphire), NOAH TAYLOR (Dick Roswell), ZOOEY DESCHANEL
(Anita Miller)
ACADEMY AWARDS 2001 OSCAR for BEST ORIGINAL SCREENPLAY (Cameron Crowe)

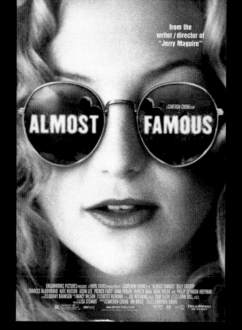

"I am a golden God."

San Diego, 1973. 15-year-old William Miller (Patrick Fugit) dreams of becoming a music critic – much against the wishes of his single mother Elaine (Frances McDormand), who believes rock music to be nothing more than the glorification of drugs and sexual dissipation. Against the odds, William's dream comes true when he meets his idol Lester Bangs (Philip Seymour Hoffman), the legendary editor of the music magazine *Creem*. Bangs is impressed by the boy's enthusiasm and commissions him to write a portrait of Black Sabbath, who are about to play in the town. At the concert William meets a pretty groupie called Penny Lane (Kate Hudson) and the musicians of the newcomer band Stillwater, who take him backstage. Before William realizes what is happening, he is accompanying the band on a tour bus through the USA for *Rolling Stone* magazine. He experiences the musicians' free and easy lifestyle at first hand, with its seductive mix of rock euphoria, habitual drug consumption, and casual sex.

As the band become more and more successful, internal tensions grow and William finds himself increasingly torn between private loyalties and the

critical distance his job demands. He becomes friends with the guitarist Russell (Billy Crudup) and falls in love with Penny Lane.

In the movies of the '90s, the '70s underwent a great revival. Like Todd Haynes's glittering glamrock film *Velvet Goldmine* (1998), many works have a nostalgic feel despite the fact that the '70s are not yet that distant in time. It is almost as if they had been submerged in some mysterious way. Such movies tend to emphasize the freedom and decadence of the decade with '70s music and fashion as a superficial acoustic and visual accompaniment. Only occasionally does a movie really communicate something of the spirit of those years, and *Almost Famous* is one of these exceptions.

Much of the movie is autobiographical. Author and director Cameron Crowe wrote for *Creem* and *Rolling Stone* as a youngster in the '70s before he turned to film, but there is never any danger that the movie will become an uncritical glorification of those times. Although he had a generous budget, *Almost Famous* is unusually simple and straightforward for its genre. Crowe makes it into an initiation story, which is told from the protagonist's point of

1 Almost famous: Kate Hudson was awarded the Golden Globe for her portrayal of elfin groupie Penny Lane.

2 Loss of innocence: the road to fame leads the band Stillwater to sell out their ideals.

3 Rock stars without glamour: compromise and middle-class limitations seep into the band's sex and drugs lifestyle (Billy Crudup and Kate Hudson).

4 The journalist and the groupie: in their naïve enthusiasm William (Patrick Fugit) and Penny embody the ideals of rock music.

5 Filmed at eye level: in contrast to other films about the music of the 1970s Crowe's film is characterized by being true-to-life.

6 Rock music as collective ecstasy: Crowe manages to bring the unifying power of rock back to life.

"A bittersweet, moving, and intelligent film and we love first of all the precise and loving way the various characters are presented." *Süddeutsche Zeitung*

"*Almost Famous* is about the world of rock, but it's not a rock film, it's a coming-of-age film, about an idealistic kid who sees the real world, witnesses its cruelties and heartbreaks, and yet finds much room for hope." *Chicago Sun-Times*

view. William's experiences are especially meaningful because everything is new for him – love, friendship, life with the band, and the American landscape. Although Crowe cannot resist some comic exaggeration, using William's perspective means he can create a lifelike portrait of scenery and figures from his intimate knowledge of the material.

In fact the musicians are presented as anything other than larger than life. Their wild lifestyle often looks like compensation and their petty jealousies and career worries reveal them to be limited and bourgeois in their outlook. The movie also tells of a time when rock music had already lost its uto-

pian force and was threatening to become an entirely commercial venture. Like Crowe's earlier film *Jerry Maguire* (1996), *Almost Famous* is about the loss of innocence and personal integrity. William and Penny Lane embody these values, and the movie uses the two outsiders to formulate its belief in the unbroken spirit of rock 'n' roll despite everything. The people who manage to retain their initial innocent enthusiasm for rock not only find themselves through the music, they also find friends for life. The movie's energetic, vital soundtrack provides a persuasive back up for this conclusion.

JH

KATE HUDSON Kate Hudson was born in Los Angeles in 1979; her mother is Goldie Hawn. She made her movie debut in Risa Bramon Garcia's ensemble comedy *200 Cigarettes* (1998). After several minor roles, Hudson's breakthrough came with Cameron Crowe's movie about musicians, *Almost Famous* (2000). Her performance as the elfin groupie Penny Lane won her a Golden Globe. Since then, the ethereally beautiful actress has appeared in Robert Altman's comedy *Dr. T and the Women* (2000), historical epic *The Four Feathers* (2002), horror flick *The Skeleton Key* (2005), and in numerous romantic comedies, such as *Raising Helen* (2004).

AMORES PERROS

2000 – MEXICO – 154 MIN. – EPISODIC FILM, SOCIAL DRAMA
DIRECTOR ALEJANDRO GONZÁLEZ IÑÁRRITU (*1963)
SCREENPLAY GUILLERMO ARRIAGA DIRECTOR OF PHOTOGRAPHY RODRIGO PRIETO
EDITING LUIS CARBALLAR, ALEJANDRO GONZÁLEZ IÑÁRRITU, FERNANDO PÉREZ UNDA
MUSIC GUSTAVO SANTAOLALLA PRODUCTION ALEJANDRO GONZÁLEZ IÑÁRRITU for
ALTAVISTA FILMS, ZETA FILM
STARRING EMILIO ECHEVARRÍA (El Chivo), GAEL GARCÍA BERNAL (Octavio), GOYA TOLEDO
(Valeria), ÁLVARO GUERRERO (Daniel), VANESSA BAUCHE (Susana), MARCO PÉREZ
(Ramiro), JORGE SALINAS (Luis), RODRIGO MURRAY (Gustavo), HUMBERTO BUSTO
(Jorge), GERARDO CAMPBELL (Mauricio), GUSTAVO SÁNCHEZ PARRA (Jarocho),
LOURDES ECHEVARRÍA (Maru)
IFF CANNES 2000 GRAND PRIX – INTERNATIONAL CRITICS' WEEK

"If you want to make God laugh, tell Him your plans."

From the first second, *Amores Perros* captivates its audience. A wild car chase sweeps through the streets of Mexico City. With daring driving maneuvers, Octavio (Gael García Bernal) tries to lose his armed pursuer. Panicked, his friend Jorge (Humberto Busto) keeps turning around to look at the gunshot wounded dog Cofi, who threatens to bleed to death on the back seat of their car. Before we can even grasp what is going on, the accident happens. At an intersection, Octavio and Jorge collide with another car. The accident not only sets the film in motion but also serves as its core. It is both the result of and the catalyst for three loosely related narratives, in which life in the Mexican capital is shown from all its sides – from the homeless to the upperclass.

The first chapter shows the events leading up to the accident. It takes place in the small-time crime scene in the poor neighborhoods of the big city. Three generations live together under one roof: Octavio and his brother Ramiro (Marco Pérez) live with their mother together with Ramiro's wife

Susana (Vanessa Bauche), and their young son. She is already expecting her second child with Ramiro. Octavio can no longer stand by and watch how his brother treats Susana. With the money he wins at dog fights, he wants to leave the city with her and her child. As a final and decisive fight ends unfairly, Octavio snaps. He stabs his opponent, flees from the dead man's gang and, in doing so, causes the accident.

The second part takes place in the world of the rich and beautiful, which so far, we have only been shown on advertisements and TV screens. The head editor Daniel (Álvaro Guerrero) leaves his wife to move in with his lover, the famous supermodel Valeria (Goya Toledo). Shortly thereafter, she is involved in an car accident and badly injured. Her career hangs in the balance. On top of that, her beloved lapdog Richi disappears, and her relationship with Daniel begins to crumble.

At the center of the final chapter is El Chivo (Emilio Echevarría). He left his wife and daughter years ago to go into hiding as a guerrilla fighter,

1   For the then 21-year-old Gael García Bernal, the role of Octavio was his big break. Today he is quite possibly Mexico's most well-known actor.

2   After the car accident, Valeria (Goya Toledo) is bedridden, her future as a model undetermined. The disappearance of her lapdog Richi makes her even sadder.

3   Present at every dog fight: the aggressive Jarocho (Gustavo Sánchez Parra). As he shoots at Cofi in the middle of a fight, Octavio snaps and stabs him.

Having let himself go, he now roams the streets of Mexico City with a pack of stray dogs and earns his living as a hit man. To El Chivo, the accident is at first nothing more than a stroke of dumb luck. As he pulls the injured Octavio from the wreckage, he manages to steal his savings undetected. He also takes the seriously injured dog Cofi and nurses him back to health. As he learns of the death of his wife, he reassesses his life and tries to reconnect with his daughter Maru, who, incidentally, is played by Echevarría's actual daughter Lourdes.

The large number of characters and events would provide enough material for one of Mexico's beloved telenovelas. Nevertheless, *Amores Perros* never feels schematic or overladen – the characters are too multifac-eted, the plot turns too unpredictable. Screenplay writer Guillermo Arriaga spins a complex web of love and intrigue, trust and betrayal, strokes of luck and blows of fate. The three stories are shown one after the other, whereas each narrative is repeatedly referred to and continued in vignettes throughout the film.

Although there is no lack of humor in its narrative style, *Amores Perros* is characterized by a pessimistic image of society. Despite their different social environments, all of the characters deal with similar problems. Absent father figures and broken families are constant themes. Just like El Chivo once abandoned his family, Daniel also leaves his wife and two young daughters. No mention is even made of Octavio and Ramiro's father. Through the

ALEJANDRO GONZÁLEZ IÑÁRRITU (*1963) AND GUILLERMO ARRIAGA (*1958)   *Amores Perros* was the first of three films that director González Iñárritu created with the writer Arriaga. While working on his first screenplay, he was able to take from his own experiences as a boy raised in the poorest neighborhood of Mexico City: at age 13, he lost his sense of smell in a street fight. The success brought the two to Hollywood, where they made their second film, *21 Grams* (2003), with stars like Sean Penn, Naomi Watts, and Benicio Del Toro. Once again, this story, which takes place in Los Angeles, revolves around a car accident, whose deadly consequences initiate a contemplation on guilt and forgiveness. It's Arriaga's radical treatment of the story's narrative form: like the pieces of a puzzle, the individual scenes gradually come together to create a picture. With *Babel* (2006), the two filmmakers brought their trilogy to a close. Although they refrained here from using a complex time structure for the three parallel plot lines, they scattered them over three continents – North America, Africa, and Asia – in order to convey the global repercussions of individual events. Once again, with Brad Pitt and Cate Blanchett, renowned Hollywood stars stood before the camera. In between, Arriaga wrote the screenplay for *The Three Burials of Melquiades Estrada* (2005), for which he was awarded best screenplay at Cannes. Subsequently, the two Mexicans went their separate ways. For *The Burning Plain* (2008), not only did Arriaga write the screenplay but directed for the first time as well. For *Biutiful* (2010), Iñárritu once again shot in Mexico and in his native language.

4   El Chivo (Emilio Echevarría) roams the big city with his stray dogs. No one would suspect that behind the facade lurks a killer.

5   On the wrong path. Ramiro (Marco Pérez) can only provide for his small family through illegal means. With his friend, he commits one robbery after the other.

6   Right before the car accident. Rage and desperation are written all over Octavio's face. With the gunshot wounded Cofi, he flees from Jarocho's gang.

"It is the work of a born filmmaker, and you can sense Gonzalez Inarritu's passion as he plunges into melodrama, coincidence, sensation and violence." *Chicago Sun-Times*

6

hit El Chivo is hired to carry out on his client's own brother, the conflict between Octavio and Ramiro is revisited.

Like the film's title already suggests, the dogs play an important role. They are the ones who either instigate a plot line's action or provide a decisive turning point. First of all, there's Cofi, whose brutal potential as a fighting dog is discovered rather by chance and with whom Octavio wins the money necessary to run away with Susana. In the last episode, Cofi also serves an important dramaturgical element. At first, El Chivo is unaware of what kind of dog he has rescued. One day, Cofi creates a bloodbath in which he kills all of El Chivo's other dogs. For the hit man, it serves as both a shock and catharsis as he recognizes in Cofi his own bestial nature.

With each new episode, the style and tone of the film change. From the racing opening sequence and dog fights to the emotional chamber drama, to the hit man's chilling episode à la Jean-Pierre Melville, the director moves effortlessly from genre to genre thus proving his multifaceted talent. For a debut film, this kind of stylistic command is remarkable. With his first attempt, Alejandro González Iñárritu created an international success. *Amores Perros* was showered with awards at countless festivals and was nominated for an Oscar for best foreign language film. In the course of this international recognition, the otherwise somewhat overlooked Mexican cinema was also introduced to a wider audience.

CZ

8

7 Still shaken from the accident, Ocatavio waits for Susana at the bus station. His dream of a future with her is crushed for good.

8 After having to have her leg amputated, Valeria stares crying through the blinds. Across the street, her last billboard advertisement is being taken down.

9 Octavio takes better care of Susana than his brother. He wants to leave the city with her and her child.

10 Valeria and Daniel's newfound happiness threatens to fall apart. She accuses him of still hanging on to his family who he left for her.

"It doesn't make any difference if you are rich or poor, handsome or ugly; we are all very vulnerable, very fragile." *Alejandro González Iñárritu*

9

10

ACADEMY AWARDS 1992–2001

1   *1991 Jonathan Demme gave a new countenance to evil, and with that won 5 Oscars.*
2   *1991 Oliver Stone and male lead Kevin Costner in search of the truth.*

1992 OSCARS

BEST PICTURE	THE SILENCE OF THE LAMBS
BEST DIRECTOR	JONATHAN DEMME for *The Silence of the Lambs*
BEST LEADING ACTRESS	JODIE FOSTER in *The Silence of the Lambs*
BEST LEADING ACTOR	ANTHONY HOPKINS in *The Silence of the Lambs*
BEST SUPPORTING ACTRESS	MERCEDES RUEHL in *The Fisher King*
BEST SUPPORTING ACTOR	JACK PALANCE in *City Slickers*
BEST ORIGINAL SCREENPLAY	CALLIE KHOURI for *Thelma & Louise*
BEST ADAPTED SCREENPLAY	TED TALLY for *The Silence of the Lambs*
BEST FOREIGN LANGUAGE FILM	*Mediterraneo* by GABRIELE SALVATORES (Italy)
BEST CINEMATOGRAPHY	ROBERT RICHARDSON for *JFK*
BEST ART DIRECTION	DENNIS GASSNER, NANCY HAIGH for *Bugsy*
BEST FILM EDITING	JOE HUTSHING, PIETRO SCALIA for *JFK*
BEST MUSIC	ALAN MENKEN for *Beauty and the Beast*
BEST SONG	ALAN MENKEN, HOWARD ASHMAN for "BEAUTY AND THE BEAST" in *Beauty and the Beast*
BEST MAKEUP	STAN WINSTON, JEFF DAWN for *Terminator 2*
BEST COSTUMES	ALBERT WOLSKY for *Bugsy*
BEST VISUAL EFFECTS	DENNIS MUREN, STAN WINSTON, GENE WARREN JR., ROBERT SKOTAK for *Terminator 2*
BEST SOUND	TOM JOHNSON, GARY RYDSTROM, GARY SUMMERS, LEE ORLOFF for *Terminator 2*
BEST SOUND EFFECTS EDITING	GARY RYDSTROM, GLORIA S. BORDERS for *Terminator 2*

3   *1991 James Cameron and his creation, which he dispatches to save humanity.*
4   *1992 No less convincing behind the camera than in front: Clint Eastwood.*

1993 OSCARS

BEST PICTURE	UNFORGIVEN
BEST DIRECTOR	CLINT EASTWOOD for *Unforgiven*
BEST LEADING ACTRESS	EMMA THOMPSON in *Howards End*
BEST LEADING ACTOR	AL PACINO in *Scent of a Woman*
BEST SUPPORTING ACTRESS	MARISA TOMEI in *My Cousin Vinny*
BEST SUPPORTING ACTOR	GENE HACKMAN in *Unforgiven*
BEST ORIGINAL SCREENPLAY	NEIL JORDAN for *The Crying Game*
BEST ADAPTED SCREENPLAY	RUTH PRAWER JHABVALA for *Howards End*
BEST FOREIGN LANGUAGE FILM	*Indochine* by RÉGIS WARGNIER (France)
BEST CINEMATOGRAPHY	PHILIPPE ROUSSELOT for *A River Runs Through It*
BEST ART DIRECTION	LUCIANA ARRIGHI, IAN WHITTAKER for *Howards End*
BEST FILM EDITING	JOEL COX for *Unforgiven*
BEST MUSIC	ALAN MENKEN for *Aladdin*
BEST SONG	ALAN MENKEN, TIM RICE for "A WHOLE NEW WORLD" in *Aladdin*
BEST MAKEUP	GREG CANNOM, MICHÈLE BURKE, MATTHEW W. MUNGLE for *Bram Stoker's Dracula*
BEST COSTUMES	EIKO ISHIOKA for *Bram Stoker's Dracula*
BEST VISUAL EFFECTS	KEN RALSTON, DOUG CHIANG, DOUGLAS SMYTHE, TOM WOODRUFF JR. for *Death Becomes Her*
BEST SOUND	CHRIS JENKINS, DOUG HEMPHILL, MARK SMITH, SIMON KAYE for *The Last of the Mohicans*
BEST SOUND EFFECTS EDITING	TOM C. MCCARTHY, DAVID E. STONE for *Bram Stoker's Dracula*

1   1993 Brought the past back to the present with unforgettable faces:
    Steven Spielberg and Liam Neeson.
2   1993 Jane Campion.

1994 OSCARS

BEST PICTURE	SCHINDLER'S LIST
BEST DIRECTOR	STEVEN SPIELBERG for *Schindler's List*
BEST LEADING ACTRESS	HOLLY HUNTER in *The Piano*
BEST LEADING ACTOR	TOM HANKS in *Philadelphia*
BEST SUPPORTING ACTRESS	ANNA PAQUIN in *The Piano*
BEST SUPPORTING ACTOR	TOMMY LEE JONES in *The Fugitive*
BEST ORIGINAL SCREENPLAY	JANE CAMPION for *The Piano*
BEST ADAPTED SCREENPLAY	STEVEN ZAILLIAN for *Schindler's List*
BEST FOREIGN LANGUAGE FILM	*Belle Epoque* by FERNANDO TRUEBA (Spain)
BEST CINEMATOGRAPHY	JANUSZ KAMINSKI for *Schindler's List*
BEST ART DIRECTION	ALLAN STARSKI, EWA BRAUN for *Schindler's List*
BEST FILM EDITING	MICHAEL KAHN for *Schindler's List*
BEST MUSIC	JOHN WILLIAMS for *Schindler's List*
BEST SONG	BRUCE SPRINGSTEEN for "STREETS OF PHILADELPHIA" in *Philadelphia*
BEST MAKEUP	GREG CANNOM, VE NEILL, YOLANDA TOUSSIENG for *Mrs. Doubtfire*
BEST COSTUMES	GABRIELLA PESCUCCI for *The Age of Innocence*
BEST VISUAL EFFECTS	DENNIS MUREN, STAN WINSTON, PHIL TIPPETT, MICHAEL LANTIERI for *Jurassic Park*
BEST SOUND	GARY SUMMERS, GARY RYDSTROM, SHAWN MURPHY, RON JUDKINS for *Jurassic Park*
BEST SOUND EFFECTS EDITING	GARY RYDSTROM, RICHARD HYMNS for *Jurassic Park*

1995 OSCARS

BEST PICTURE	FORREST GUMP
BEST DIRECTOR	ROBERT ZEMECKIS for *Forrest Gump*
BEST LEADING ACTRESS	JESSICA LANGE in *Blue Sky*
BEST LEADING ACTOR	TOM HANKS in *Forrest Gump*
BEST SUPPORTING ACTRESS	DIANNE WIEST in *Bullets Over Broadway*
BEST SUPPORTING ACTOR	MARTIN LANDAU in *Ed Wood*
BEST ORIGINAL SCREENPLAY	QUENTIN TARANTINO, ROGER AVARY for *Pulp Fiction*
BEST ADAPTED SCREENPLAY	ERIC ROTH for *Forrest Gump*
BEST FOREIGN LANGUAGE FILM	*Burnt by the Sun* by NIKITA MICHALKOV (Russia)
BEST CINEMATOGRAPHY	JOHN TOLL for *Legends of the Fall*
BEST ART DIRECTION	KEN ADAM, CAROLYN SCOTT for *The Madness of King George*
BEST FILM EDITING	ARTHUR SCHMIDT for *Forrest Gump*
BEST MUSIC	HANS ZIMMER for *The Lion King*
BEST SONG	ELTON JOHN, TIM RICE for "CAN YOU FEEL THE LOVE TONIGHT" in *The Lion King*
BEST MAKEUP	VE NEILL, RICK BAKER, YOLANDA TOUSSIENG for *Ed Wood*
BEST COSTUMES	LIZZY GARDINER, TIM CHAPPELL for *The Adventures of Priscilla – Queen of the Desert*
BEST VISUAL EFFECTS	KEN RALSTON, GEORGE MURPHY, STEPHEN ROSENBAUM, ALLEN HALL for *Forrest Gump*
BEST SOUND	BOB BEEMER, GREGG LANDAKER, DAVID MACMILLAN, STEVE MASLOW for *Speed*
BEST SOUND EFFECTS EDITING	STEPHEN HUNTER FLICK for *Speed*

1996 OSCARS

BEST PICTURE	BRAVEHEART
BEST DIRECTOR	MEL GIBSON for *Braveheart*
BEST LEADING ACTRESS	SUSAN SARANDON in *Dead Man Walking*
BEST LEADING ACTOR	NICOLAS CAGE in *Leaving Las Vegas*
BEST SUPPORTING ACTRESS	MIRA SORVINO in *Mighty Aphrodite*
BEST SUPPORTING ACTOR	KEVIN SPACEY in *The Usual Suspects*
BEST ORIGINAL SCREENPLAY	CHRISTOPHER MCQUARRIE for *The Usual Suspects*
BEST ADAPTED SCREENPLAY	EMMA THOMPSON for *Sense and Sensibility*
BEST FOREIGN LANGUAGE FILM	*Antonia's Line* by MARLEEN GORRIS (Netherlands)
BEST CINEMATOGRAPHY	JOHN TOLL for *Braveheart*
BEST ART DIRECTION	EUGENIO ZANETTI for *Restoration*
BEST FILM EDITING	MIKE HILL, DAN HANLEY for *Apollo 13*
BEST MUSIC	DRAMA – LUIS ENRIQUE BACALOV for *The Postman*
	MUSICAL, COMEDY – ALAN MENKEN, STEPHEN SCHWARTZ for *Pocahontas*
BEST SONG	ALAN MENKEN, STEPHEN SCHWARTZ for "COLORS OF THE WIND" in *Pocahontas*
BEST MAKEUP	PETER FRAMPTON, PAUL PATTISON, LOIS BURWELL for *Braveheart*
BEST COSTUMES	JAMES ACHESON for *Restoration*
BEST VISUAL EFFECTS	SCOTT E. ANDERSON, CHARLES GIBSON, NEAL SCANLAN, JOHN COX for *Babe*
BEST SOUND	RICK DIOR, STEVE PEDERSON, SCOTT MILLAN, DAVID MACMILLAN for *Apollo 13*
BEST SOUND EFFECTS EDITING	LON BENDER, PER HALLBERG for *Braveheart*

3   *1996 The return of the melodrama: Anthony Minghella and Ralph Fiennes.*
4   *1996 Sceptical looks from the Coen Brothers.*

1997 OSCARS

BEST PICTURE	THE ENGLISH PATIENT
BEST DIRECTOR	ANTHONY MINGHELLA for *The English Patient*
BEST LEADING ACTRESS	FRANCES MCDORMAND in *Fargo*
BEST LEADING ACTOR	GEOFFREY RUSH in *Shine*
BEST SUPPORTING ACTRESS	JULIETTE BINOCHE in *The English Patient*
BEST SUPPORTING ACTOR	CUBA GOODING JR. in *Jerry Maguire*
BEST ORIGINAL SCREENPLAY	JOEL COEN, ETHAN COEN for *Fargo*
BEST ADAPTED SCREENPLAY	BILLY BOB THORNTON for *Sling Blade*
BEST FOREIGN LANGUAGE FILM	*Kolya* by JAN SVERAK (Czech Republic)
BEST CINEMATOGRAPHY	JOHN SEALE for *The English Patient*
BEST ART DIRECTION	STUART CRAIG, STEPHANIE MCMILLAN for *The English Patient*
BEST FILM EDITING	WALTER MURCH for *The English Patient*
BEST MUSIC	DRAMA – GABRIEL YARED for *The English Patient*
	MUSICAL, COMEDY – RACHEL PORTMAN for *Emma*
BEST SONG	ANDREW LLOYD WEBBER, TIM RICE for "YOU MUST LOVE ME" in *Evita*
BEST MAKEUP	RICK BAKER, DAVID LEROY ANDERSON for *The Nutty Professor*
BEST COSTUMES	ANN ROTH for *The English Patient*
BEST VISUAL EFFECTS	VOLKER ENGEL, DOUGLAS SMITH, CLAY PINNEY, JOSEPH VISKOCIL for *Independence Day*
BEST SOUND	CHRIS NEWMAN, WALTER MURCH, MARK BERGER, DAVID PARKER for *The English Patient*
BEST SOUND EFFECTS EDITING	BRUCE STAMBLER for *The Ghost and the Darkness*

1   1997 The final instructions before the big scene: James Cameron and his two leads.
2   1997 James L. Brooks and the third star of the film.

1998 OSCARS

BEST PICTURE	TITANIC
BEST DIRECTOR	JAMES CAMERON for *Titanic*
BEST LEADING ACTRESS	HELEN HUNT in *As Good As It Gets*
BEST LEADING ACTOR	JACK NICHOLSON in *As Good As It Gets*
BEST SUPPORTING ACTRESS	KIM BASINGER in *L.A. Confidential*
BEST SUPPORTING ACTOR	ROBIN WILLIAMS in *Good Will Hunting*
BEST ORIGINAL SCREENPLAY	MATT DAMON, BEN AFFLECK for *Good Will Hunting*
BEST ADAPTED SCREENPLAY	BRIAN HELGELAND, CURTIS HANSON for *L.A. Confidential*
BEST FOREIGN LANGUAGE FILM	*Karakter* by MIKE VAN DIEM (Netherlands)
BEST CINEMATOGRAPHY	RUSSELL CARPENTER for *Titanic*
BEST ART DIRECTION	PETER LAMONT, MICHAEL FORD for *Titanic*
BEST FILM EDITING	CONRAD BUFF, JAMES CAMERON, RICHARD A. HARRIS for *Titanic*
BEST MUSIC	DRAMA – JAMES HORNER FOR *Titanic*
	MUSICAL, COMEDY – ANNE DUDLEY for *The Full Monty*
BEST SONG	JAMES HORNER, WILL JENNINGS for "MY HEART WILL GO ON" in *Titanic*
BEST MAKEUP	RICK BAKER, DAVID LEROY ANDERSON for *Men in Black*
BEST COSTUMES	DEBORAH L. SCOTT for *Titanic*
BEST VISUAL EFFECTS	ROBERT LEGATO, MARK LASOFF, THOMAS L. FISHER, MICHAEL KANFER for *Titanic*
BEST SOUND	GARY RYDSTROM, TOM JOHNSON, GARY SUMMERS, MARK ULANO for *Titanic*
BEST SOUND EFFECTS EDITING	TOM BELLFORT, CHRISTOPHER BOYES for *Titanic*

3   1998 All the world is a stage: John Madden giving instructions to the actors.
4   1998 Nothing makes him lose his cool: Spielberg while shooting.

1999 OSCARS

BEST PICTURE	SHAKESPEARE IN LOVE
BEST DIRECTOR	STEVEN SPIELBERG for *Saving Private Ryan*
BEST LEADING ACTRESS	GWYNETH PALTROW in *Shakespeare in Love*
BEST LEADING ACTOR	ROBERTO BENIGNI in *Life Is Beautiful*
BEST SUPPORTING ACTRESS	JUDI DENCH in *Shakespeare in Love*
BEST SUPPORTING ACTOR	JAMES COBURN in *Affliction*
BEST ORIGINAL SCREENPLAY	MARC NORMAN, TOM STOPPARD for *Shakespeare in Love*
BEST ADAPTED SCREENPLAY	BILL CONDON for *Gods and Monsters*
BEST FOREIGN LANGUAGE FILM	*Life Is Beautiful* by ROBERTO BENIGNI (Italy)
BEST CINEMATOGRAPHY	JANUSZ KAMINSKI for *Saving Private Ryan*
BEST ART DIRECTION	MARTIN CHILDS, JILL QUERTIER for *Shakespeare in Love*
BEST FILM EDITING	MICHAEL KAHN for *Saving Private Ryan*
BEST MUSIC	DRAMA – NICOLA PIOVANI for *Life Is Beautiful*
	MUSICAL, COMEDY – STEPHEN WARBECK for *Shakespeare in Love*
BEST SONG	STEPHEN SCHWARTZ for "WHEN YOU BELIEVE" in *The Prince of Egypt*
BEST MAKEUP	JENNY SHIRCORE for *Elizabeth*
BEST COSTUMES	SANDY POWELL for *Shakespeare in Love*
BEST VISUAL EFFECTS	JOEL HYNEK, NICHOLAS BROOKS, STUART ROBERTSON, KEVIN MACK for *What Dreams May Come*
BEST SOUND	GARY RYDSTROM, GARY SUMMERS, ANDY NELSON, RONALD JUDKINS for *Saving Private Ryan*
BEST SOUND EFFECTS EDITING	GARY RYDSTROM, RICHARD HYMNS for *Saving Private Ryan*

1   *1999 Sam Mendes casts his unerring gaze on our life-long lies.*
2   *1999 Spectacular images: Andy and Larry Wachowski.*

2000 OSCARS

BEST PICTURE	AMERICAN BEAUTY
BEST DIRECTOR	SAM MENDES for *American Beauty*
BEST LEADING ACTRESS	HILARY SWANK in *Boys Don't Cry*
BEST LEADING ACTOR	KEVIN SPACEY in *American Beauty*
BEST SUPPORTING ACTRESS	ANGELINA JOLIE in *Girl Interrupted*
BEST SUPPORTING ACTOR	MICHAEL CAINE in *The Cider House Rules*
BEST ORIGINAL SCREENPLAY	ALAN BALL for *American Beauty*
BEST ADAPTED SCREENPLAY	JOHN IRVING for *The Cider House Rules*
BEST FOREIGN LANGUAGE FILM	*All About My Mother* by PEDRO ALMODÓVAR (Spain)
BEST CINEMATOGRAPHY	CONRAD L. HALL for *American Beauty*
BEST ART DIRECTION	RICK HEINRICHS, PETER YOUNG for *Sleepy Hollow*
BEST FILM EDITING	ZACH STAENBERG for *The Matrix*
BEST MUSIC	JOHN CORIGLIANO for *The Red Violin*
BEST SONG	PHIL COLLINS for "YOU'LL BE IN MY HEART" in *Tarzan*
BEST MAKEUP	CHRISTINE BLUNDELL, TREFOR PROUD for *Topsy-Turvy*
BEST COSTUMES	LINDY HEMMING for *Topsy-Turvy*
BEST VISUAL EFFECTS	STEVE COURTLEY, JOHN GAETA, JANEK SIRRS, JON THUM for *The Matrix*
BEST SOUND	DAVID E. CAMPBELL, DAVID LEE, JOHN T. REITZ, GREGG RUDLOFF for *The Matrix*
BEST SOUND EFFECTS EDITING	DANE A. DAVIS for *The Matrix*

3 *2000 Steven Soderbergh.*
4 *2000 Ang Lee maintains his bird's-eye view.*

2001 OSCARS

BEST PICTURE	GLADIATOR
BEST DIRECTOR	STEVEN SODERBERGH for *Traffic*
BEST LEADING ACTRESS	JULIA ROBERTS in *Erin Brockovich*
BEST LEADING ACTOR	RUSSELL CROWE in *Gladiator*
BEST SUPPORTING ACTRESS	MARCIA GAY HARDEN in *Pollock*
BEST SUPPORTING ACTOR	BENICIO DEL TORO in *Traffic*
BEST ORIGINAL SCREENPLAY	CAMERON CROWE for *Almost Famous*
BEST ADAPTED SCREENPLAY	STEPHEN GAGHAN for *Traffic*
BEST FOREIGN LANGUAGE FILM	*Crouching Tiger, Hidden Dragon* by ANG LEE (Taiwan)
BEST CINEMATOGRAPHY	PETER PAU for *Crouching Tiger, Hidden Dragon*
BEST ART DIRECTION	TIM YIP for *Crouching Tiger, Hidden Dragon*
BEST FILM EDITING	STEPHEN MIRRIONE for *Traffic*
BEST MUSIC	TAN DUN for *Crouching Tiger, Hidden Dragon*
BEST SONG	BOB DYLAN for "THINGS HAVE CHANGED" in *Wonder Boys*

GENERAL INDEX

All those involved in a film's production are mentioned.
The movie titles are indicated in bold, production companies
in italics, and the film genres are highlighted by dashes.
Numbers in bold refer to a glossary text.

GENERAL INDEX

GENERAL INDEX

GENERAL INDEX

GENERAL INDEX

GENERAL INDEX

GENERAL INDEX

ABOUT THE AUTHORS

Ulrich von Berg (UB), *1955, degree in American and Media Studies. Many years' experience as a movie journalist in all branches of the media. Editor and author of various books on film. Lives in Berlin.

Philipp Bühler (PB), *1971, studied Political Science, History, and English Studies. Film journalist; works for various daily newspapers, online media, and educational media publications. Lives in Berlin.

Malte Hagener (MH), *1971, Professor of Media Studies, specializing in film history, theory and aesthetics, at the Philipps University of Marburg. Main research areas: film theory and history; media education. Author of an introduction to film theory (with Thomas Elsaesser) and *Moving Forward, Looking Back: The European Avant-garde and the Invention of Film Culture, 1919–1939*, Amsterdam, 2007. Lives in Marburg.

Steffen Haubner (SH), *1965, studied Art History and Sociology. Many academic and press articles. Runs an editorial office in Hamburg. Lives in Hamburg.

Jörn Hetebrügge (JH), *1971, studied German Literature. Author and journalist of many articles on film. Lives in Berlin.

Annette Kilzer (AK), *1966, degree in Theatre Studies, German Studies, and Philosophy. Film journalist and writer, author of numerous press articles and books on, among others, the Coen Brothers, Bruce Willis and Til Schweiger. Lives in Berlin.

Heinz-Jürgen Köhler (HJK), *1963, film & TV journalist; author of many academic and press articles. Lives in Hamburg.

Steffen Lückehe (SL), *1962, film gallerist, manages the film archive and video library "Mr. & Mrs. Smith". Author of many articles in various magazines. Lives in Mannheim.

Nils Meyer (NM), *1971, studied German Literature and Politics, trainee at the Evangelische Journalistenschule in Berlin, research assistant in Dresden, editor in Bremen. Articles for print, radio, and television. Works as a public relations officer. Lives in Hanover.

Olaf Möller (OM), author, translator, program curator. Film journalist, writes for the national press. Lives in Köln.

Anne Pohl (APO), *1961, active as a journalist since 1987. Author of numerous academic articles. Lives near Hamburg.

Burkhard Röwekamp (BR), *1965, researcher at the Institute for Contemporary German Literature and Media at the Philipps University in Marburg. Has taught numerous courses and published many articles on the aesthetics and theory of contemporary film. Lives in Marburg.

Markus Stauff (MS), *1968, PhD, media scientist, teaches at the Media Studies department of the University of Amsterdam. Key research areas are digital television, media sports and cultural studies. Author of many academic articles and several books. Lives in Amsterdam.

Rainer Vowe (RV), *1954, PhD, historian, teaches at the Institute for Film and Television Studies at the Ruhr University in Bochum. Numerous articles on the history of cinema and television. Lives in Bochum.

Christoph Ziener (CZ), *1980, studied Art History and Medieval History. Main research areas: film history and North European art of the Early Modern Age. Lives in Dresden.

ACKNOWLEDGEMENTS

As the editor of this book, I would like to thank all those who invested so much of their time, knowledge and energy into the making of this book. My special thanks to **Martin Holz** and **Florian Kobler** from TASCHEN for their coordination work and truly amazing ability to keep track of everything. Thanks also to **Birgit Eichwede** and **Andy Disl** for their ingenious design concept that gives pride of place to the pictures, the true capital of any film book, and to **Herbert Klemens** of Filmbild Fundus for his assistance in procuring the master images.

Then, of course, I am hugely indebted to the authors, whose keen analyses form the backbone of this book. Technical editing was conducted with the accustomed thoroughness by **Malte Hagener** and **Heinz-Jürgen Köhler**. **Benedikt Taschen**, who not only agreed to produce and publish the series, but enthusiastically followed each volume's progress from start to finish. My personal thanks to him and everyone else mentioned here.

CREDITS

The publishers would like to thank the distributors, without whom many of these films would never have reached the big screen:
ARSENAL, ARTHAUS, BUENA VISTA, C/I VERTRIEBSGEMEINSCHAFT, COLUMBIA TRI STAR, CONCORDE, CONSTANTIN, HIGHLIGHT FILM, JUGENDFILM, KINOWELT, NIL FILM, PANDORA, POLYGRAM FILMS, PROKINO, SCOTIA, SENATOR, TOBIS, 20th CENTURY FOX, UIP, WARNER BROS.

ABOUT THIS BOOK

The 144 films selected for this book represent a decade of cinema. It goes without saying that this particular selection is based on a decision that could have turned out differently. Each film is presented in an essay, and additionally accompanied by a glossary entry devoted to an individual person or a cinematographic term. To ensure optimal access to this wealth of information, an index of films is provided at the beginning of each volume, while a general index can be found in the back of Vol. 2.

IMPRINT

Endpapers / Pages 1, 748–749 **LOST HIGHWAY** / David Lynch /
SENATOR FILM / OCTOBER FILM; Pages 2–3, 6–17, 386–387 **THE SILENCE OF
THE LAMBS** Jonathan Demme / COLUMBIA / TRI-STAR / ORION PICTURES.

Photographs: Filmbild Fundus Robert Fischer, München
ddp images, Hamburg (Pages 81–85, 511–515, 581–587, 741–747)
Heritage Auctions/HA.com (Pages 22, 30, 42, 46, 56, 62, 66, 76, 80, 92,
98, 110, 120, 124, 132, 138, 146, 150, 162, 168, 172, 176, 188, 192, 214,
218, 222, 228, 234, 254, 262, 268, 278, 284, 288, 292, 296, 304, 308,
316, 320, 324, 330, 334, 344, 354, 362, 372, 378, 394, 398, 402, 408, 414,
418, 424, 436, 448, 454, 458, 482, 490, 496, 506, 510, 526, 532, 538,
550, 562, 566, 582, 588, 594, 624, 630, 634, 644, 652, 666, 672, 680, 692,
702, 718, 722, 726, 730, 736)
The Kobal Collection, London/New York (Page 182)

Editorial Coordination: Martin Holz and Florian Kobler, Cologne
Technical Editing: Malte Hagener and Heinz-Jürgen Köhler, Hamburg
English Translation: Deborah Caroline Holmes, Vienna (Texts), Harriet Horsfield
in association with First Edition Translations Ltd, Cambridge (Introduction),
Katharine Hughes, Oxford (Captions)
Production: Ute Wachendorf, Cologne
Design: Sense/Net, Andy Disl und Birgit Eichwede, Cologne
www.sense-net.net

Texts: Ulrich von Berg (UB), Philipp Bühler (PB), Malte Hagener (MH),
Steffen Haubner (SH), Jörn Hetebrügge (JH), Annette Kilzer (AK),
Heinz-Jürgen Köhler (HJK), Steffen Lückehe (SL), Nils Meyer (NM),
Olaf Möller (OM), Anne Pohl (APO), Burkhard Röwekamp (BR),
Markus Stauff (MS), Rainer Vowe (RV), Christoph Ziener (CZ)

To stay informed about upcoming TASCHEN titles, please request our magazine at www.taschen.com/magazine or write to TASCHEN America, 6671
Sunset Boulevard, Los Angeles, CA 90028, USA; contact-us@taschen.com;
Fax: +1-323-463-4442. We will be happy to send you a free copy of our
magazine, which is filled with information about all of our books.

© 2012 TASCHEN GmbH
Hohenzollernring 53, D–50672 Köln
www.taschen.com

Printed in South Korea
ISBN 978-3-8365-3263-1